REVOLUTIONARY MEDICINE

EXPERIMENTAL FUTURES

TECHNOLOGICAL LIVES, SCIENTIFIC ARTS,
ANTHROPOLOGICAL VOICES

A series edited by Michael M. J. Fischer and Joseph Dumit

P. Sean Brotherton

REVOLUTIONARY
MEDICINE HEALTH AND THE
BODY IN POST-SOVIET CUBA

DUKE UNIVERSITY PRESS DURHAM AND LONDON 2012

PUBLISHED WITH THE ASSISTANCE OF THE FREDERICK W.
HILLES PUBLICATION FUND OF YALE UNIVERSITY.

To my parents, Ivan and Delcita Brotherton

CONTENTS

*Walking along the streets of the formerly posh suburbs of
Havana, I am always struck by the contrast between the old
and new, now fused together. The streets resemble a bricolage of
different centuries, and each house I pass seems to reveal a new
style, era, or simply an invention born of necessity. Romanesque
pillars painted in soothing pastel colors, now faded, complement
large windows and crumbling balconies that contrast with
decorative rusting ironwork and gardens in disarray. It is not
uncommon to find a bust of the Cuban independence fighter José
Martí standing proudly in the center of many of these gardens,
an image of his head and a revolutionary slogan engraved on a
small plaque partly shrouded by encroaching weeds.*

*In contrast to this serene image is the blaring sound of American
pop music coming out of 1950s-model Fords and Chevrolets with
large Sony or Panasonic speakers from the U.S.-dollar store
placed strategically in the cars' rear windows. The booming,
repetitive bass and synthesized voices remind me that, despite
appearances, we are in the new millennium. Laundry hanging
out of ornate colonial windows and the buzzing sound of
pressure cookers softening the daily fare of* frijoles negros *(black
beans) are accompanied by the shrill laughter of brightly
uniformed children on their way home from school. People
standing in a winding queue in front of the local* bodega *(ration
store) converse, laugh, and share a collective sigh, as most of the
daily rations fail to arrive or simply run out. Unbothered by a
river of water flowing from a broken pipe in the street, people
smile obligingly as a passing tourist snaps a photo of what is,
for him, a novelty: Cubans lining up for bread. These are the
participants in the making of history, as it passes by in a series
of rhythmic beats.*

ETHNOGRAPHY OF
CONTRADICTIONS

In a crowded theater in Havana in the summer of 2000, as I sat watching the Cuban-directed and Cuban-produced movie of the year, *Un Paraíso bajo las estrellas* (A paradise under the stars)—incidentally, this is also the motto of the Tropicana, the infamous Cuban cabaret that features voluptuous dancing girls—the audience roared with laughter and shouted comments about the unfolding drama. One part of the movie that generated a particularly vociferous response was the demise of one of the secondary characters, who, while arguing with his neighbors, slipped off a bridge and fell to his death, standard fare in a Cuban soap opera. What was most remarkable about this death, however, was the character's rebirth.

During his funeral, his ex-wife, a Cuban living in Spain, arrived with her arms weighed down with shopping bags and boxes and dressed in the latest designer wear. The center of attention immediately shifted from the deceased to the newly arrived *cubana de afuera* (Cuban living abroad) and her declaration that she had brought *regalitos* (little presents) for everybody. While the mourners surrounded her, the deceased, not to be left out of the general mayhem of gift distribution, suddenly awoke.

The mourners, stunned into disbelief, began to question him. "What happened?," they cried out. Responding quite matter-of-factly he stated, "When I got to Heaven, they wouldn't let me in because the entrance fee was in *divisa* [U.S. dollars]." Rejoicing in his rebirth, the mourners silently accepted the reality that the afterlife is merely an extension of everyday life, in which access to divisa shapes lives and experiences differentially. The audience in the theater screamed out in jest, *"Vaya, no es fácil!"* (It is not easy!). A woman sitting next to me shook her head and grumbled, "This country is shit." A man yelled out, "*Oye* [listen], there is nothing left in this country that isn't in divisa!"

In Cuba today a deep discontent runs beneath the reiteration of revolutionary catechisms. In myriad ways Cubans are beginning both to voice serious concerns and to poke fun at the situation in which they find themselves. Whereas once official state rhetoric served as a political summons to rally the population, even if superficially, the conspicuous reemergence of haves and have-nots, defying the socialist discourse of egalitarianism, leaves the government exposed to widespread criticism at unprecedented levels, often in public forums. As the state continues to defend its socialist aspirations, individual citizens, long accustomed to the basic necessities and the few extra luxuries furnished by the revolution, are starting to feel the effects of a prolonged economic crisis now that this material well-being is no longer guaranteed. More important, citizens are beginning to question and challenge the rebirth of a class-stratified economy in which possession of divisa indexes differential access to basic goods and services and to rampant consumerism by the privileged few who reside in the upper layer of this multi-tiered economy.

Like other spheres of Cuban society, the health care system has been at the center of recent macroeconomic transformations, such as the socialist government's pursuit of a dual economy using Cuban pesos and U.S. dollars (now substituted by *pesos convertibles*).[1] This book examines how these reforms characterize some of the implicit contradictions of everyday life and, importantly, shape individuals' experiences with institutions of the state. Nowhere are these contradictions more evident than in Cuba's socialist health policies, which are currently undergoing revisions, experiencing constraints, and meeting obstacles as the country's current financial woes pose serious challenges to the state's ability to keep the underlying principles of the socialist government intact.

While many social scientists have examined public health care in Cuba, none have ethnographically explored how health reform might be analyzed in terms of larger economic and political considerations, many of them external to Cuba, as well as in terms of changing practices in the everyday lives of citizens. To address these concerns, I ground this book in what I call an ethnography of contradictions, and, in order to map such an ethnography, I advocate a theoretically promiscuous approach, one that is wedded not to a single theoretical camp or framework, but to an engagement with a diverse body of recent scholarship on the anthropology of the state, critical-interpretive medical anthropology, and postcolonial and postsocialist studies. Such an approach is necessary in order to analyze an ethnographic context—contemporary Cuba —that has occupied multiple positions throughout history: from Spanish colony (1493–1899) to capitalist democracy under the tutelage of U.S. domination (1902–59) to socialist state (1959–present).

Shortly after arriving in Havana in July 2000 to begin my formal field research, I set off early one morning to meet a professor named Liliana Menendez from the Ministerio de Salud Pública (Ministry of Public Health, MINSAP). I had met Menendez a year earlier while visiting a close friend of mine who worked in her office. I was pleasantly surprised to find out that she was an avid reader of medical anthropology literature, and she immediately expressed an interest in my research. Having sent my proposal earlier for her review, I was eager to get feedback. She agreed to meet me in her small office, located in a crumbling building in the city center that also served as a residence for students. After we exchanged formal greetings and sat down she pulled out a copy of my proposal.

Before launching into her discussion, she stated, "These are only suggestions, but I think you should strongly consider them." She circled the phrase "governable subjects" in the opening paragraph. "My dear," she said, laughing playfully, "this language is simply too strong." Switching to a more serious tone, she queried what exactly I meant by such a phrase. "Are you suggesting Cubans are manipulated like objects by the state?" she asked pointedly. She was skeptical of my references to various theorists, in particular, Michel Foucault, and said one could interpret my research intentions in Cuba as being overly critical of the socialist government. The state review board, she stated, shaking her head, would never approve such a study.

She pulled out a scrap of paper and began to draft a new proposal, one which, she stated, would be of "greater scientific interest" and, importantly for state reviewers, appropriate in the Cuban context: a comparison of the "cultural models of health care" in the United States, Canada, and Cuba. Excitedly, she sketched out a chart with three columns: on the left was Capitalism–United States; on the extreme right of the page was Socialism–Cuba; and in the middle was a Mixed–Model–Canada. She seemed impressed by the new "culturally appropriate" project she had drafted and once again stressed that the new project was only a suggestion. As I maintained an expressionless face throughout her frenzied sketching and exclamations that the project was of "vast interest," she finally looked up at me and gauged that I was not terribly enthusiastic. "You are aware that several social scientists have been removed from Cuba, aren't you?" she queried. Her comments had a ring to them that made me feel I was privy to some kind of secret information. After forty minutes of explaining the importance of a sound methodology, as opposed to anthropological methods, which she disparagingly referred to as "simply hanging out," she finished drafting the new proposal. By her account, it followed the grant guidelines set out by the Pan American Health Organization, a format, she indicated, that state reviewers responded to well. Handing me several sheets of paper, a draft of my "new project," she wished me good luck. After thanking her for her help, I left her office with the clear sense that I had my work cut out for me.

Several days after my encounter with the professor from the MINSAP I spoke with a close friend of mine, a Cuban physician, who was completing a master's degree in biostatics. He offered to work with me to make my proposal acceptable to the officials of the MINSAP. "Your language is too theoretical," he complained. The physician worked with me for two days to help me transform my original proposal into a project infused with positivist language that harkened back to my second-year university organic chemistry lab reports. After reading over the proposal, the physician was convinced it was "scientifically solid" and, in his view, could actually say something beyond a limited context; that is to say, he proudly concluded, it was "statistically significant." The revised proposal would have had me working in eight *consultorios* (family doctor's offices), randomly selected across the city, and carrying out extensive survey-like research with, at a minimum, several hundred people. Moreover, the new project was devoid of the hallmarks of anthropological research methods—extensive participant observation and semistructured interviews—and purposefully avoided political issues.

Unwilling and unable to carry out such a large-scale project, I decided to seek out a social science research institution. I had a lucky break when, after repeatedly being told by various government officials that any study of medicine in Cuba, social or otherwise, is the sole responsibility of the MINSAP, I finally got an appointment with a social science professor who was recommended to me by a friend of a friend. I sat down with the professor, who I later found out was a high-ranking member of the Communist Party. He examined my original proposal and my curriculum vitae and, to my surprise, expressed great interest in my project. "It is obvious that the MINSAP will not understand the kind of research you are doing," he stated. "You are not studying medicine per se but examining the practice of medicine as your object of study." "At this institution," he continued amicably, "I am sure you will find we are very open-minded." He offered me numerous references and contacts with medical professionals and personally took on the responsibility of calling the people who could secure my student research visa. In less than a week a local ethnological research institution officially sponsored my field research, with no changes to my original proposal.

In a country beleaguered by bureaucratic red tape, matched by a population conditioned by years of having to possess multiple layers of documentation, the mere existence of a Cuban form of identification made things easier for me in certain respects. My "Temporary Foreign Resident in Cuba" identification booklet, which listed biographical information, citizenship, parents' names, address in Cuba, and institutional affiliation, served as a point of reference of sorts, flagging that a state entity was essentially responsible for me. In effect, the booklet granted me access to a plethora of institutions, including libraries, research centers, hospitals, and clinics, and authorized me, as a person living in the country, to socialize and interact with Cubans in ways that normally arouse the suspicion of authorities, who often treat such interactions as signs of prostitution, hustling, or general illegality.

However, as a foreign researcher, I was also aware that the socialist government had demanded over the years that various social scientists, among other researchers, leave Cuba for carrying out what government officials believed was "questionable research practices."[2] As if reading from the pages of George Orwell's novel *1984*, I did have fleeting thoughts of the omniscient Big Brother state watching and controlling my every move and action and that of the populace. For the most part, this was not my personal experience of Cuba, although some individuals did interact with me in ways that reinforced the rumors that the populace was being watched and followed by a ubiquitous state. For example, a small percentage of people I interviewed whispered, refused to be taped, or went to great lengths to arrange interviews in out-of-the-way places.

My most troubling experience involved several interviews I conducted with family physicians in Havana, all of whom were recommended to me through my Cuban host research institution. This experience made me rethink my methodological approach and wonder whether I had dismissed the notion of Big Brother too quickly. During several of the interviews with family physicians, I was surprised to find a striking similarity among their responses to my questions. They were reminiscent in both cadence and content of Fidel Castro's popular speeches, and I thought I had fallen prey to the official harangue of prescribed state discourse—what many Cubans refer to as *el teque* (literally, a spinning top).[3] The physicians' responses, replete with discussions of the successes reflected in Cuba's vital health statistics and peppered with accolades for the country's family physician and nurse program, which is popularly understood as being the product of Castro's innovative thinking, shared critiques of what was to blame for recent changes to the Cuban health care system: the withdrawal of Soviet aid and the U.S. embargo against Cuba, popularly known as *el bloqueo*.

I wondered whether my affiliation with my host institution, which in theory was a nongovernmental organization (NGO) but for all intents and purposes was managed and run by the Ministry of Culture, had cast me in a specific light. I could well have been perceived as an official of the state. It was clear that several of the interviews, previously arranged through my Cuban advisors, had set the stage for a particular kind of interaction. In effect, any effort to secure my informants' anonymity was impossible. Having carried out extensive preliminary fieldwork in Havana since 1998, I had, by the time my formal research began in 2000, already built up a large informal network of friends and acquaintances, many of whom were family physicians. I was well aware, from attending many gatherings with this eclectic group of people, that heated debates and discussions on numerous topics, political and otherwise, were commonplace in certain situations. The physicians I encountered who were toeing the party line in formal interviews were the exception rather than the rule.

Having carried out extensive formal and informal interviews among the general public, I encountered a diverse range of opinions and experiences, particularly in regard to the public health system. Were these physicians, who had been recommended to me by my host institution, just feeding me state rhetoric? A close Cuban friend of mine made an astute point that helped shed light on my dilemma. As he put it, two kinds of people typically flock to Cuba. The first group, the idealists, come to Cuba in search of the image of Ernesto "Che" Guevara, and they have a romanticized vision of Castro and socialism. The second group, he suggested, are the critics, who arrive in Cuba in droves to point fingers, cast doubt, and castigate the socialist government. Unfortunately, as my friend further pointed out, while some individual citizens may happily bare their souls without thinking twice, many state professionals, especially physicians, are in a different position. They are more conscious, he suggested, of the way in which open dissent may have negative consequences for their careers, particularly as they work so closely with the government. This is a risk, he added, that many physicians are unwilling to take with people who have not demonstrated themselves to be *de confianza* (trustworthy).

My final decision to branch out and pursue interviews with physicians recommended through informal contacts, rather than through my sponsoring institution, was prompted by one event in particular. Marisol Domínguez, a forty-eight-year-old family physician recommended to me by a Cuban professor at my host institution, had agreed to do a series of interviews with me and offered to let me visit her consultorio. Arranging to meet her at her house for our first interview, I found the experience to be revealing in many ways. Domínguez responded to all of my questions in monosyllables, and I had decided that the interview was a complete failure. Toward the end of our conversation, I asked her to tell me about some of the challenges she faced in her work as a family physician. I also asked her to comment on any improvements she felt were needed in the current primary health care system.

Looking noticeably uncomfortable, Domínguez asked, "You do know our Comandante is the mastermind behind this current program, don't you?" She paused and then added, "I believe the program is ideal, and no changes are needed." Upon further questioning about how her consultorio was affected by the recent shortages of food and medicine in Cuba, she became visibly disturbed and adamantly stated, "Nobody in Cuba is without adequate food or medicines. If people are telling you that, they are absolute lies." Taken a little aback by her hostile response, I inquired about the general shortages that many of the ordinary citizens I had interviewed complained of. "Well, yes," she admitted, "we have some shortages, but they are getting better. Surely you do not want to focus on this topic when we have accomplished so much in Cuba." I made it clear I was not on a fact-finding mission to identify only the faults in the system or to criticize the government, but to put in context recent changes in the health care system caused by social and political shifts in Cuba. Seemingly unimpressed by my explanation, Domínguez concluded, "Cubans are prone to exaggerate things, especially with foreigners."

My formal meeting with Domínguez was similar to several others I had with people I refer to as low-level bureaucrats—social workers, MINSAP officials, and so on—who were recommended to me through my host institution. Rather than dismiss these interviews as mere rhetoric, I include them alongside other interviews, many of which involved informants with whom I had developed long-term relationships, such as those I met in 1998 or 1999. Others warmed up to me only after repeated interviews and extensive participant observation. I do acknowledge, though, that Domínguez's comments about the questionable interaction between foreign researchers and exaggerating Cubans have a certain ring of truth, however limited.

Throughout my fieldwork it was not uncommon for some informants to drop by my house or to call on me, often to complain extensively about their various experiences with the primary health care system or about one physician in particular. For example, one woman I had interviewed insisted that I put on a doctor's lab coat and sneak into the maternity hospital where her niece had been admitted in order to witness firsthand the abhorrent conditions. I declined. Several people unmistakably had an agenda, one which they believed matched what they thought was my own: to identify faults in Cuba's health care system in order to undermine the socialist government. When these individuals had positive experiences with their family physician or state officials, I was not called upon to chronicle those events. Not attempting to censor the experiences of my informants, I nevertheless had to use my own strategies and tactics sometimes in order to tease out the underlying and multiple truths in people's everyday experiences.

For example, several individuals painted images of starvation and at times complained that the state had not provided basic monthly rations, such as meat or fish. When I asked to see their state ration books (*libreta*), which I justified by stating that I was merely curious, meat and fish products were indeed provided.[4] I asked people to explain the discrepancies in their stories. "But those are not the choice parts of the meat," many of them would claim, or "Yes, we got fish last week, but it was in a can." The notion of starvation, in this context, was the inability to eat culturally appropriate foods. Moreover, other individuals complained of having no access to U.S. dollars yet smoked a particular brand of cigarettes that was sold only in this currency. When I asked them how often they smoked, on average, several individuals indicated they smoked a pack a day. The popular brands of cigarettes for sale in U.S. dollars sell for anywhere between fifty cents and one dollar per pack.

Therefore, some people were smoking from fifteen to thirty dollars' worth of cigarettes per month. Yet by their own accounts they did not have access to U.S. dollars. These are only some of the many discrepancies among the multiple realities of people's lived experience. Ethnographic research, in this context, is the best way to address the many nuances and contradictions of contemporary Cuban life.

I owe a huge debt of gratitude to the many people and institutions that have made this book possible. First and foremost, I offer my heartfelt thanks to the many individuals and health professionals who participated in my research. While they cannot be named, all of the informants invested a great deal of trust in me by inviting me into their homes and lives. Without their personal experiences and opinions of everyday life, this book would have lacked the complexity and sensitivity necessary to analyze contemporary Cuban life.

I thank my host institution in Havana and the Cuban Ministry of Culture (MINCULT), which made this research possible. Special thanks to the international relations specialist office at the MINCULT, which efficiently processed my multiple entry and exit visas throughout my extended stay on the island. I would like to thank my Cuban research assistants, who assisted me with the immense task of transcribing the reels of taped interviews. Throughout the years, they have been tireless in their communications via e-mail to keep me up to date on current events in Cuba. While they cannot be named, I trust they know I am forever grateful. In addition, I also want to thank all of the informal research assistance offered to me by a vast network of Cuban friends who made my numerous visits to the island eventful. I greatly appreciate their support and their trust, which facilitated the crucial field contacts required for this research.

I would also like to express my gratitude to the different academic communities and individuals that have inspired and nourished my intellectual and professional growth throughout the past decade. I would like to thank Margaret Lock, whose supervision of an early phase of this project, as a dissertation, was influential in the development of my interests in anthropology of the body and critical-interpretive medical anthropology. Lock's rigorous academic standards and thought-provoking scholarship have both challenged and inspired me to be a better scholar. Thanks are also due to Allan Young, Kristin Norget, and Phillip Oxhorn, who all lent intellectual support and guidance for earlier stages of this project. I am also indebted to

Stacy Leigh Pigg, who served as the external reviewer of my dissertation. Her astute, insightful comments proved pivotal in transforming the dissertation into a book.

I would also like to express my sincerest gratitude to Vinh-Kim Nguyen. I cannot thank him enough for the support and encouragement he has provided throughout the years and, more recently, in the completion of this book. I am forever indebted to him for his pep talks and, invaluably, sharing his house, books, great food, and critical theory talks over espresso. Though the ideas discussed in this book are my own, many emerged as I tested them out on Vinh-Kim's critical ear. He is an exceptional scholar and an equally exceptional friend.

I also owe a huge debt to my colleagues in the Department of Anthropology at Yale University, especially those who provided helpful feedback on various parts of this manuscript in our SoCLA workshop. I am especially grateful to Kamari Clarke, Marcia Inhorn, Inderpal Grewal, Catherine Panter-Brick, William Kelly, Helen Siu, and Richard Bribiescas for their extended discussions with me, mentorship, and overall guidance. Thanks are also due to colleagues and friends whose support and debates throughout the years have been influential in fleshing out my arguments, especially Danaydes Albondiga, Naomi Adelson, Jafari Allen, Malcolm Blincow, Raimundo Cruz, Sabrina Doyon, Narges Erami, Alberto Espinosa, Andre Farquharson, Julie Feinsilver, Sandra Hyde, Junko Kitanaka, Rosa Maria Osorio, Josue Pratts, Ihosvany Hernandez Gonzalez, Ariana Hernandez-Reguant, Robert Lorway, Kristin Peterson, Alberto Roque, Zakia Salime, and Audra Simpson. I owe special thanks to Adriana Premat for her friendship, collegiality, and intellectual generosity. Despite the geographical distance separating us at times, she has been a constant source of support throughout the entire writing of this book manuscript, from it is original conception to the final product.

I am also thankful for the invaluable feedback provided on different chapters of this manuscript by various academic audiences: at Case Western Reserve University; Centro de Investigaciones y Estudios Superiores en Antropología Social (CIESAS-DF, Mexico); Cornell University; Duke University; Michigan State University; University of California, Davis; Universitat Rovira i Virgili (Tarragona, Spain); and Western Michigan University.

An earlier version of chapter 6, "*Turismo y Salud*," appeared in *American Ethnologist* 35(2) (2008), 259–74.

I am indebted to my parents, Delcita and Ivan Brotherton, and to my sisters, Lori, Nadine, Brigette, and Jennifer. As my sisters put it, I am the "spoilt one" and must thank my parents for what I prefer to call "indulging me," even when they were skeptical as to where all this "anthropology business" was going. Special thanks to my sister Lori, who also shares a passion for anthropology and critical theory and who visited me in the field on several occasions. She has been subjected to more discussions of social theory than I am sure she cares to admit. Her grounded advice and comments are always well received.

I would also like to gratefully acknowledge the generous financial support received for various stages of this research by the Wenner-Gren Foundation for Anthropological Research Inc., the International Development Research Centre of Canada, Social Sciences and Humanities Research Council of Canada, the Frederick W. Hilles Publication Fund at Yale University, and generous financial support from internal grants at Yale University and Michigan State University.

I would also like to acknowledge the superb editorial assistance provided by Anitra Grisales. I am also greatly appreciative of the help of Norma (Angie) Jaimez in helping to format and cross-check the manuscript.

And, of course, this book would not be possible with the support and guidance of the staff at Duke University Press, particularly Ken Wissoker, Jade Brooks, and Bonnie Perkel. I am also grateful to the two anonymous readers for their detailed reports.

Tracing the deep, furrowed lines that branched out from slightly under her nose and created a crease on either side of her mouth, María Luisa laughed apprehensively. The permanent frown of etched lines temporarily transformed.

"They appeared right at the height of the *período especial*," she remarked. These were not mere signs of age or the vain complaints of a woman of a certain age who no longer looked the way she used to, she commented. Instead, "these *cicatrices* [scars]" were the embodied proof of living through the worst years of Cuba's economic crisis of the early 1990s. Shuffling through her bag, she quickly produced her *carné de identidad* (state identification card). "This is what I looked like at the beginning of the crisis," she proudly exclaimed. The card was issued in 1988. She was thirty-five then. The face that stared back from the crumbled blue carné had little resemblance to the frail figure that sat before me.

Looking around suspiciously, she continued in a barely audible tone: "El Barba"—she rubbed her chin to indicate the beard of El Comandante, Fidel Castro—"doesn't like people to tell things the way they are. But I can't lie. People here are going through a terrible crisis." The crisis had changed everything, she lamented: "My body is still suffering from the effects of the período especial. Since then, things have never been the same."

Using her body as a diagnostic map, María Luisa walked me through her many ailments: a case of optic neuropathy in 1993, which resulted in a prolonged period of temporary blindness. She found out circuitously from a friend who had access to the international media that foreign presses were reporting severe nutritional deficiencies as the cause.[1] Only later did her doctor intimate that this was, indeed, the cause. Shortly thereafter she started experiencing flare-ups of gastritis, severe migraines, body aches, and fatigue, all of which she medicated through a combination of prescription pills. To make matters worse, she added, because the local state pharmacies were increasingly unable to fill prescriptions, even for aspirin, she was often forced to rely or impose on her friends, friends of friends, and the *bolsa negra* (black market) to fill the void.

As an accountant affiliated with the Institute of Cuban Radio and Television prior to the crisis, María Luisa had lived what she described as "a privileged existence." She had traveled to Moscow on several occasions as a student during the Soviet period. Fluent in Russian and French, she had also worked part-time as a translator, which sometimes allowed her to tour the island with foreign dignitaries. Recognized for her involvement in revolutionary activities, including her work with the Federation for Cuban Women, the government awarded her an apartment in a beautiful colonial building in the Santos Suárez neighborhood of Havana, well known for its striking architecture.

However, within Cuba's supposed new social order, everyday life was now inverted, María Luisa conceded. The frequent blackouts, crumbling local transportation system, empty pharmacies, massive lineups for the few basic necessities (those still provided), and the politics of passively watching foreigners enjoy the now-popular socialist resort island and not being able to participate were simply too much for the average person. In an exasperated tone she added that Cubans had come to expect a certain standard of living, similar to that of people in other economically developed countries: "Is this not what *la Revolución* was for?"[2]

This book charts diverse narratives, such as María Luisa's, that relate to the body and health in order to explore the Cuban government's changing policies and objectives in the primary health care sector. These narratives speak to the myriad ways in which the specter of the Soviet past and the uncertainty of the island's political future have served as potent signifiers of the nation's vulnerability, particularly as the withdrawal of Soviet aid and the magnified effects of the U.S. embargo manifest at the level of individual bodies and reverberate through the multiple spheres of quotidian life.

In 1991 the government declared, "Socialism is under siege" and formally announced the beginning of the Período Especial en Tiempos de Paz (Special period in time of peace, hereafter, período especial). The logic of everyday life in post-Soviet Cuba was radically transformed under the rubric of "wartime measures in times of peace." Operating in many ways as a "state of exception,"[3] government policies institutionalized corrective measures by creating new and refining older policies (migration laws, banking practices, employment categories, and access to basic needs and services, to name a few) as part and parcel of a general program of economic recovery and revival.[4] In 1991 Julio A. García, the former head of the Cuban Chamber of Commerce, described the Communist Party's logic behind these changes: "We have to think like capitalists but continue being socialists."[5] As implied by García's statement, the island started charting a new course for the social, political, and economic survival of the country's socialist revolution.

Over the past decade scholars and political commentators have continued to debate whether the período especial, as a transitory phase, has officially ended in light of the country's improving economic indicators in the late 1990s. Yet the rush to demarcate a beginning and an end obscures the lasting affective and corporeal dimensions of how this period was imprinted on people's bodies; in particular, how it was embodied through physical and mental ailments, palpably and materially experienced through deep senses of loss, betrayal, disillusion, and longing. The redefining of the socialist state through the lens of crisis directly influences the multifaceted ways in which individual Cubans in Cuba construct narratives about bodily and psychological health through the vagaries of social, economic, and political change.

Such narratives form an active part of people's imagination and circulate in multiple registers: real, imagined, symbolic, material, state-sponsored, and personal. They are also mobilized to variously construct notions of victimhood, social suffering, martyrdom, patriotism, resilience, resistance, and physical pain. These narratives serve as an Archimedean point for broader debates and discussions, often invested with great emotional intensity, on bodily health, the health of the nation, and the role of the political in defining both. The crisis narrative, therefore, becomes a way to discuss the complex dynamics that have historically influenced Cuban culture and shaped the construction of *cubanidad* (Cuban national identity).[6]

Based on more than a decade of field research (1998–2010) conducted in the city of Havana, this book chronicles the experiences of family physicians, everyday citizens, public health officials, and research scientists participating in the country's primary health program, central to what is known as the Programa del Médico y la Enfermera de la Familia (MEF, Family physician and nurse program).[7] This program calls for family physician-and-nurse teams to live and work in small clinics known as *consultorios* on the city block or in the rural community they serve.[8] Through an ethnographic exploration of the relationship between health policy (of which the MEF program is an example) and individual experiences, I explore two central themes.[9] First, I focus on how state policy, enacted through the government's public health campaigns, has affected individual lives and changed the relationship among citizens, government institutions, public associations, and the state. Second, I look at how the collapse of the Soviet bloc and the strengthening of the U.S. embargo are changing the relationship between socialist health policies and individual practices; specifically, I discuss how these changes have redefined the way in which state power becomes enacted through and upon individual bodies.

Combining historical, epistemological, and ethnographic modes of analyses, this book is divided into three parts. Part I explores how, in a context of growing economic scarcity in the health sector, individual citizens, who have highly medicalized understandings of their body, negotiate the role of the state in providing health and social welfare and their own personal desires to seek comprehensive health care, increasingly at their own expense. Part II takes up a historical examination of the mechanisms and practices through which power relations operate in the primary health care system. Through a discussion of various public health campaigns, with their emphasis on treating both the individual and social body, I explore the relationship between health ideology as an explicit discourse and as lived experience. Finally, part III considers how the country's shifting state policies and external global factors have interacted with each other to change the course and practice of health and medicine in the island nation.

A GENEALOGY OF INDIVIDUAL BODILY PRACTICES

The analysis presented throughout this book is informed and shaped by what I call a *genealogy of individual bodily practices*. For the purposes of this book, I define individual practices as the complex ways in which individuals communicate, improvise, enact, and revise ideology.[10] Yet the task of genealogy, according to Michel Foucault, is to expose a body totally imprinted by history.[11] Genealogy provides an empirical methodology by which to explore the truth claims individuals make regarding the knowledge they have of themselves, their bodies, and society at large, while at the same time understanding such knowledge as a relation of power.[12] By unraveling the multiple historical layers that contribute to bodily formations, both culturally and materially, a genealogy of individual bodily practices offers an analytical lens through which to examine the lived experience of bodies. This approach addresses three interrelated ethnographic and theoretical concerns.

First, it reveals how individuals embody the past in creating and re-creating the present. This makes legible how bodies operate in particular fields, or *doxas*; that is, sentient bodies are products of embodied knowledge that are shaped by historical events, unconscious beliefs, and learned behavior and values. Ultimately, this influences people's actions and thoughts. Second, my approach emphasizes that while we cannot take for granted that self-directed agency is everywhere, neither can we assume that subjects do not try to modify, manipulate, or escape the effects of those forces that construct them.[13] In this way, it draws attention to multivalent individual and group responses to the changing nature of state power. These responses are complex, blurred, and fractured and at times function in the form of pragmatic behavior, bodily reform, or the quotidian practices of routine actions.[14] Finally, a genealogy of individual bodily practices offers a theoretical lexicon to examine the sometimes contradictory and overlapping relationships among the individual practices of everyday citizens, economic reform, and state power.[15] In this way, it reworks the customary model for understanding state power as imposing itself on the subject who, weakened by its force, comes to internalize or accept its terms.[16] My approach, rather, stresses that state power "can only achieve an effective command over the entire life of a population when it becomes an integral, vital function that every individual embraces and reactivates on his or her own accord."[17] This approach, then, seeks to create a "history of the present" or "to create a history of the different modes by which, in our culture, human beings are made subjects."[18] It advocates that comprehending how bodies are being imagined and reimagined in Cuba's post-Soviet context is to treat them as a palimpsest by situating the present and its pasts side by side so that they can be seen and interpreted simultaneously.[19]

Since the revolution in 1959, many of the practices employed by the state and by individual Cubans, particularly during the período especial, have obvious continuities with the past. In this respect I argue that the revolution was in fact not revolutionary in the sense of provoking a dramatic shift in ideas and practice. Rather, I suggest that one must understand the contemporary interaction and competition among different ideological principles as the ongoing expression of years of political struggle, which has historically existed between sectors within the island's population.[20] In an attempt to address this approach, I have integrated the narratives of several of my interlocutors throughout the text as a way of presenting their personal lived experiences and accounts of historical and current events in Cuba.[21] Each personal account, I argue, represents a separate genealogy that reflects a complex web of values, ideas, and, ultimately, lived experience before and since the Cuban revolution.

Cuba's socialist revolutionary period, also known as the Período Revolucionario Socialista (1959–present), has used health as a defining characteristic of its reform. Underpinning this commitment was the notion that the health of the individual is a metaphor for that of the body politic, effectively linking the bodies of individuals to the political project of socialism and its governmental apparatuses. Since 1959 the country's socialist health ideology, in part predicated on the idea that health care is a basic human right, has been successful both at the level of ideology and in practice. This health ideology operated as a form of biopower that regulated "social life from its interior, following it, interpreting it, absorbing it, and rearticulating it."[22] These all-encompassing health campaigns effectively produced a new kind of medicalized subjectivity in Cuba, one in which a prolific network of health professionals has encouraged the citizenry to become increasingly attuned to biomedical understandings of what constitutes bodily health and physical well-being.[23] One of the results of embracing this subjectivity has been the increasing reliance on biomedical intervention and innovation. Physicians and their patients, particularly those who are ill, became much more invested in a politics of hope, whereby the power of biomedicine, infused with a millenarian quality, takes center stage as the primary therapeutic answer.[24] The socialist health care doxa has saturated people's everyday lives and mundane practices, producing state-fostered expectations and feelings of entitlement to a particular form of biomedical health care.

With the advent of the período especial, the state embarked on a new kind of biopolitical endeavor that sought to divert the moral expectations, assumptions, and entitlements of the citizenry away from the cradle-to-grave social welfare model so painstakingly cultivated over three decades to be more in line with the forces of market capitalism. The state's slow withdrawal from certain sectors in the political economy of health care demanded that individuals engage in a complex web of practices to mitigate the increasing pressures of daily life.[25] These practices, often classified as *lo informal*, depend on a network of client-based relations with individuals known as *socios* (informal partner or affiliate), or an "economy of favors."[26] These activities include, but are not limited to, the bolsa negra, which trades in goods stolen from state enterprises; involvement in legal and illegal small private businesses for profit (known as *cuenta propia* and *el bisne*); and hustling and prostitution (commonly referred to as *jineterismo*).

Under a system characterized by *sociolismo*, as opposed to *socialismo*, social relationships are no longer strictly defined by state politics or affiliations, but by personal contacts and socios framed by access to material resources like medicine, food items, and luxury goods and to specialized services, including unofficial access to health care services and supplies. Sociolismo was exacerbated by the legalization and circulation of the U.S. dollar shortly after the crisis began, a step which has effectively destabilized the state's ability to control wealth and income disparity within the population.[27] In terms of health care, people increasingly engage in lo informal to obtain foreign currency (*divisa*) or, more recently, its equivalent, *pesos convertibles*, often as proactive strategies to seek out therapeutic recourses that the state can no longer provide for. On the one hand, I argue that individual citizens with access to foreign currency are increasingly (and ironically) becoming active health consumers in a climate of ever more scarce resources. On the other, I argue that individual bodily practices reflect an expanding "therapeutic itinerary" in which individuals seek out diverse avenues, both state sponsored and informal, in biomedical, spiritual, and alternative medicine to achieve personal fulfillment of their notions of health and well-being.[28]

STATES OF CRISIS

While significant social and politico-economic changes in the country's biopolitical project have led to the proliferation of individual practices, including those in the health sector, I argue that this does not signify an outright withering of state power. The political flurry surrounding the announcement in 2006 of Castro's undisclosed health crisis best exemplifies this, albeit in the abstract. The crisis led to renewed speculation about the future of Cuba after Castro, particularly as international media outlets and political and cultural theorists alike metonymically linked the survival of the Cuban state to the aging socialist leader.[29]

This discursive imaginary of the state, however, feeds into a specific kind of moral economy that adheres to the dyadic model of the transition from the strong state to the weak state.[30] To this end, Castro's bodily health became a metaphorical battleground for the staging of a visceral politics of the withering state. From the early 1960s to the present, analysts have imagined the reified strong state in Cuba as a static entity in which the visibility of state power is often linked to a form of authoritarian governmentality. This exertion of power is enacted on decidedly nonliberal subjects, for example, through the jailing of political dissidents and the systematic surveillance and harassment of those people deemed *la lumpen*, or the underclass.[31] Contrary to this depiction, an emerging body of literature in Cuban studies has argued that ordinary Cubans have increasingly engaged in informal practices to mitigate the escalating pressures on daily life and that this development has largely weakened state power and eroded the government's political order.[32] Ethnographically, then, how can one reconcile and account for these competing state imaginaries?

To address this question, I draw a distinction between state power and state regulatory authority.[33] This differentiation "seems a more precise manner of taking on the state as an anthropological object, and . . . accounts, in some respects, for the contradiction between the expansion of unregulated activities, which seems to indicate a loss of state control, and the continuity of state power in spite of it all."[34] The very contradiction of states makes them ethnographically productive objects of analysis.[35] This book addresses state power not as a monolithic function, but as a proliferation of strategies that shape individual experiences.[36] Such an approach allows one to explore how everyday practices in the health sector culturally constitute the state as a dispersive network of multiple actors, institutions, and bureaucratic processes.

Recent studies of the state have suggested that "when practices that violate laws are accepted as the norm and have a legitimacy that is not the state's, they are often called 'informal practices.'"[37] Equally important, though, is how one theorizes an understanding of a state that actually creates spaces of informality in which such practices thrive. Moreover, through what theoretical framework can one analyze these spaces when they are used as state-sponsored economic strategies to tap into individual wealth accumulation? For example, the divestment in state-sponsored services and social welfare to private corporations speaks to Marxist theories of "accumulation through dispossession."[38] But what are the microdynamics of these marginalized or dispossessed spaces? How can these spaces also be theorized as generative or as "productivity in the margins," whereby individuals' lives are not strictly determined by an all-powerful capital or lack thereof, but are also manipulated in ways that become important for the formation of new fiscal subjects?[39] Within this analytical framework, individual bodily practices "are fundamentally linked to the state and are even essential to the very recomposition of state power in present conditions of extreme austerity."[40]

This book challenges the popular perception that lo informal, as constituted through individual bodily practices in the health sector, is a kind of Achilles heel of Cuban socialism. This belief assumes that lo informal is a subversive element percolating through and chipping away at the artifice of socialism and, in the process, exposing a linear movement toward a predetermined end: liberal capitalism and democratic politics.[41] These practices are not a political index of the demise of the state, occupying the shadows or margins of everyday life. Rather, they are an integral and vital part of the basic subsistence patterns for many Cubans. Furthermore, this is a reality the state can neither deny nor compete with. To a certain degree, individuals must rely on the informal economy to fill in the gaps that have resulted from the deterioration of government social welfare programs. Within this context, individual bodily practices that effectively integrate formal and informal economies play an important role in the maintenance of Cuba's health care system and, more generally, contribute to the daily functioning of the country's modern welfare state.[42]

STATISTICAL FETISHISM AND DOCILE BODIES

As one walks along the waterfront or tours the hospitals, schools, and monuments in the neighborhoods of Havana, one sees billboards advertising the successes of the revolution, as if, in the words of the fiction writer Cristina García, "they were selling a new brand of cigarettes."[43] Covering the sides of buildings and erected on movie-sized screens, these enormous signs contain such various aphorisms as "Millions of children in the world die of curable diseases, none of them are Cuban"; "The weapons of the Revolution are our ideas"; "We believe in socialism now more than ever before"; or "Hey Imperialist. We have absolutely no fear of you." The messages conveyed by these clever forms of political rhetoric are open to multiple interpretations. One message, deeply rooted in the demarcation between Cuba's past and present, suggests the power of "political will" to reinvent history. Another, perhaps less subtle, expresses the socialist government's anxiety over convincing the Cuban citizenry and the rest of the world that the revolutionary project is working. In the case of Cuba's primary public health system this is particularly true.

In 2000 the widely circulated Health Report of the World Health Organization (WHO) ranked the world's health care systems according to an overall index of performance and responsiveness based on, among other things, vital health statistics. The WHO Health Report ranks Cuba 39th among 191 countries surveyed, whereas the United States is ranked 37th, suggesting that there is no link between gross domestic product (or health expenditures) and health outcomes. The report's ranking of the small island nation with a socialist-based economy, rare in today's global capitalism, is of great theoretical and practical relevance.

In one respect Cuba's success in the field of health reform, most celebrated in international development circles, helps boost the egos of Cuban Communist Party officials, who find moral solace in these tangible results of years of revolutionary fervor and sacrifice. Hinging on the success of their public health reforms and corroborated by concrete health outcomes, as evidenced in their health statistics, Cuba became, as Castro made clear, "a bulwark of medicine in the Third World."[44] In this way Cuba has gained the status of a kind of antimodel for the development logic that fuels the top-down structural adjustment policies so common in contemporary Latin America and the Caribbean. Several of Cuba's best-known public health successes, such as the island's low HIV/AIDS transmission rates, low infant mortality rate, and longer life expectancies at birth, have led a vast number of scholars to conclude that even in the face of scarce material resources the country has managed to achieve First World health outcomes through strong political will.[45] This argument is an important one. For example, in many countries of Latin America and the Caribbean, structural adjustment policies, for the most part funded and implemented through international bodies such as the World Bank and the International Monetary Fund, have spelled financial ruin and deepening poverty, leaving large segments of the population without basic health care.

Nonetheless, scholars who follow this line of thinking are blinded by what I call a kind of statistical fetishism, a heightened focus on ideological models and measures of health in place of more nuanced accounts of the complex interrelationships among the individual practices of health care professionals and ordinary people, health policies, and state power.[46] Ultimately, this form of fetishism serves a specific purpose: Cuba's health care statistics provide a "model of" and a "model for" reality, to borrow the famous dictum of the anthropologist Clifford Geertz, but do not constitute a critical examination of what those numbers reflect or, more important, how they are produced. In one respect, scholars have analyzed Cuba's health statistics as models of the health of the body politic, while others have used Cuba's health statistics as models for or alternatives to the status quo in international development circles.[47]

For purely heuristic purposes, I would organize the abundant studies of Cuba's public health system in two groups: the first generally describes the relationship between the individual and the state as one characterized by "hyper-vigilant medical police" who exercise control on "over-observed and over-disciplined bodies."[48] Interpreting Cuba's public health system through the lens of the social control thesis, the studies cast the Cuban citizenry as unwitting actors in an unfolding play of disciplinary technologies.[49] This approach suggests that state health policies such as increased health surveillance of the population inevitably shape, regulate, and control people's everyday practices and experiences. The second group, hoping to breathe life into Che Guevara's original project of "exporting revolution," promotes the Cuban model for health reform on an international scale.[50] In doing so, these studies fail to address how the conditions of the Cuban revolution are materially, culturally, and historically situated.

In the end, both groups reify an uncritical statistical approach in which individuals are perceived as passive subjects of state rule; in short, individuals become a caricature of Foucault's idea of "docile bodies," bodies manipulated and controlled in the management of the population. This process is further driven by international governing bodies such as the WHO, which explicitly link global agendas to local practices and circulate health statistics as a means to rank and classify the countries of the world on a scale from developed and First World, on one extreme, to underdeveloped and Third World on the other. Cuba, when viewed through such a polarized lens, becomes an enticing case study. But what do the statistics actually reflect? More important, what light can the numbers shed on the so-called anomaly of Cuba, a country in which, to quote a popular Cuban saying, "people live like the poor, but die like the rich." I believe the answers to these questions can be found by exploring how "statistics tell stories. They are techno-representations endowed with complex political and cultural histories. . . . One should be able to analyze counting in terms of its political conse-quences, the way in which it reflects the crafting of subjectivities, the shap-ing of culture, and the construction of power—including what these figures say about surplus material and symbolic consumption in those parts of the world that think of themselves as developed."[51]

Only by examining the interrelation of economic, ideological, and geo-political discourses in the development of Cuba's contemporary public health system can one address the ways in which these discourses articulate and construct an image of a healthy nation. Specifically, one can see how Cuba's vital health statistics, as a reflection of the success of the country's socialist project, have become part of a larger web of power relations. These relations feed into the geohistorical categories of First, Second, and Third World, whereby Cuba attains the status of a celebrated anomaly: "the Third World country with First World health indicators." Embedded within this "development discourse," to borrow Arturo Escobar's (1995) terminology, Cuba's health statistics become trapped in an epistemological conundrum, one that not only discursively but also materially constructs certain realities, while simultaneously excluding others.

This book draws attention to the individuals and animate social pro-cesses, or "social life," to which these health statistics refer.[52] In it, I shift the analytical gaze away from docile bodies—individuals who are acted upon through regimens of discipline—to an account that examines how individ-uals are active subjects operating in specific sociopolitical and historical contexts. In breaking from the "avalanche of printed numbers," the analysis that unfolds in each chapter begins the important task of interrogating how Cuba's health statistics are in fact part of a broader social and political project.[53] This project has its historical roots in Cuba's socialist health ideol-ogy, in epistemological changes to their approach to public health, and in the governing of the population.

Part I

BIOPOLITICS IN THE SPECIAL PERIOD

The sculpted head of the Cuban independence fighter José Martí being refurbished in
a neighborhood of Havana for the 26th of
July celebrations. Brotherton © 2002.

THE BIOPOLITICS
OF HEALTH

In Cuba, health care is free. But when you go to the family doctor, the clinics, or the hospitals there are generally no medications, no disinfectants, no cotton, and some-times no needles. If you need to be admitted to the hospital, you have to bring your own sheets, a towel, and a fan because there is no air conditioner, or it is broken. For the most part, you have to find a way to get the medications you need if they are not available, which is often the case, even the most basic drugs, such as aspirin. But, yes, health care is free. . . . In this country, the government goes on and on about how "nobody is without access to health care from the most advanced to most basic." But, really, if it were not for the people *luchando* [struggling] you would really see what our health care system actually provides. We are the ones, *el pueblo* [the people], that make the sacrifices so Fidel can give his grandiose speeches about how wonderful our health care system is!

Marianna Díaz Rodríguez, accounting assistant,
born in Havana in 1951

Since the crumbling of the Soviet bloc in 1989, Cuba's socialist health care system has been affected by market-based reforms and the government's pursuit of a dual economy in U.S. dollars and Cuban pesos. These new economic reforms, complicated by the U.S. government's tightening of eco-nomic sanctions against Cuba, have undermined individual health by affect-ing the availability of food, medicines, and equipment.[1] For example, the term *la lucha* (the struggle) joined a legion of other terms in the early 1990s within a growing body of idiomatic phrases known as *cubanismo*, specialized terms or phrases either invented or commonly used that have taken on new meanings in the post-Soviet context. The term *la lucha* addresses the multi-ple ways in which individuals are dealing with the widening gap between their current standard of living and the formal state apparatus aimed at addressing the material well-being of the populace. Often used in response to "How are things?," "Estoy en la lucha" (I'm struggling) has become a way of describing the personal hardships of everyday life. Díaz Rodríguez, bitterly ironic, expresses her frustration with the Cuban state's increasing problems in providing adequate health and social services. Rather than focus on Cuba's health accomplishments as defined through the widely published vital health statistics, I want to critically examine the role of individual Cubans and professionals who are luchando to achieve their health care goals and who generate these statistics. This approach requires a shift from the macro- to the micropolitics of health, which necessarily moves the discussion away from an examination of the state as an entity that acts on individual bodies toward an examination of the multiple on-the-ground social processes that shape and influence Cuba's contemporary primary health care system.

MACROECONOMIC CHANGE

One of the major differences I have noticed after the *período especial* is the health situation of our country. While, generally, I think things have gotten better in terms of overall health after 1993, there have been major shortages in medicines, distribution of medicine, and basic medical supplies. However, I still maintain that health, on an individual level, is still better in the 1990s, despite the economic crisis, than in the 1980s. If you look at the basic health statistics you see that individual health has actually improved, with the average life expectancy increasing. These are indicators of the health of our country. I also strongly believe these numbers are a reflection of the work of our health care professionals and their effectiveness, despite many hardships. I think one of our strongest programs in Cuba has been the maternal-infant health program. The education for maternal and infant health care has been growing steadily over the past forty years. Our infant mortality figures nationally are seven or eight [per ten thousand live births], generally below seven. This is a reflection of the strength of our primary public health programs.

In my hospital, for example, we have the majority of necessary medicines and almost all of the antibiotics, or at the least the necessary primary materials to produce them in Cuba. We receive the primary materials mainly from Europe. However, as you know, there are some lines of antibiotics that are very expensive for us to produce. If possible, we usually get some of these medicines through donation. For example, I am treating a patient now for whom I managed to get a treatment that lasts fourteen days, and the antibiotic cost U.S. $100. Now this is just one case, but you know that such an expense for the average Cuban is impossible. However, through international dona-tions and working through *socios*, you can find solutions.

Javier Valdéz, Director of Primary Health Care Research in
Plaza of the Revolution City Hospital, born in Havana in 1963

As Valdéz notes, physicians, like individual citizens, are not immune to the struggles of everyday life in the período especial, and many of the strategies and tactics health professionals employ, such as working through socios and transnational connections, suggest that the revolutionary work ethic is now merged with a pragmatic engagement in the informal economy. With the advent of the período especial in the early 1990s, the structural reforms implemented in the face of mounting macroeconomic changes directly af-fected the political economy of the health sector. Buffered for over three decades by highly favorable terms of trade with the former Soviet Union and the countries of the Council for Mutual Economic Assistance, or COMECON, that had been major catalysts in the country's social development, Cuba was now faced with a severe economic crisis.[2] This crisis was triggered and compounded by Cuba's nearly complete dependence on the Soviet Union and by the economic embargo the U.S. government had imposed on Cuba more than forty years earlier. Between 1984 and 1989, 77 percent of Cuba's export trade was attributable to sugar, and nearly 70 percent of its import–export trade was with a single country, the Soviet Union.[3] As a result of the Soviet collapse and the U.S. embargo, between 1989 and 1993 the country's gross domestic product fell 35 percent, and exports declined by 75 percent.[4]

In the aftermath of the Soviet withdrawal from Cuba a complicating fac-tor was the U.S. government's tightening of economic sanctions against Cuba in the 1990s. The so-called Torricelli-Graham Act of 1992,[5] also known as the Cuban Democracy Act, and then the Helms-Burton bill[6] of 1996 made clear that the intent of U.S. foreign policy toward Cuba was to foster the socialist government's defeat through what U.S. Sen. Jesse Helms called "a final push over the brink."[7] In late December 1997 Vice President Carlos Lage of Cuba estimated that the U.S. embargo and other political factors cost the Cuban economy U.S. $800 million a year, equivalent to about 20 percent of Cuba's current import bill.[8] The economic crisis threatened the survival of the Cuban revolution, particularly in regard to its continued commitment to basic human needs. However, the economic crisis also undermined health by affecting the availability of food, medicines, and equipment, and this subsequently challenged the developments achieved in public health.[9]

The MINSAP reports that between 1989 and 1993 the total expenditures in hard currency in the health sector went from U.S. $227 million to $56 million. In 1990 the country imported approximately U.S. $55 million in medical and pharmaceutical products, while by 1996 this figure had dropped to U.S. $18 million, a decrease of around 67 percent. An agricultural and nutritional crisis also affected the health of the population, as a critical shortage of petroleum and the growing scarcity of replacement parts for antiquated Soviet technology brought the agricultural industry to a grinding halt in the early 1990s. Food production plummeted.

An often-cited case of the nutritional crisis was the outbreak in 1993 of an epidemic of neuropathy, which caused thousands of people to temporarily lose their vision (see introduction). This outbreak was due in part to nutritional deficiencies resulting from the dropping per-capita daily food consumption, which fell from 3,100 calories in 1989 to fewer than 1,800 in 1993.[10] In the early 1990s a decline in medical and pharmaceutical imports seriously compromised many physicians' treatment options. As a result of a reduction in therapeutic options, increasing numbers of nonfunctioning medical devices, and equipment shortages in the country's hospitals, the capacity of secondary and tertiary institutions to undertake high-technology procedures decreased markedly. For instance, the political scientist Thad Dunning (2001) studied the effects of the período especial on the ability of hospitals in the city of Santiago de Cuba to perform major surgeries. He found that between 1989 and 2000 the number of surgeries decreased by 46 percent in selected hospitals. Dunning hypothesized that this trend was reflective of the overall decrease in high-tech procedures being performed in other hospitals throughout the country.

The withdrawal of Soviet aid and the deleterious effects of the U.S. *bloqueo* have been linked to such negative trends as massive shortages in pharmaceutical drugs and medical supplies.[11] In 1997 the American Association for World Health sponsored a study of the impact of the embargo on health and nutrition in Cuba. The study suggested that while 1,297 medications were available in Cuba in 1991, physicians in 1997 had access to only about 889 of them, many of which were available only intermittently.[12] The strengthening of the embargo in the mid-1990s resulted in drastic changes in Cuba's ability to trade with foreign countries. Despite the U.S. Department of State's contention that the embargo against Cuba did not prohibit U.S. companies and their subsidiaries from selling medicines and medical supplies to the Cuban people, the same report failed to address the almost insuperable bureaucratic barriers imposed by U.S. legislation.[13] Laws imposed by the U.S. government, which require multiple levels of bureaucratic approval to export goods to Cuba, result in inordinate delays, increased costs, and limited access to some of the most important medicines and medical products. The added expense of imports for public health due to the embargo cost the Cuban government an estimated U.S. $45 million in 1993.[14] From this perspective, the bureaucratic obstacles put in place by the U.S. government amount to a de facto embargo on important medicines and medical supplies.[15]

Strangely, despite the significant macroeconomic changes affecting Cuba's health sector, the country's basic health indicators continued to increase over the course of the período especial. For example, between 1990 and 2001 the infant mortality rate declined from approximately 11 to 6 deaths per 1,000 live births, and life expectancy improved slightly between 1990 and 2001, from 75.22 to 76.3. Given this seeming paradox in Cuba's health care system, I reiterate Dunning's question: "How did the health-care system, which was deeply compromised by economic contraction, nonetheless produce an improvement of basic health indicators?" (2001, 1). Dunning provides one of the most compelling attempts to explain health care outcomes by examining patterns of resource allocations in the context of state spending and Cuba's dual monetary economy. He argues that from 1989 to 1999, the quantitative success in basic health indicators can be attributed to the state's concentration on resources for "health care within the internal, Cuban-peso dominated sector" and "the expansion of the family doctor system, primary care and other low-tech but human-capital intensive investments" (2001, 1). This idea resonates with the opinions of several health professionals I interviewed, who suggested that Cuba's vital health statistics, the infant mortality rate being the most widely referenced, was an embodiment of their hard work and daily sacrifices. However, while persuasive, this argument has several limitations. The focus on resource allocation in the form of human capital is one aspect of a much more complex series of processes. The MEF program is dependent on salaried family physicians working within the peso economy, who are essentially clinicians and who in most cases have very little equipment or medicine at their disposal. The MEF physicians' primary goals are health promotion and disease prevention, and their role is to identify health problems that can be referred to more specialized institutions. In this respect, the expansion of the MEF program at best played an influential role in maintaining Cuba's basic primary health statistics, if only because of these physicians' efforts to mobilize communities around health education (for example, the education campaigns geared toward infant and maternal health).

The relationship between the increasing role of medical intervention (or between the level of expenditures in health care) and mortality and morbidity rates are questionable.[16] Vital health statistics are influenced by several factors, including, but not limited to, nutrition, sanitation, the general standard of living, and medical care.[17] In this respect, an analysis of Cuba's resource allocation and funding patterns neglects other important factors that occurred in Cuba from 1989 until the present, namely, the role of individual Cubans in negotiating their own health and well-being. Rather than falling prey to statistical fetishism or an analysis of the achievements of the health sector as if they existed in a vacuum, one must look beyond the raw numbers achieved in Cuba's population health profile. The período especial called into question the moral legitimacy of the state, and it had indelible social and political consequences for both the revolutionary government and the popular support citizens and health professionals gave it.

One area among many that could considerably influence the health sector was the everyday practices of individual Cubans who, during the same period, were ingeniously maneuvering through other sectors of the economy that were undergoing state reform; for example, the legalized circulation of dollars, changes in U.S. legislation allowing remittances to be sent to the island, the opening of U.S.-dollar stores, the expansion of pharmacies and international clinics that catered to tourists and Cubans alike, and changes in laws allowing Cubans who lived abroad, especially Cuban Americans, to visit their friends and families on the island.[18] Within this broader context it becomes apparent that the very fabric of Cuban society, including the practice of medicine, was undergoing broad social and political changes.

In the following vignettes, I examine the various ways in which individual Cubans and primary health care physicians are negotiating macroeconomic changes in their everyday lives. I present the experiences of individuals in their designated health area (*área de salud*) that is attended to by MEF

Biopolitics in the Special Period

physician-and-nurse teams stationed in small clinics known as *consultorios del médico de la familia.* The vignettes reflect a growing reality among a number of people whose access, or lack thereof, to foreign currency has shaped their everyday experiences in the city of Havana.

CONSULTORIO SAN LÁZARO

Living in a small two-bedroom apartment with her mother, husband, and son in a rundown area of central Havana, Isabella Esparza discussed how her daily struggles with the primary health care system resulted from the massive changes brought about by recent macroeconomic problems and the widespread corruption that had ensued. Her mother, Adelfa Castillo Esparza, was paralyzed on the left side of her body and in need of regular checkups and medication. Castillo was unable to walk, so the family physician had to visit her house on his local afternoon rounds. As Esparza stated,

> I can't take my mother to the consultorio because she cannot walk, and to carry her there I have to bring the wheelchair down three flights of stairs. Then, I would have to carry my mother down. Of course, for whatever emergency, I call the consultorio. Sometimes they come. Other times, they tell me they cannot come. More often than not, they do not actually come. When they arrive, they often do not have a stethoscope or equipment to take blood pressure. It is like, why come then? I understand, though, there is no motivation to do the work they are supposed to do. Imagine, they make four hundred pesos per month. That is about twenty dollars in *divisa*, which is not enough to buy anything. The médicos work with nothing. The conditions they work in are horrendous. They often do not have papers to write out prescriptions, worse yet, they know the drugs are not available, and so they cannot solve the most basic problems that physicians should be able to solve. I have never solved any of my mother's health problems at the médico de la familia. The médicos are just like us; they have to take the *camello* [a long bus mounted on a flatbed truck] and make a living. There is no incentive to go door to door anymore.
>
> If it wasn't for my friend Robercito, who works at one of the major hospitals and basically works out everything, you know, from behind—that is how things work now—what would I do with my mother? My aunt in Miami is really the one who sends my mom the money to buy the foods for her special diet, and the drugs and sterilized needles I need to inject her medication. I

have learned to administer the drugs myself. That is what things have come to these days. Do you understand me? I think when the médico de la familia was started up, it was able to do its job because at that time the equipment for sterilization and the basic medical tools were readily available for physicians to do their jobs effectively. However, you have to remember in 1984, when the program started, there was not an economic crisis. The year the economic crisis began in 1990, things started to fall apart. After the período especial, the médico de la familia couldn't do injections because there were no sterilized needles; there was no alcohol for disinfection; if you needed cotton or bandages you had to bring your own. Slowly, the médico de la familia no longer solves our problems.

Esparza's narrative reflects the concerns of several of the citizens I interviewed, including the family physicians themselves. As several family doctors made clear, they are forced to work with severe limitations and, at times, feel that their role is more that of a social worker than a health care provider. As one physician in Esparza's neighborhood said, "People do not respect us like they did before. Now, we cannot solve even the most basic problems. I have to look into patients' eyes and say, 'Sorry, I do not have needles,' or 'Maybe you can get a relative who lives abroad to send you this certain kind of medication.' For me, these are hard things to say. Basically, you have to learn to invent something out of nothing." This physician, however, was blunter than several other physicians I interviewed, who evaded the topic by choosing to use oblique phrases like, "We make do" or "Things are tough, but Cubans are notoriously inventive."

Rather than passively accept the massive shortages of important medications and supplies, however, Esparza was very methodological in her ability to ensure her mother's health care. Having given up her job as a factory worker several years earlier to take care of her mother full-time, Esparza has been fastidious in making contacts at various institutions and pharmacies in order to help facilitate her mother's care. Esparza had created a socio in strategic places. She would take coffee to a local pharmacist, who in return would save her the essential drugs that she needed, when available, to be purchased in Cuban pesos. As an anthropologist, I was not exempt from being part of Esparza's network of contacts. She often called on me to purchase prescription drugs at international pharmacies by using my passport (see chapter 6). In addition, when I was in Canada Esparza managed to

Biopolitics in the Special Period

write me through her son's university e-mail address, asking me to bring a range of medicines and medical supplies, several of which I was unable to obtain without a prescription. Instead of consulting with her designated family doctor for regular checkups, as stipulated in the MEF program, Esparza would call her friend, a physician in a large hospital in the city center, and get him to attend to her mother personally.

Subsidized peso taxis, historically designated for taking patients to the hospital for their health appointments, were now involved in the thriving private informal economy and operated as *boteros* (illegal taxis that charge ten to twenty pesos to go between specific locations), so Esparza relied strictly on tourist taxis that charged in U.S. dollars to pick her and her mother up from her house, take them to the hospital, and then drop them back at home. For a small tip (*propina*), the tourist taxi drivers would often help her mother up and down the stairs of her apartment building. Dependent on the monthly remittance from her aunt in Miami, who sent anywhere from eighty to one hundred dollars a month, Esparza washed clothes and cleaned apartments for people in her building to earn extra money to meet her mother's health care needs. Esparza's husband, a *militante* (Communist Party member) and a former member of the Fuerzas Armadas Revolucionarias (FAR), was unhappy that his wife was working, essentially as a maid, and constantly reminded her that the government had worked years to overcome such class-based inequalities.

Frustrated, Esparza argued that despite her informal activities she was still a *revolucionaria*, but her mother's health came before politics. On the various occasions that I spoke with Esparza, she would always respond to my standard greeting, "How are you?" with her characteristic phrase, "I am still here, my dear, luchando." Esparza's son was in his last year of university and was studying immunology. Legally, he could not work while registered in school, and he, too, was dependent on the remittances sent from Miami to buy his school clothes, books, and meals at school. The end of every month, when Esparza's son picked up the Western Union money transfer from her aunt in Miami, was always fraught with tension for Esparza. As she remarked, her son demanded more and more money to purchase brand-name clothes and shoes, now sold at the dollar stores (*shopin*). While critical of her son for trying to "live like a capitalist," Esparza was upset that the state was selling overpriced consumer goods in U.S. dollars to a population that was, for the most part, officially paid in Cuban pesos. As she said, the state has created unreasonable and in many cases unobtainable desires among young people. Esparza remarked that young people, in addition to a growing number of adults, wanted the consumer goods that were increasingly visible in contemporary Cuban society. "In the 1970s and 1980s," she said, "everybody basically had the same kinds of things with little variation. People had Soviet-style boots, the same kind of pants and shirts, and so on. But now, we have kids with brand-name clothes sent from their relatives abroad and American movies every weekend on TV, with the latest stuff. These things have an influence on el pueblo."

Esparza's husband, Ramón Crespo, a fifty-five-year-old retired military lieutenant, despite his assertion that he did not want to be formally interviewed because he did not have much experience with the health care system, often participated indirectly by offering a sort of armchair commentary while, on one occasion, he sat watching a baseball game on television. Asking to speak to me one day, Crespo offered me a glass of aged whiskey, sat down with me, and explained why people in general, particularly young people, should value *la Revolución*. Crespo, who had no relatives living outside of Cuba—something he was proud of—had great disdain for his wife's extended family that had fled Cuba to the United States in the early 1960s and often referred to his wife's relatives in Miami as the *gusanera* (worms).[19] Crespo made it clear that the remittances his wife's aunt sent were strictly for his mother-in-law's health care needs, and he saw none of that money. In fact, he refused to allow his wife's family to come to his home when they visited from the United States, and he refused even to greet them on the phone when they called. Crespo argued that although the Cuban government was going through a hard time, in recent years things were slowly changing for the better.

Unable to live on his state pension, Crespo, with the help of the FAR, had recently returned to work as a manager of a distribution warehouse for a popular chain of state-run stores. His company regularly awarded him vouchers—material incentives to reward him for his good work. The vouchers could be redeemed in dollar shops and allowed him to purchase electronic goods, bedroom furniture, and, more recently, a new washing machine, all for Cuban pesos at one-for-one U.S.-dollar prices. For example, his new washing machine, valued at two hundred dollars, was purchased with a voucher for two hundred Cuban pesos (ten dollars). The government cared, he argued, for those who worked well and were dedicated *revolucionarios*.

Crespo was involved in several of the mass organizations and regularly participated in voluntary labor campaigns. Throughout the years, the local Comité de Defensa de la Revolución had presented him with various medals and certificates of accomplishment for his revolutionary activities. The problem with the health care system, Crespo noted, was the deteriorating values of health professionals, who were tempted by desires for material wealth and had fallen into the trap of making money on the side through informal practices.

Esparza, whom I interviewed on several occasions without her husband present, felt that her husband was out of touch with the reality of el pueblo. She said the state was taking care of select people, especially Communist Party members and people in the military. However, as she said, while she was fortunate to have some material luxuries provided through her husband's job, the rest of el pueblo was left to fend for itself. In prerevolutionary times, Esparza remarked, her mother was an associate of the Spanish insurance scheme known as *mutualistas* (see chapter 3).

> In those days, my mother was attended to by La Covadonga Hospital, which la Revolución renamed Salvador Allende Hospital after the assassinated Chilean president of the same name. I recall when I was six or seven my mother had a uterine infection and was treated there. Everything was beautiful and the staff provided you with everything, including well-cooked meals and clean linen. I am not a racist, but blacks were not allowed in specific sections of the La Covadonga, and there were certain standards of hygiene. Now, if you go to the same hospital you need to bring a bottle of bleach to clean the floor and you see roaches everywhere. My mother went there two years ago and the service was horrible! I would never go back.[20]

Esparza's discussion reflects her critical stance on the state's current inability to provide equitable social and health welfare; however, she is also nostalgic and optimistic about the semiprivatized health care system that existed in the prerevolutionary period, in which, as she stated, "You got what you paid for."

Esparza's and her husband's experiences reflect the challenges faced by individual citizens in the context of massive social and economic changes. Esparza is torn between her commitment to la Revolución and her firsthand experiences with a health care system that is rife with massive shortages and that has required her to become increasingly vigilant in working through socios to secure services and resources in a system overrun by informal practices. However, although Crespo has less direct experience with the health care system, his narrative is equally important. The ideas and values he discusses reflect sectors of the Cuban population that, despite tremendous social upheaval, hold steadfast to the objectives of la Revolución and see the recent turn of events as a temporary product of the effects of U.S. influence—an influence, Crespo argues, facilitated by the return of Cubans living abroad and the money they send to promote capitalist values in an attempt to subtly undermine la Revolución.

CONSULTORIO LAS VEGAS

María Menendez, a family physician in her late thirties working in a neighborhood in the municipality of Plaza of the Revolution, was assigned to a relatively affluent área de salud (health area). Popularly known as Las Vegas, Menendez's área de salud was made up of about six hundred people, the majority of whom were involved either directly or indirectly with the tourist economy. Menendez remarked that a large percentage of her patients have family members living abroad, which made her job easier. As she stated, "Cuban people always have a socio who can resolve their problems in one way or another, so really my job is to identify the problem and let them work to find the solution. Really, that is all I can do." I was in a privileged position for carrying out research in the consultorio Las Vegas because I lived in close proximity to many of Menendez's patients and encountered them daily in the market, at the local dollar store, or, more often than not, buying prized food items from the same vendors in the private informal economy.

The neighborhood of Las Vegas had a high concentration of people with access to U.S. dollars, perhaps because it is was home to foreigners who live in state-licensed housing; it also had many wealthy apartment owners who earned as much as four hundred to six hundred dollars a month renting out their homes. For these reasons the area was a prime target of various vendors in the private informal economy. A regular topic of discussion in Las Vegas was the availability of various foods and medicines from informal contacts recommended by word of mouth to different clientele. In the building where I lived, for instance, several of my neighbors had put vendors at ease in my presence by informing them that *"está en confianza"* (he can be trusted). Although I was a stranger and a foreigner, they knew I was not going to report them to the authorities.

Biopolitics in the Special Period

As word spread to other vendors in the area, I ended up purchasing the majority of the food I consumed at my front door, from men and women selling everything from first-grade beef, lobster, and shrimp to milk powder, cheese, and eggs. All of these products were sold at prices considerably cheaper than at the local dollar stores, although in many instances the items being sold, for example, state-regulated lobster and beef, would bring jail sentences should the vendor be caught. At first I was uncomfortable making these transactions, but I quickly got over any conflicts of conscience, especially seeing that the local shopin carried a selection of liver, gizzards, chicken backs and legs, canned goods, milk, beverages (alcoholic and otherwise), and other packaged consumer goods that were often overpriced and, according to the labels, already expired. The other option, the diplomatic store (*diplotiendas*), was a considerable distance away, and the prices there were often exorbitant. While I was less concerned with purchasing medicine and medical supplies, as a *persona de confianza* I quickly tapped into the reality that Las Vegas was also home to a large-scale informal economy of people selling *pastillas* (pills), which were often stolen from the local pharmacies or were sent from abroad in their original packaging. These medications were usually sold per pastilla, with the foreign-produced drugs and nongeneric brands being sold at significantly higher prices.[21]

In one local pharmacy, a forty-five-year-old woman I interviewed, Margarita Pérez, who lived in my building, tried to buy vitamins without the required prescription and was told they were sold out. However, the pharmacist added, there was another brand of vitamins available for ten pesos, if she was interested. Pérez, knowing full well that the normally subsidized vitamins and drugs, which rarely cost more than one to two pesos, were being appreciably hiked in price, decided it was the best way for the pharmacist to turn a blind eye to the fact that she had no prescription. I regularly bought cold and flu medicine and antihistamines, several of which theoretically needed prescriptions, directly from the peso pharmacies. I often simply asked for what I wanted and, if asked for a prescription, made up some excuse about not going to the doctor; I usually paid anywhere from ten to forty pesos, depending on the pharmacist.

This routine, Pérez claimed, was common. However, she argued, it also undermined centrally planned resource distribution. As people seek out drugs, medical supplies, and other health-related supplies and services in other health areas, the local pharmacies, clinics, and hospitals find themselves burdened with heavy caseloads and dwindling supplies that are often funneled into black market networks and not to those individuals who follow official channels. Pérez later stated, "I do not understand how the state can say drugs are not available when some of these very drugs are made in Cuba. It is like you go to the local pharmacy with the prescription, and they say sorry, we do not have that in stock. Then you walk one block and people are selling the very same drugs, made in Cuba, on the street! Where are they getting the drugs? You understand, people are stealing the stuff and everybody knows."

Several of the individuals I interviewed in Menendez's área de salud were regularly both buyers and sellers of pharmaceutical products and medical equipment. Often bringing the doctor *regalitos* (little presents), many of these patients stressed that the gifts were tokens of appreciation because Menendez often prescribed medicines that she knew were not available in local Cuban pharmacies—at least, not for sale in pesos. Meybol Tomas, a sixty-five-year-old diabetic who lived in Menendez's área de salud, for example, made frequent visits to consultorio Las Vegas with her foreign-purchased medications. Tomas wanted Menendez to translate the complicated instructions and warnings on the package from English into Spanish. Furthermore, she wanted Menendez to advise her on the other medications her overzealous relatives in Miami had sent her, which, they indicated, "were also good for diabetes." Tomas, unlike many of the other residents I interviewed for this book, was cautious before taking too many drugs based on word-of-mouth advice. Menendez used these visits to stress the importance of diet and exercise in Tomas's daily routines. As Menendez indicated, "My consultorio is packed, and it is often to give people advice on how to use the drugs they already have in their possession. I always warn them of the dangers of self-medicating, but historically, Cubans have been known for their obsession with taking pills for everything."

Many of the physicians were well aware of the proliferation of informal trading in pharmaceutical drugs and medical supplies. This situation, they noted, resulted in increased self-diagnosis and self-medication. For example, a large percentage of the individuals I interviewed bought their medications without a medical prescription, directly from the black market (*bolsa negra*), many without consulting a family physician. This is not to suggest, however, that this process of self-diagnosis and self-medication does not have serious consequences. For example, the dangerous misuse of antibiotics or the reality that a serious medical problem may go undetected and untreated was troubling. Surprisingly, though, many of the interviewees stated that they felt comfortable with this way of doing things and saw themselves as active consumers in addressing their individual and family health needs. The family physicians of many of these people were used as a means to an end in a complex network of contacts, often reduced to writing prescriptions and advising people on the correct usage of various medications.

Several of the physicians also used consultations to admonish their patients for naively self-medicating without the physician's direct instructions. The physician's admonishments, for the most part, fell on deaf ears, as individuals increasingly claim control of their own health care needs. For instance, the health expenses of those people I interviewed who had access to U.S. dollars ranged from ten to eighty dollars per month for the purchase of medication, vitamins, and other health-related products. Those individuals who tended to spend more money on health care expenses also tended to suffer from chronic illnesses such as asthma, diabetes, or cardiovascular-related problems. These individual health care expenses are significant when put in the context of the average official state salary of a Cuban, which in 2001 was approximately 180 to 200 Cuban pesos per month ($8 to $10). Individuals I interviewed made it clear that they were increasingly forced to seek out U.S. dollars, whether through remittances or the informal economy, to meet individual and family health care expenses. This practice is supported by national studies of Cubans in the diaspora that examined their intended purposes for sending remittances to the island. They were found to be, in declining order of importance, health care needs, consumer goods purchases, home improvements, and small-scale business ventures.[22]

It would be unfair to suggest that individual Cubans do not have health care options in the Cuban peso economy and must instead resort to private informal activities. To lose sight of some of the health care system's achievements would be misleading. One woman I interviewed, Eva Castañeda, a fifty-four-year-old woman who lived in a remote rural area an hour outside of Havana, had undergone a heart-valve replacement two years earlier. Having no access to U.S. dollars, she expressed little interest in politics and stated that, despite being poor, she still had access to health care, from the most basic to the most advanced. She added, "The kind of surgery I got would have cost nearly $20,000 in the States." She mentioned this several times, repeating what her doctors had told her at the Cardiology Surgical Hospital in Havana, where her surgery was performed. While relatively apathetic toward la Revolución, she openly criticized the U.S. government and was convinced—on the basis of images from documentaries, frequent on Cuban television, that feature the U.S. government's problems with drugs, racism, illiteracy, and health care—that a person like her was better off in Cuba. In the more than one hundred interviews I carried out in various municipalities, all the individuals expressed respect and admiration for a health care system that did not have barriers based on gender, race, income level, occupational status, religious affiliation, or sexual orientation. What upset people was the disintegration of the quality of services provided, including the sporadic availability of important drugs and medical supplies, compounded by long waits and increasingly unsympathetic health professionals.

My personal experiences of Cuba's local health care system, as opposed to an international clinic, provides a good example of the severity of complaints being expressed by individual citizens. One evening, suffering from a severe allergic reaction to a strange mildew that emerged from an old Russian air conditioner in my bedroom, I arrived in the emergency room at the local Calixto Garcia Hospital and went directly to the ear, nose, and throat specialist. Despite the insistence of a friend who had accompanied me that I invent a more Spanish-sounding name so that, as a foreigner, I would not be charged the U.S. consultation fee, I resisted. The Cuban government offered free medical and dental assistance to students who are classified as temporary foreign residents, which I was at the time. Clearly, the deteriorating appearance of the hospital and the dismal-looking examination room paled in comparison to the ultra modern U.S dollar international clinics. Appearances aside, the specialist attending me conducted the physical exam with great care, writing extensive notes on a piece of scrap paper and determined that I had inflamed sinuses. She prescribed antihistamine nasal drops and sent me on my way. I picked up the medication, manufactured in Cuba, at the hospital pharmacy for seventy-five *centavos* (less than five U.S. cents) and left the hospital less than fifteen minutes after entering. My symptoms were gone within three days.

While my Cuban friend profusely apologized for the conditions of the hospitals and recommended that I go to the international clinic for more personalized and friendly attention, I told him I could only dream of being attended to in an emergency room in a hospital or even a doctor's office in Canada in such record time. While my experience is anecdotal, it is nonetheless important to stress that, despite some of the changes brought about by the período especial, the health care infrastructure and human resources remain in place. Furthermore, those individuals with no access to U.S. dollars are not simply left without basic health services. The circulation of foreign currency, however, has meant that individuals who have access to dollars can now strategically exploit the two-tiered health care systems: one in dollars and the other in pesos.

PRAGMATIC STRATEGIES AND
NEW AND OLD SUBJECTIVITIES

In this period of the building of socialism, we can see the *hombre nuevo* [new man] being born. **Ernesto "Che" Guevara,** *Man and Socialism*

The Cuban ethnologist Miguel Barnet has recently bemoaned the arrival of a "new type of Cuban . . . a sort of anachronism," resulting in people "who want to be capitalists but don't know what a capitalist is. [They] want to imitate the Cuban of the 1940s and 1950s, but with the achievements of socialism" (1995, 30). Barnet's pronouncement is clear: the birth of this hombre nuevo in Cuba's current social and political milieu is a step backward. I argue the opposite. The emergence of these new subjectivities, what I call *pragmatic subjectivities*, is expressed by individuals negotiating and, in some cases, manipulating the very contradictions of the state itself. In this respect, the recent economic crisis has served as a catalyst for the emergence of new subjectivities and the reemergence of old ones in the island's changing social and political landscape. Despite this shifting terrain, the Cuban government has been adamantly opposed to describing the current sociopolitical climate in the country as late socialism, let alone as postsocialist.

The increasing reliance on social relations, or *sociolismo*, has redefined and challenged the historic relationship between the individual, the family, and the state. Individual citizens forging social relationships based on material interests have reformulated some of the informal values of Cuba's prerevolutionary past, as Barnet notes above, and have combined them with a pragmatic twist to confront the new challenges of everyday life. The rise of such pragmatic subjectivities, maneuvering through the vicissitudes of the state's crumbling welfare system, are shaped by gender, local classifications of race, and local and translational ties to relatives and friends, both on and off the island. They are also, most certainly, historical narratives of the intimate and corporeal ways in which the past is embodied and rearticulated in the present.

Prior to 1989, 94 percent of the workforce in Cuba was employed in state enterprises; workers were divided into about twenty salary categories with fixed remuneration matched by subsidized consumer goods. By 1996 the percentage had shrunk to 78, and a significant portion of the population had moved into the private, mixed, and cooperative sectors. Relatively high amounts of market-based wealth and power began to be concentrated in the hands of a small group of people, especially in economically expanding regions such as those catering to tourists. Cuba's economy of remittances also contributed notably to the growing income disparity among groups in the population.[23] Official figures estimate that remittances increased from a reported fifty million dollars in 1990 to over nine hundred million in 2005, representing a large infusion of foreign currency circulating in the hands of individual Cubans during the período especial.[24]

In spite of the government's assurances that socialism was still intact, the unintended consequences of the new reforms in the health sector and beyond have created a situation wherein Cubans without regular access to dollars now look with envy at the minority, who can enjoy the fruits of the dollar economy.[25] The reality created by this situation leaves many individuals bitter, especially those who have dedicated their lives to la Revolución and have now witnessed the removal of barriers to the development of economic inequality. Such disparities have threatened to resurrect the social divisions between different ethnic groups in Cuba. Cubans of color are not only less likely to have relatives who have emigrated, a source of dollars through remittances, but are also, owing to a resurgence of racial discrimination and prejudice, less likely to be hired in many of the joint-venture businesses operating in Cuba, backed by foreign investors.[26]

It would be impossible to discuss these events without addressing the way in which la lucha of everyday life is increasingly and disproportionately gendered. As the state slowly receded as the sole provider of the political economy of health care, women have been increasingly forced to fill this role in their homes. Historically, state public health campaigns of the past, infused with paternalist language, comforted expectant mothers and their families with phrases such as "For This Child That Is To Be Born. We are all caregivers."[27] At that time the message was clear. The state would assume the primary responsibility for the welfare of the citizenry as a right to which they were guaranteed. The moral character of past state campaigns carries considerably less material and rhetorical authority in the present day, particularly as women are forced to navigate formal and informal networks in pursuit of their families' basic needs. The gendering of la lucha speaks to the limitations of the socialist government's policies concerning gender equality in the workplace and at home. Historically, the vestiges of entrenched gendered practices and gender inequality in Cuban society were at the forefront of the country's mandate for socioeconomic development. While the country made considerable headway in ameliorating many of these inequalities, many undoubtedly remained, if only under the radar.[28] They are now more pronounced and solidified.

The population, which had grown accustomed to the privileges provided by the cradle-to-grave health and social welfare system, which was intimately tied to social and economic equality, is now witnessing a chipping away of the foundations of that system. As a result, individuals are becoming active in addressing and administering their own health care needs and, despite the state's disapproval of these practices, they pragmatically rationalize their actions by drawing on the state's socialist discourse of access to health care as a basic human right. People view themselves as filling in the gaps created between the state's rhetoric of health and social welfare and its inability to actually provide these services. In many instances, *lo informal* in the health sector, as constituted through individual bodily practices, operates in parallel with the objectives of the state's health care programs: for example, in seeking necessary medications and medical supplies through remittances and socios. In other instances, individuals undermine the institutions of the state by siphoning limited resources away from official channels to informal networks, which leads to increases in self-medication and autonomous practices.

The state's withdrawal from various sectors of the economy, not simply health care, has encouraged the development of informal practices and alternative forms of social networking, which are gradually replacing the state as the sole means of addressing the problems of everyday life.[29] These sinuous ties that weave diverse groups of people together, crosscutting personal, institutional, familial, state-sponsored, and private spheres, constitute the micropolitics of health. They have become part and parcel of the so-called normal functioning of Cuba's socialist health care system. In recent years Castro's pronouncement that "socialism is under siege" and his calls for the population to luchar, have been effective in the health sector, although the results have not unfolded in a teleological fashion. It has become increasingly difficult to disentangle practice from ideology as individuals, physicians, and health officials juggle multiple subjectivities in the pursuit of positive health outcomes. While it is self-evident that many individuals luchan for their own bodily health and physical well-being and for those of their family members, what is less evident is the way in which these practices contribute to the perception that Cuba's primary health care system is a success.

Biopolitics in the Special Period

EXPANDING THERAPEUTIC ITINERARIES

At the very beginning of my formal research in Cuba in July 2000 I rented a small apartment in a quiet residential area of Havana. The owner of the apartment, Trinidad López, a sixty-year-old retired nurse, was eager to rent to me, although she did not have a state license to legally rent to foreigners. Hoping to avoid paying the high rental tax to the state, she explained to her inquisitive neighbors that I was her *sobrino* (nephew) from the countryside. Packing up a few of her things, she left me a set of keys and instructed me not to open the heavily barred front door to strangers. In the event that I absolutely had to open the door, for instance, to pay the electricity or water bill brought by the door-to-door state collectors, she told me to speak as little as possible and direct the collectors to her neighbor's apartment. Her neighbor, whose outdoor patio was adjacent to my own, was aware that I was a foreigner, despite López's claims that I was related to her. Her neighbor went along with the act and politely turned a blind eye to the holes in her story.

As if to test López's explicit instructions not to open the front door, her neighbor and persistent friends always came knocking in hopes of getting her advice or a chance to discuss the eight-foot Santería altar built into the closet of my bedroom. The altar, always full of offerings and holding over fifteen round ceramic jars, each representing a particular *orisha* (syncretic Yoruba-Catholic saint), required frequent propitiation and maintenance. While I had initially thought of the ritual objects in my closet as not being relevant to my research into the primary health care system, it was obvious from the visitors to my apartment, who often gave detailed explanations of what they were hoping to obtain by consulting with López, that, for them, issues of health and well-being were intimately interconnected with spiritual and material well-being. It was not until several weeks later, when I acquired my state research visa and moved into a new apartment building that was registered with the state housing authorities, that López's altar in the closet took on greater meaning. Again, I saw people coming in and out of my new building to consult with one of my neighbors, Angela Ulloa, a *santera*, or practitioner of Santería, to solve both health-related and spiritual problems.

MAMÁ OCHÚN

I met Angela Ulloa in an unconventional manner.[1] One day, as she was washing sheets on her back terrace, which was parallel to my own, we struck up a conversation on the nuisance of the people selling black market goods at our doors. An older woman, Ulloa was vivacious and used crude body language to express her points, often punctuating her rough street Spanish with English phrases for my benefit. She was born in Santiago de Cuba in 1938 and in 1960 moved to Havana with her husband, who was a former rebel fighter in the M-26-7 (the 26th of July Movement), also known as a *combatiente*. The revolutionary government had awarded Ulloa and her husband an apartment in the fashionable Havana municipality of El Vedado, one of the many apartments vacated by wealthy urbanites in the mass departure shortly after *la Revolución*.

Although she had little formal education beyond high school, Ulloa had little difficulty after moving to Havana, she told me, in integrating her life into the revolutionary movement and taking advantage of the many benefits such integration entailed, including retraining and adult education. Shortly after her arrival in the city she started working as the director of the janitorial staff at a local hospital. She kept one secret, though: she and her husband were both active practitioners of Santería. Being a believer, or *creyente*, in Santería meant that she and her husband had to be discreet about their faith in certain circles. Ulloa made clear that during the first thirty-five years of the revolution, that is, until the mid-1990s, one could not readily admit in public to being both a creyente and a *militante*. If discovered, such practices would be strongly frowned upon by the socialist revolutionary government and ultimately would result in some form of sanction by the party, if not the outright revocation of one's membership.

In the early 1960s, in line with scientific atheism—as part of the transition to communism—the government declared Cuba to be an atheist state and

Biopolitics in the Special Period

began a gradual program of repression of religious groups. For example, the Roman Catholic Church and other religious institutions were severely marginalized, and practitioners were forced to worship in private, often secretly. A rare collection of ethnographic studies by the anthropologist Oscar Lewis and his team of researchers details the everyday experiences of life in a Havana shantytown, providing one of the most personal accounts of life before and after the revolution.[2] The individual oral histories presented in these studies reflect the vibrancy and importance of religious forms, such as Santería, also known as the Rule of Orisha, or La Regla de Ocha, a syncretic complex of African beliefs and traditions and Roman Catholicism.[3] Since many slaves from Africa arrived in Cuba as late as the mid-nineteenth century, their African past was only a generation old at the time of independence. The Lewis studies chronicle how individuals, marginalized by the poor physical conditions of their squatter settlements, confronted the harshness of family life as well as the integral role Santería played in shaping their life experiences. The oral life histories also reveal the high levels of racial discrimination that prevailed in the prerevolutionary era. For example, the shantytown Lewis studied was believed to be a stronghold of *santeros* and perceived by many wealthier city dwellers to be associated with high levels of criminality, filth, and disease. This association was, in part, a colonial legacy that linked the terms *Africa* and *blackness* with inferiority, degeneration, disease, and contagion.[4]

Shortly after the revolution, Santería was dismissed as a folkloric practice and an impediment to the project of modernity and was valued only for its redeeming qualities in the form of public cultural performances. Santería, however, never required the institutional infrastructure of Catholicism and continued to exist in private throughout the revolutionary period. For example, Ulloa and her husband, like López, had a small hidden altar in one of the closets of their apartment. Despite the difficulties involved, they tried to maintain a close relationship with their orishas (pantheon of gods). The orishas, Ulloa noted, were very demanding and needed to be propitiated frequently. Meanwhile, life grew increasingly difficult for Ulloa. Her marriage became shaky because of her husband's alcoholism and the physical abuse she suffered as a result of it. Ulloa also discovered during that time that she was unable to have children, and she felt increasingly separated from her family in Oriente.

As an active member of the Federación de Mujeres Cubanas (Federation of Cuban women, or FMC) and a local delegate of the Comité de Defensa de la Revolución (CDR) in her municipality, Ulloa stated that she became less dependent on having a man around the house for economic security, companionship, and so on. If anything, she noted, la Revolución was liberating in many respects because it gave people, particularly women, options. The majority of men, she argued, remained set in their ways, despite the revolutionary teachings that stipulated the egalitarian delegation of tasks, both inside and outside of the home. Women still carried the burden of domestic chores, in addition to revolutionary commitments, and this situation only made her marriage worse. As she stated, she did not want to be a housewife. More specifically, she had no children, and she was not going to be like her mother and be defined solely by her husband. Rather, Ulloa asserted, she would live her life alone and in the way she deemed appropriate, without the added burden of living with a domineering husband.

Divorcing her husband after twenty years of marriage, Ulloa sought a *permuta* (exchange) to switch her two-bedroom apartment for two separate one-bedroom apartments to enable her to start her life independently.[5] Securing a small one-bedroom apartment a block away from her former home, she began seriously dedicating her life to the secret worship of her orishas. She had lived the double life of a *revolucionaria* and creyente for many years, but the economic crisis of the 1990s marked a turning point in her life: "I could no longer live the hypocrisy of what it meant to be a revolucionaria." The economic crisis, she stressed, had forced creyentes, who often worshiped in secret, to become bolder in their desire to worship openly. Ulloa further noted that during the height of the economic crisis in 1993, the rhythmic sound of *batá* drums, the sacred drums used in Afro-Cuban rituals, could often be heard in the late afternoons before the sun set on her normally sedate residential community. The rhythmic Afro-Cuban drumming was luring the orishas to the mundane world, where santeros were asking their patron saints for help and guidance.[6] Also noticeable during the height of the economic crisis, she said, was a growing number of santeros in public places, both new and old adherents, often decorated in bright beaded bracelets and wearing necklaces that were visible outside their state uniforms. Seeking out protection to ensure their well-being from their respective orishas, individuals brazenly appeared in the streets of Havana, Ulloa said, adorned in the consecrated white- and blue-beaded chains for

Biopolitics in the Special Period

Yemayá or the red and white beads for Changó. Creyentes, she noted, were slowly beginning to openly proclaim their faith.

El Estado (the state), Ulloa stressed, appeared to react complacently to the reappearance of blatant religious accoutrements. Ulloa and several other santeros I interviewed agreed that it was a widely held belief that Castro was the son of Changó (*el hijo de Changó*), an orisha known for being a fierce warrior and the embodiment of virility.[7] In fact, Ulloa noted, police, physicians, and well-known party members, among other state officials, were regular participants at various Santería gatherings from the very beginning of la Revolución. The practice of Santería, Ulloa remarked, could not simply be explained away as the superstitious beliefs of an ignorant group of poor Afro-Cubans. The practitioners, she stressed, were from all walks of life. As was evident from the many gatherings Ulloa held that I personally attended, there was no clear sociodemographic profile that could accurately describe the diverse group of participants I encountered regularly in her living room.

In 1993 Ulloa retired and started to collect her state pension. Suffering from severe asthma and diagnosed with hepatic cirrhosis, she found that her health was rapidly deteriorating. The state, she declared, had failed her. Food items for her special diet, normally provided through her ration card, were increasingly unavailable for longer periods of time. Crucial things like an inhaler to control her asthma and vitamins and medicines to help alleviate the effects of her deteriorating liver function were quickly disappearing from local peso pharmacies—only to reappear, she added, at exorbitant prices in the *bolsa negra.* "People were becoming desperate and things were becoming critical for many people," she said. "People were drinking sugar water at the height of the special period, in 1993. That was one of the worst years of my life. If you wanted anything of value, you had to start buying it in *divisa*," she said. "I remember my doctor asking me if I had any friends abroad who could send me the important medicines I needed. I asked the doctor why—the government is supposed to provide these things. Everything was changing and the poor like myself, who had nobody abroad, were suffering."

Ulloa had always relied on the orishas for spiritual guidance. However, now she was looking to them for something more concrete: to meet her material needs. She recalled the day she asked her orishas for help: "When I stood in front of my beautiful Ochún, I said, Mamá Ochún, I need help because I earn 127.40 Cuban pesos a month [U.S. $6], and with the special diet I have, and the drugs I need to buy, the money I have won't suffice. I don't have kids, and I can only ask my brother for money for so long before he says, 'Sorry, my sister, I don't have any more money to give you.' " Asking the *carcacoles* (a form of divination) to predict her future, Ulloa was comforted that Ochún would protect her. Help for Ulloa, she believed, came two months later in the form of an *extranjero* (foreigner) from Brazil. Rolando, an elderly man, had arrived in Cuba to become initiated into the religion of Santería. Angela met Rolando at his initiation ceremony.

In Rolando's ceremony it was determined he was a son of Ochún (also known as the Virgen de la Caridad del Cobre), the Yoruba and Santería goddess of sweet waters (river), love, and money, and the patron saint of Cuba. Naturally, Ulloa declared, they were drawn to one another because they shared the same patron saint, but, as she made clear, there was nothing sexual between them. Immediately after their friendship began, Rolando, a former federal judge in a small province of Brazil, started sending Ulloa from fifty to one hundred dollars a month, in addition to sending all her necessary medications and vitamins. With the influx of money, Ulloa grew fiercely religious. As she remarked, she was no longer willing to hide her faith in the closet and instead built an altar in her living room and started to worship her orishas openly. As she stated, she wanted to dedicate her life to Ochún and the other orishas.

Recalling another critical time in her life when she fell ill, Ulloa explained that she went to the hospital first but also consulted with her *padrino* (godfather or spiritual advisor in Santería), who looked after her spiritual well-being. Her padrino, in turn, used caracoles to diagnose and provide her with a spiritual therapeutic recourse. "I had faith that Ochún would not abandon me," she noted. She still believed in the "hard sciences," that is, biomedicine, but she also believed strongly that one could follow the treatment regimen for each tradition without any internal contradiction. "One system of belief is as important as the other," Ulloa stated, adding, "My doctor is aware that I am a santera. She is aware that I also seek out the advice of my padrino, and there is nothing she can do about it. The government cannot tell me what to believe. Take a look outside. How many people do you see at work, or more generally walking around the streets, dressed all in white with the beads openly around their necks? These are new initiates to Santería, and there are many, and the number of creyentes is growing. Before, when the

Russians were here, this would be unheard of. Now, people need something to believe in. The *santos* will answer our prayers." This is because the state, Ulloa added, had stopped fulfilling its function, which she defined as providing citizens with the basic material necessities for life.

I visited the homes of several individuals who claimed to be atheist, and it was evident that some were uncomfortable discussing their religious beliefs; often they had small glasses of water, a typical offering to the saints, with flowers and candles strategically placed behind doors or on high shelves in their apartments. Moreover, when I attended several *fiestas de santos* (a party celebrating the day one became initiated into Santería), many of my apparently atheist friends, who claimed they were only there for the food and drink, danced correctly in step to the various Afro-Cuban rhythms and spoke with specialized knowledge with other santeros on the various ways one could appease a specific orisha. When I finally asked several of these supposed nonbelievers why, if they were not creyentes, they were interested in learning about these things, they admitted that they did not want to "tempt fate." Several people pointed out that it couldn't hurt if an orisha would help give them an edge when confronting the problems of everyday life.

Several of these same individuals stated that, informally, they were "pragmatic religious practitioners"; in other words, there was no harm in drawing on religion in times of crisis, as people the world over do. "It works," stressed a close friend of mine, a young physician and Communist Party member who aggressively defended la Revolución at every opportunity. He argued that Santería was another option for seeking out personal health and well-being. The inspiration for his renewed faith, he later revealed, was his mother's recent bout with cancer, which he believed was cured after she was initiated into Santería. At the time of his mother's illness hospitals did not have the proper drugs to administer chemotherapy, despite the physician's desperate attempts to work through *socios* to guarantee her stay in one of the best hospitals in Havana. His family members, who lived three hours outside of Havana, had not been creyentes before, but turned to Santería as an alternative.

In 2007, when I paid a visit to Trinidad López, who acted as a *madrina* (godmother) to a large network of younger santeros, she said she was a little surprised to find an increasing number of people turning to Santería in hopes of finding quick solutions to their problems, like asking the saints to help them "get papers to get out of Cuba." "The orishas," she remarked ironically, "do not work in immigration." Although she spoke reservedly, López was nonetheless adamant that Santería could not be strictly reduced to a religion of give and take, in which people conducted magic spells to produce positive results. Building a relationship between oneself and las orishas, she stressed, is only possible with time. While an increasing number of people were becoming santeros, she noted, there was unfortunately no quick fix to their problems. López was a little disturbed by the apparently causal relationship between the recent economic crisis and the visible presence of creyentes.

This link between the increasing numbers of people being initiated into Santería and the crumbling of the state's provision of social and material welfare has been recognized before. The ethnomusicologist Katherine Hagedorn, who examined the aesthetic and ritual significance of Afro-Cuban Santería, argues that "the chance to *resolver* one's material problems is directly related to the swelling ranks of Santeros and Santeras in Cuba" (2001, 220). The term *resolver*, Hagedorn contends, implies relying on an informal network of people, both living and deceased, who may help resolve everyday problems. In this way, individuals from the spiritual world are added to one's network of socios. Beyond material necessity, however, which is not necessarily considered profane, as I was informed by various participants in Santería, one repeatedly propitiates the orishas in order to seek guidance and protection and to find solutions to everyday problems in the here and now, as well as for spiritual assistance in the future. I was told repeatedly in numerous interviews that increasing numbers of individuals are proclaiming a faith in Santería because it provides a tangible means to seek out immediate physical and spiritual well-being. The ability to change one's current life conditions is in opposition to clerical religions such as Catholicism or, increasingly in Latin America and the Caribbean, evangelical Christianity, both of which focus more on spiritual redemption and the afterlife.[8]

As was evident after Pope John Paul II's visit to Cuba in 1997, during which he publicly condemned both the socialist government for curtailing religious expression in Cuba and the United States for its embargo against the island, religious spiritualism has been gaining ground in recent years.[9] The Roman Catholic Church began to experience a resurgence of followers. The Cuban government previously espoused a militant atheism and embodied Marx's dictum that "religion is the sigh of the oppressed creature, the feeling of a heartless world, and the soul of soulless circumstances. It is the

FIGURE 1. Medicina tradicional y natural (MTN) pharmacy in Havana. Brotherton © 2006.

[opiate] of the people."[10] The state now turns a blind eye to open religious worship. I interviewed several physicians and one MINSAP official who were skeptical of religious healing and viewed people's return to *curanderos*, or what they termed *brujeros* (witch doctors), with disdain; however, I suspect that given the current climate of scarce resources in Cuba, they thought that spiritualism could also divert people's attention from growing economic inequalities. Yet one could equally argue that many of the individuals seeking out Santería for health and well-being would have done so previously, if the state had not carried out a passive campaign to eradicate this religious practice as "witchcraft." Given that Santería existed as an informal practice both before and after la Revolución, it is difficult to discern a single underlying motive behind the recent visible reemergence of santeros.[11] To date, no published study has systematically addressed medical pluralism in Cuba and, in particular, the role of Santería in people's health-seeking behavior in the *período especial.*[12]

The state's reluctance to denounce the return to religious practices is directly related to the ease and openness with which individuals are now exploring the health options available to them, without fear of state reprisal. In the following case study I explore how, in the context of the período especial, the socialist state, rather than individual citizens, is actively promoting the use of *Medicina tradicional y natural* (natural and traditional medicine, MTN) as part of a strategy, presented as benevolent, to offer the population more health care options (see figure 1).

While modernization campaigns throughout the world, including in Cuba, have resulted in the preeminence of scientific medicine, most commonly associated with biomedicine and also known as cosmopolitan medicine, the eradication of natural and traditional approaches to medicine in many parts of the globe has proven difficult: "Economic necessity has, of course, been a driving force in sustaining this situation."[13] But in Cuba the revolutionary government has attempted, with partial success, to eliminate the class-based inequalities that denied people access to cosmopolitan medicine—irrespective of individual cultural beliefs toward different medical traditions—and has carried out various campaigns to marginalize medical traditions like herbal medicine, for example, that diverge from what the government believes is evidence-based medicine.

PRACTICING *"MEDICINA VERDE"* (HERBAL MEDICINE)

Miguel Nuñez, a thirty-four-year-old physician who pursued his medical training through the FAR, was stationed in various posts for the FAR as a military physician until the late 1990s, when he asked to be discharged. At that time, Nuñez wanted to pursue his research interests in the study of medicinal plants. This interest, he stated, was stimulated in part by a study he conducted for the FAR in the mid-1990s on the knowledge of medicinal plants among curanderos and santeros throughout the island. His study received a warm welcome among FAR scientists, although the general scientific community in Cuba still looks upon these practices as a form of quackery. However, Nuñez noted that FAR scientists had been carrying out clinical investigations of medicinal plants since the mid-1980s as a strategy to prepare the country for the possibility of war.[14]

Finding his role in the FAR limiting, Nuñez, who had worked closely as a personal physician for several high-ranking military officials and Communist Party members, requested to be transferred to one of the many state research facilities. Several weeks after his request, the FAR coordinated a research position for him at a research institute run by the Ministry of Science, Technology, and the Environment (CITMA), formed in 1994. Nuñez stated that the FAR had been very good to him, even awarding him an apartment in a prized area of the city center overlooking the waterfront. Nuñez's tastefully decorated apartment was formerly the home of another well-known research scientist who had defected while at a scientific conference in Mexico, eventually making his way to Miami. "I am a *revolucionario*," Nuñez told me, making it clear that, unlike the apartment's former owner, he was dedicated to la Revolución and for this reason deserved the luxuries afforded him by the state. Nuñez believes that the FAR was being especially generous to him in view of his relatively young age, perhaps in recognition of his unique credentials: his title as a physician of MTN. He completed a master's degree in this specialty in 1996. At the time, he was one of few people who specialized in this area and was trained in Cuba, as opposed to abroad, where this form of specialization is more common.

In 1991 Nuñez was part of a unique group of physicians who benefited from the MINSAP's broadening of a narrower vision of science and medicine to incorporate the use of herbal remedies and therapeutic regimes into the biomedical model. This was accomplished under the newly devised Programa para el Desarrollo y la Generalización de la Medicina Tradicional y Natural (Program for the development and generalization of natural and traditional medicine). An executive report issued by the MINSAP in 1996, "Analysis of the Health Sector in Cuba," outlines the rationale for the newly devised program:

> The strategic objective of the National Health System is to give priority to the development of natural and traditional medicine. The "Program of Development," initiated in 1991, includes the search for active medicinal principals of plants, their clinical testing, and the subsequent generalization of the results so that they can be progressively incorporated into the techniques and procedures of the East Asian medical tradition. For the development of these activities, we have created a multisector commission that is presided over by the MINSAP and that integrates the Ministry of Agriculture and the Ministry of Science, Technology and the Environment, among others.[15]

While the MINSAP's strategic rationale behind the development of Cuba's program for MTN focused strictly on scientific inquiry, a report produced by the MINSAP in 1999 puts the recent developments in a more historical and socioeconomic context:

> Among recent trends in the practice of contemporary medicine around the world, one especially stands out: the inclusion of natural and traditional medicine [MTN]. The professional practice of MTN is not an alternative based on simple economic necessity, a solution to, say, a shortage of medical supplies. It is a true scientific discipline. We must study to perfect MTN and develop a lasting tradition by demonstrating its ethical and scientific advantages. This medical tradition can help correct the inequalities between poor countries and highly industrialized countries that have produced a worldwide pharmaceutical monopoly.[16]

The MINSAP reports show that natural and traditional medicine, which was previously marginalized by the state as an "occult science," is now being strategically pursued. However, conspicuously absent from the MINSAP reports was any mention of the reality of massive shortages in pharmaceutical drugs and medical supplies that resulted from the cessation of Soviet aid after 1989 and the strengthening of the U.S. blockade. The strategic pursuit of MTN is discussed in terms of the scientific efficacy of these practices, with no mention of the state's inability to provide pharmaceutical products, as it had previously done. As what constitutes scientific medicine in the global scientific community has changed, contributing to a new regime of truth, MTN in Cuba has become an acceptable and justifiable therapeutic avenue. As the MINSAP report further indicates, "MTN **does not constitute a form of alternative or complementary** therapy developed in response to economic problems. Rather, it is a discipline of scientific medicine."[17]

However, despite MINSAP's disclaimers, it is important to examine, from a historic perspective, the shift in the MINSAP's official policy. Nuñez provides a more detailed explanation of the reasons underlying the MINSAP's changed approach to MTN:

> I will say this, but I believe it needs to be said responsibly. The período especial was definitely a catalyst for self-reflection within MINSAP and other institutions of the state. Cuba is a poor, Third World country and without a financial backer such as the Soviet Union, we have to face certain realities that are characteristic of our kind of economy. When the MINSAP started to develop programs based on natural and traditional medicine in 1991, only a small percentage of people actually believed in it. I don't think it was difficult to convince people over time, since these traditions existed before la Revolución. Meanwhile, the international scientific community evolved over time, and I think MINSAP started to realize, in the decade of the 1990s, that well-respected institutions such as the WHO had approved thousands of projects for investigation with respect to natural and traditional medicine.
>
> Before 1959 *el pueblo* was syncretic and actively used natural and traditional remedies. But for certain reasons—I guess we can say errors committed by la Revolución—these practices were denounced as "primitive." La Revolución saw these practices as a kind of witchcraft [*oscurantismo*]. What happened in 1959, 1960, and 1961, at the beginning of la Revolución, was that all of the pharmacies with medicinal plants disappeared or were eradicated.

Biopolitics in the Special Period

Beyond that, all of the traditional healers such as curanderos and brujeros, who had a poor scientific reputation in the eyes of the state, were pushed underground. Of course, you could never say that the popular uses of these kinds of treatments stopped. Doctors and professionals are quite familiar with grandmother's home remedies. But at the institutional level, the direct actions of MINSAP, which controlled all levels of medical care and practice, including control of research within the country, effectively eradicated what we call popular medicine at the institutional level. If health professionals were found to be engaging in unorthodox medical practices, such as recommending herbal remedies to their patients, MINSAP would not take away their degrees, but it would sanction them. You also have to remember that, at that time, Cuba had significant ties with countries in the Soviet bloc. Our pharmacies were chock full of pharmaceutical products from these countries.

I am sure that there are still health professionals in the upper levels of the MINSAP—people above the age of forty or fifty—who during the past thirty or so years were prohibited from using "popular medicine" and were never trained in it. I think these are the doctors, trained at the height of la Revolución, who are most disappointed to see a return to these forms of medical practice. However, the newer generations, trained in the late 1980s and 1990s, have confidence in these medical traditions. And you can see the older generations welcoming these practices because, quite frankly, they never stopped using them in private.

As Nuñez attests, he was convinced that the resurgence in MTN practices was, in part, associated with the country's decline in foreign pharmaceutical imports. While the knowledge of natural and traditional medicine is increasingly widespread among primary health physicians in Cuba, Nuñez was the only physician I interviewed for this book who had specialized in MTN. In the early 1990s, in an attempt to promote the use of MTN, the MINSAP distributed a national formulary and educational materials on "green [that is, herbal] medicine," compiled by seventeen scientists in medicine and biology, which was sent to practitioners throughout the country. Among other things, these documents discussed the pharmacological basis of traditional herbal remedies. Similar MINSAP materials were also directed at the general population. Local pharmacies featured colorful illustrated posters with the plants' popular medicinal names, their scientific names, and a description of their medicinal properties. In addition, all of the local pharmacies started to carry a

FIGURE 2. *Huerto* (garden) of medicinal plants. Adriana Premat © 2001.
Reprinted by permission.

limited selection of bottled herbal remedies for sale in Cuban pesos. Not surprisingly, while the majority of the pharmacies I visited had a limited selection of pharmaceutical medicines, they carried a wide selection of herbal remedies for a variety of ailments, including treatments for colds, upset stomachs, and some antiparasitic lotions for external application.

The state's promotion of MTN has been mixed. While several of the citizens and medical practitioners openly embraced the integration of MTN, the majority I interviewed saw the medicina verde as a clear sign that the state was trying to cover up for a lack of pharmaceutical products it had been promoting zealously for over forty years. For example, when I visited a physician named Louis Pérez in his *consultorio*, known as Los Molinos, he had a dwindling supply of allopathic treatments, which meant he often had to send his patients directly to the local polyclinics for routine injections because, at times, he didn't have even the necessary needles. According to the MINSAP, the consultorio should have approximately twenty-six types of medicine on-site.[18] Pérez's consultorio had less than half of the medicines on the stipulated list. A small, unkempt plot of land on the side of the consultorio was used to grow a sparse garden of medicinal plants (such as that shown in figure 2). These herbal remedies, Pérez explained, supplemented and in some cases supplanted the dwindling supply of drugs he had at his disposal.

"Some are actually quite useful," he offered sardonically. He claimed that with the right knowledge of medicina verde, a physician could make efficacious treatments.

Unfortunately, the majority of the doctor's patients were proving hard to convince when it came to taking the herbal remedies. "When they come to *el médico* they want pills and needles. Generally speaking, if they want to use medicina verde they do not need to come and see me. I believe most Cubans are aware of herbal remedies either through word of mouth or from older family members," the doctor said. A patient I interviewed was frustrated after a visit with Pérez: "I go to the doctor for antibiotics to treat an infection and he gives me aloe vera or some kind of herbal calming tea. What on earth am I suppose to do with this? Yet I go home and watch Fidel on TV sending our doctors all around the world and providing free medical care. You can bet those doctors have the necessary drugs and equipment to take care of their patients. But what about us, *los cubanos*? All of these sacrifices? And for what, I ask?" A large percentage of the individuals I interviewed, while not against MTN, would not substitute them for the apparent wonders of pharmaceutically based medicine. Not surprisingly, many of the interviewees who were born and raised in the sixties, seventies, and eighties and were trained under the revolutionary pedagogy were forthrightly resistant to MTN. However, several older people I interviewed, including several santeros, had always incorporated herbal remedies into their religious practices and were convinced of the efficacy of MTN and even of acupuncture. A more systematic study would be necessary to identify specific trends that might throw light on the relationship between an individual's perceptions of MTN, on the one hand, and age and religious beliefs, on the other.

All the primary health care physicians I interviewed had a basic knowledge of MTN, in part because all medical graduates, including nurses and dentists, are required to attend training courses in MTN. Among the family physicians I worked with, several had to tend to small medicinal gardens, if grudgingly, that were located alongside their consultorios (figure 2). While few of the primary health care physicians were thrilled about their added responsibility as gardeners, in several instances community members, as part of the popular participation of the community in health-related affairs, had organized collectives to tend the herbal gardens. Nuñez elaborated on some of the challenges the new MTN program has faced from physicians and the wider community:

The problem with the MEF program is that some of the médicos are not convinced of the use of medicinal plants, despite the fact that they have been well educated on them and understand their correct usage. There are other médicos, on the other hand, who do not know how to properly use medicinal plants. For example, some doctors believe that the popular use of medicinal plants sets a dangerous precedent. For example, people who do not know how to use these medications may take toxic dosages or experience secondary side effects because they don't understand the correct dosage and the specific ways in which MTN must be taken. In this respect, we have our work cut out for us. We still need to educate el pueblo more. These are traditions that have existed for years, but in Cuba we can't expect to learn them overnight.

We don't have the experience of the Chinese, who have over five thousand years of practice. But while people still see a certain degree of conflict between Western medicine and traditional medicine, I don't doubt that they could coexist in Cuba. I believe that traditional medicine can actually be complementary to Western medicine. If you approach the matter intelligently, you can seek out both traditional and Western medicine and basically exploit the positive characteristics of each. In this way, individuals can ultimately obtain the same final results. We have had help from advisors in Cuba over the past ten or twelve years—Chinese, Vietnamese, Koreans, and some Canadians—who are very well known.

Look at acupuncture, which arrived in Cuba around the 1960s. It was not very strong at that time, but slowly it has gained momentum. By the 1990s, acupuncture had become a strong tradition in Cuba. In my opinion, it is because it was a Chinese tradition and people could more easily believe in a tradition that was backed by history. There is a popular saying in Cuba, "If a Chinese doctor can't save you, nobody can." This saying emerged because Cubans believe the Chinese to have a very strong history in the development of medicine. However, medicinal plants have a unique history in Cuba. In Cuba, herbal remedies are associated with the black curanderos of Africa, and so you can see that people question the competency of those practitioners because of their racial origin. How could black Africans know anything about medicine, is what people think in the general population.

Nuñez provides a historical context in which to trace the influences on individuals' perceptions of various medical traditions. Several individuals I interviewed, while willing to try acupuncture because of its proven history as a form of Chinese traditional medicine, were more skeptical of Cuba's fledgling herbal medicine program. The fact that herbal medicine in Cuba has been associated with the historic practices of the Afro-Cuban population has added to people's unwillingness to embrace it. Although the MTN program is being marketed to the population as the evolution of Cuba's health sector, the reality that the state's ideological shift in approach to basic medicine occurred just as the island was undergoing massive shortages in medicines and medical supplies seriously calls into question whether this strategic move was not a form of economic pragmatism. A more systematic study is needed to arrive at a definitive conclusion.

MEDICAL PLURALISM AND STATE-SANCTIONED SOCIAL WELFARE

Alberto Guerrero, a fifty-four-year-old physician and a former research scientist specializing in drug-transport mechanisms, worked as a family physician in a local polyclinic in a municipality of Havana. Suffering from stress, insomnia, and body aches and pains, Guerrero had been unable to get an accurate diagnosis for his medical problems. He was frustrated by the regular battery of tests he was subjected to and was recommended by another physician to an MTN and alternative-health clinic in Havana. He described his experience as follows:

> The doctor looked me over and used her hand to get a feel for my energy. She concluded that I was a violet person. Yes, violet, the *color*. The doctor asked me if I would think in violet. Of course I was a little taken aback. Another physician then entered the room, and he immediately stated he could feel my negative aura. He massaged the aura that was apparently emanating from my body and declared that I needed to be spiritually cleansed. When the consultation was over, the doctor very officiously wrote out a prescription for several herbal remedies, and another page outlining the specific uses, and dosages to be taken, and what I should do to cleanse my spirit. When I got the hell out of there, I thought, "Is this what medicine has been reduced to in Cuba?"

The recent trend in using such questionable treatments in Cuba, similar to the trends occurring in other industrial countries, in one respect is disheartening, but also refreshing. The average Cuban out there has no access to U.S. dollars and has limited options when it comes to buying the drugs at the international pharmacies or getting them sent from abroad. These alternative and herbal clinics are there to make these people feel better. Some people swear on their life that they actually work. The government, of course, likes this because it means people are not complaining about what it is not providing. The government is supposedly giving el pueblo options for medical treatments, when really what it is doing is hiding the fact that it does not have the financial resources to provide the population with pharmaceuticals or, worse, is selling them on the international market.

On a positive note—and I say this as a former research scientist—the recent crisis has opened the door to all kinds of innovative medical research, which the government previously did not permit. For example, I know a scientist—a good friend of mine—who is studying the effects of healing the body through positive thinking. Imagine! Of course, don't think the older established scientific community in Cuba is happy about all of this. Like me, they think all this MTN and alternative therapy stuff is rubbish.

While Guerrero is fairly critical of the recent promotion of MTN in the health sector, he views this recent trend as a kind of opiate of the masses, meant to appease the population when the state has nothing else to offer. In this sense, the state's promotion of MTN and its loosening of restrictions on religious practice, whether seen as positive or negative developments, must also be viewed as a pragmatic strategy employed by the state. It has emerged in part from the necessity of providing the population with health options and, ultimately, of shifting some of the responsibility for health and social welfare from the state onto the individual. For example, the anthropologist Steve Ferzacca, who examined health governance in the changing political context of Indonesia, argued that medical pluralism was employed as a form of state rule "disguised as state-sanctioned social welfare."[19] Extrapolating on Ferzacca, I argue that one must question the degree to which the promotion of MTN and alternative medicine, as Guerrero points out, is offered as a means to placate a health-conscious population that is slowly realizing that the state can no longer provide the same level of health care services as it did in the past.

The período especial has created a climate that allows individuals greater freedom to pursue natural, traditional, and alternative (and spiritual) therapy. However, as is clear in other highly visible spheres of the health sector, the state has been reluctant to relinquish control of some health policies. For example, maternal and infant care programs still mandate institutional childbirth and do not recognize traditional birth attendants, or midwives.

Biopolitics in the Special Period

The Cuban government has made choices that are not all visibly driven by economic pragmatism, though this is not to suggest that a strategy is not involved. Since the early 1960s Cuban leaders have envisioned physicians as being akin to soldiers, though armed differently, in the island's historic battle against disease and suffering. For example, in an address to the nation in 2002, Castro argued, "Health care is one of the most sensitive areas through which our enemies tried to hurt our people. It is very logical that we Cubans aspire to lowering infant mortality; to extending the average life expectancy of every citizen; to combating disease; and combating death. There is no aspiration more legitimate than this one."[20] The implementation of public health programs provided the state with quantifiable means, like the infant mortality rate and increasing life expectancies at birth, by which to measure success and bolster domestic and international recognition of the revolutionary achievements of the state. In the process, the government expended considerable capital—financial, social, political, and symbolic—in strategically defining the terms and parameters of what constituted bodily health and physical well-being.

Part II

SOCIALIST GOVERNMENTALITY, PUBLIC HEALTH, AND RISK

Use me. . . . Cooperate with me to keep the
city clean and healthy. Source: *Bohemia,* 26
February 1965: 108.

3

MEDICALIZED SUBJECTIVITIES

During my research I was regularly struck by the descriptive language people used to speak about their bodies and health. I met countless individuals, of different educational backgrounds and ages, who could discuss with a relatively advanced biomedical vocabulary the etiology and treatment of various illnesses; for example, the various kinds of parasites one can be exposed to, the symptoms one exhibits, and the specific drugs and dosages required to treat such infestations. Most people knew the names of drugs, either by their generic or brand name, the class of drug they belonged to (e.g., whether an antibiotic, anti-inflammatory, or hypertensive), and the corresponding treatment regimen. Moreover, many people were equally literate in translating the drug names of North American brands, mostly sent by relatives in the United States, to the equivalent drugs manufactured in Spain, Italy, or France and in mastering a dizzying array of treatment plans and dosages.

Many of the individuals I worked with throughout the course of my research had large collections of pharmaceutical drugs and medical supplies that far exceeded the contents of the average first-aid kit (figure 3). A woman who I interviewed at her home proudly pulled out her medicine drawer to show me how well equipped she was for any unexpected illnesses. Her collection included an array of *pastillas* (pills), including different classes of prescription drugs such as hypertensives, antibiotics, diuretics, and painkillers as well as ointments, needles, sterile water, and gauze. This type of collection was not uncommon in the building where I lived. If I so much as coughed or complained of a headache I was offered a spectrum of medications and subjected to ad hoc medical diagnoses from my neighbors, all of whom had a small pharmacopoeia in their homes. One of my neighbors, a nurse at a local hospital, was unhappy with how skinny I looked and con-

FIGURE 3. A personal collection of medicine, ointments, needles, and gauze of one of my informants. Brotherton © 2002.

vinced herself that I needed Vitamin B-12 injections to give me more energy and, hopefully, a more robust appetite. In her attempts to convince me she would often appear unannounced at my door with a disposable needle and packaged vitamin in hand. Since I was a foreigner and presumably flush with dollars, "there was no excuse to be thin in Cuba," she regularly complained. Cubans, she often playfully noted, "like people with meat on their bones." Rather than changing my diet and lifestyle, medical intervention in the forms of injections or vitamins was, according to her, the answer to my apparent problem.

Beyond skillfully negotiating pharmaceutical prophylaxis and therapeutic options, many people I interviewed were equally invested in a biomedical culture in which medicalized understandings of the body were concomitantly couched within larger conceptual framings of scientific advancement and socialist modernity. Years of state-sponsored public campaigns, policies, and practices had resulted in highly medicalized understandings of what constitutes health and physical well-being. The creation of these medicalized subjectivities is the product of a historically, socially, and politically contingent way of seeing the individual and social body as populations in need of management. For instance, the early revolutionary period, characterized by a large population that had been historically dispossessed of basic medical and health services, made it possible for the revolutionary government to incorporate large masses of individuals into health-reform campaigns. These reforms, which were synonymous with the betterment of all in the socioeconomic transformation of Cuban society, were increasingly linked to the construction of a socialist society. However, consistent with the vision of socialist society was the increasing focus on science and medicine as rational means of developing the country.

It is impossible to speak of the Cuban revolution as being external to the revolution in the health sector. To consider the two phenomena as separate events would fail to address "the confrontation between real people, armed with ideas and politics, and the concrete problems that are thrust upon them by history."[1] A brief genealogy of Cuba's public health revolution will serve to draw attention to changing governmental apparatuses involved in delivering postrevolutionary health services and, in turn, to the changing relationships among citizens, government institutions, public associations, and the state. This changing individual-society-state dynamic represented a distinctive shift in the art of governing the island's population, requiring the mobilization of a new armature of techniques and practices that set out to craft a socialist citizenry that was as explicitly political as it was corporeal. The body figured prominently as the battleground for the deployment of strategies and policies to develop and expand an efficient public health system, one that required an increasing degree of state intervention, management, and protection and that reinforced the infrastructure and institutions necessary to create, regulate, and produce "governable subjects."[2]

RECONCILING HISTORY (1902–1958)

A cursory review of the public health services in the prerevolutionary context, the *período burgués*, or bourgeois period (1902–58), serves as an important counterpoint for subsequent analysis. My concern here is not to enter into a semantic and statistical tug-of-war to reconcile descriptions of Cuba's prerevolutionary health services, or what Quiroga calls "two distinct memories of the process," the "official" and the "dissident."[3] My objective, rather, is to highlight how a particular political discourse was mobilized to create and transform subjectivities. Comprehending the history of the public health system requires placing specific events, people, and experiences in context. The postrevolutionary government's strategy to create healthy bodies, which entailed broadening the definition of individual health to integrate health care into the overall socioeconomic development of the country, has served as an important source of political legitimacy in official public health discourses.

Located ninety miles south of Miami, lodged between the Gulf of Mexico and the Caribbean Sea, Cuba was settled by Spain in 1493 and used primarily as a naval base. Following the introduction in the seventeenth century of sugar plantations worked by African slave labor, as occurred in many of its

Caribbean neighbor countries, Cuba's monoculture export economy prospered; the United States, the dominant economic power in the region, was its main trading partner. However, strained relations between Spain and the United States culminated in the U.S. government's occupation of Cuba after the second war of independence (1894–98). The United States imposed a military government on the island from 1899 until 1902. Under the Platt Amendment to the new Cuban constitution of 1902, the United States retained the right to intervene in the Republic's affairs, and it exercised this right on several occasions, namely, in 1906–9, 1917, and 1921.

A series of administrations characterized by instability, authoritarianism, and gangsterism marked the period from independence in 1899 up until the 1930s. Although Cuba abolished slavery and gained its independence, the cultural underpinnings of colonialism remained important factors in the postcolonial subjugation of the island nation under U.S. tutelage. In 1933 a rebellion by students and army officers brought Fulgencio Batista Zaldívar, who was backed by the U.S. government, to power. From 1934 until 1936 Cubans lived under a virtual military dictatorship.[4] The Batista government, aided in part by U.S. corporate interests in Cuba, did little to reduce the problems of structural violence associated with the highly class-stratified Cuban society. For example, the pervading social injustice and material inequalities that characterized the período burgués were best depicted in the various social and political actors who were involved in Cuba's sugar cane industry: the military, the bourgeoisie, domestic and foreign corporate interests, and the exploited worker. As other scholars have noted, the place of the sugar industry in Cuba's history reveals the profound local and global interactions that shaped the production, extraction, and consumption of this commodity and helped determine the social and political trajectory of the inhabitants of the island.[5]

Given the widespread poverty that prevailed in the período burgués, in 1959 the revolutionary government inherited what Fidel Castro called an "overdeveloped capital in a completely underdeveloped country."[6] Public health services during the período burgués reveal a system characterized by uneven distribution of and access to medical services, determined by social class, urban and rural locations, and ethnic differentiation. An abundance of literature on the prerevolutionary period describes a health care system that was profit-oriented and focused on the diagnosis and treatment of diseases rather than on their prevention through education and other services essential for the long-term improvement of health.[7] The diversity in health care access and quality resulted in a high concentration of privately owned clinics that provided health care services for the few people who lived in the cities and who could afford it. Consequently, physicians in private practices tended to serve only the upper-middle and upper classes.

In addition, a system called the mutual benefit societies, also known as *mutualistas*, consisted of exclusive hospital plans organized to serve the descendants of people from specific geographic regions of Spain, who paid monthly membership dues similar to medical insurance collectives. In 1948 this self-financed system served about 20 percent of the population and had about 242 clinics and hospitals. The mutualista system incorporated approximately 1.4 million associates and had an annual budget of 40 million pesos, twice that of the state budget, admitting only those members enrolled in their health programs.[8] Except for the program's exclusionary politics, the mutualista system represented one of clearest antecedents for what was later to become Cuba's socialized health care system.[9] Perhaps owing to the relative success of the mutualista system before 1959, Cuba's health profile and its health care delivery system were fairly good when compared to the health statistics of other developing countries in the region.[10] Cuban health statistics from the late 1940s and early 1960s indicate that it "appears to have been (in terms of health and sanitation) a healthier place in the Batista years than most contemporary representations of this period imply."[11]

However, the aggregate statistics masked enormous regional, racial, and class inequalities.[12] For instance, in 1959 more than 60 percent of Cuba's population of 6.5 million had virtually no access to health care. Given that more than 50 percent of the doctors and 70 percent of hospital facilities were in the capital province of Havana, where costly services catered to the fortunate few, the people of rural Cuba and the majority of the urban poor went unserved. This segment of the population depended on the few state-run services,[13] which were so corrupt, as suggested by interviews I conducted with people who experienced this period firsthand, that even admissions to hospitals were bestowed in exchange for favors or bribes to politicians.[14]

All of the above factors resulted in high morbidity and mortality rates for curable and preventable diseases such as polio, malaria, tuberculosis, and intestinal parasitism.[15] The general state of public health care for many

Cuban citizens in the período burgués is described in Castro's speech "History Will Absolve Me," given in his defense of 1953 before the Batista government's magistrate, where he stated the following:[16]

> Only death can liberate one from so much misery. . . . Ninety per cent of rural children are consumed by parasites, which filter through their bare feet from the earth. Society is moved to compassion when it hears of the kidnapping or murder of one child, but it is criminally indifferent to the mass murder of so many thousands of children who die every year from lack of facilities, agonizing in pain. . . . They will grow up with rickets, with not a single tooth in their mouths by the time they reach thirty; . . . and will finally die of misery and deception. Public hospitals, which are always full, accept only patients recommended by some powerful politician who, in turn, demands the electoral votes of the unfortunate one and his family so that Cuba may continue forever in the same or worse conditions.[17]

While undoubtedly serving as an evocative and highly stylized performance, Castro's landmark speech, whether taken as political rhetoric or as a true reflection of on-the-ground realities, articulates how inequitable access to medical services and facilities in the período burgués was a pivotal theme in mobilizing popular support for his movement. This discourse resonated with many individuals who were on the margins of Cuban society and, as Castro suggests, were placed there as a result of a range of political and cultural factors that created difference according to ethnicity, social class, and geographical location.

THE BODY AS A BATTLEGROUND

Soon after the revolutionary army arrived in Havana, Castro and his supporters, most prominently his brother Raúl Castro and Che Guevara, transformed the Cuban economy from one of entrepreneurial capitalism to a centrally planned system. Castro united various political groups to form the Organizaciones Revolucionarias Integradas (ORI) to spearhead this transformation of Cuban society. These changes, including land reforms, the nationalization and socialization of private property,[18] and campaigns to reduce illiteracy sought to equalize the vast disparities of resources, wealth, and education in Cuban society.[19] Many Cubans who were against the government's initial changes fled to the United States, in particular many of the business and professional classes and those closely associated with the

Socialist Governmentality and Risk

former Batista government, known as *batistianos*. In 1960, in response to Cuba's new policies, the U.S. government quickly imposed a partial embargo on Cuban imports. Almost a year later, in January 1961, in response to the Cuban government's expropriation of assets worth over one billion dollars belonging to U.S. enterprises, the United States severed relations with Cuba and extended the partial embargo to all goods, including food and medicine. The severity of the embargo may be gauged from Cuba's trade figures for 1959, in which 74 percent of all trade was with the United States. Cuba, left with no viable economic alternative, turned to the Soviet Union for trade and military protection. This relationship was formalized in 1972, when Cuba became a member of the Council for Mutual Economic Assistance. Cuba entered a period of hostile relations with the United States, framed by the geopolitics of the Cold War.[20]

While Castro's revolutionary government had not professed an adherence to a particular ideological framework earlier, Cuba's alliance with the Soviet Union heralded the growing importance of the Soviet model of socialism in Cuba's politico-economic organization and political ideology. For instance, when, in the early 1960s, under the tutelage of the Soviet Union, the Castro government started to make advancements in implementing public health programs, increased education, and the reduction of economic disparities, the revolutionary government also began to affirm Marxist-Leninist principles. In 1964 the Castro government formed the Partido Comunista de Cuba (PCC).[21] A new constitution, approved by referendum in 1976, replaced the one suspended when Batista fled in 1948. The new constitution describes Cuba as a socialist workers' state in which the entire population owns the basic means of production. However, the socialist government went beyond the oft-quoted Sovietization of Cuba and sought to socialize the populace by creating the *hombre nuevo* (new man). These cadres of men and women were to work together with the revolution to realize the collective vision of Cuba as a state of the people.

In the late 1960s and particularly in the early 1970s official state discourse in Cuba was steeped in Marxist-Leninist and Guevarist principles. Castro, drawing on Marx, portrayed communism as the highest, most ideal stage of development surpassing the earlier stages of feudalism, capitalism, and socialism. Echoing Marxist thinking, Castro advocated that under communism people would contribute according to their capacity and be rewarded according to their need. Following Lenin, Castro envisioned that a "vanguard party," the PCC, would facilitate this radical transition to communism.[22] For example, in the early 1960s Che Guevara strongly criticized the Soviet model of development for its bureaucratic and technocratic nature. Instead, Guevara advocated a strategy for economic, social, and political development to deepen and expand the role of the working people in Cuba. The ubiquitous revolutionary slogan of the time was *"¡Patria o Muerte!"* (Homeland or death!), which sought to implement the notion of heroic sacrifice (*numancia*) and the worker's dedication to the nation or the Cuban people (*el pueblo cubano*). In line with this vision, the worker was exhorted to labor for society rather than for personal gain.

Rather than work for material rewards, workers were to labor out of a sense of moral commitment. For their dedication, individuals were to be recognized with pennants, flags, and titles. During the Year of Solidarity in 1966, Castro stated, "If we want people to remove the dollar sign from their minds and from their hearts, we must have men who have gotten rid of their own mental dollar signs."[23] In line with these statements, the Castro government nationalized and expanded social services. Education, medical care, social security, day care, and most housing were provided free of charge, with access to them designed to be more equitable and need-based than ever before.[24] Seeking to dismantle the former class-based privilege and elitism of the prerevolutionary era, the new government drew on the utopian ideas of Marx and on Cuba's independence hero José Martí to break down barriers between manual, nonmanual, and intellectual labor. City dwellers and professionals were encouraged to voluntarily participate in seasonal agricultural labor, mainly in sugar production. Such activities, the government argued, would blur, if not eliminate, the contentious divide between consumer and producer, between bourgeoisie and proletariat, and help to create a communist consciousness (*conciencia*).

As part of the general initiative to incorporate the masses (*las masas*) into the revolutionary transformation, the Castro government created new organizations that brought people together on a territorial and functional interest-group basis. For example, the Comités de Defensa de la Revolución (CDRs),[25] the Cuban Women's Federation (FMC),[26] and the Cuban Labor Federation (CTC)[27] were just three of many organizations that encouraged the adult population to actively participate in revolutionary reform. Youth were organized into political groups during their schooling; primary school children formed the Cuban Pioneer's Union, and older students belonged to the Fed-

Socialist Governmentality and Risk

eration of Secondary School Students, the University Students' Federation, and the Union of Young Communists. The formative role of these organizations was, and still is, to instill the values of the revolution and, in turn, loyalty to the "vanguard party," that is, the PCC.[28] These organizations were officially recognized as the heart of "socialist civil society" and actually operated as "transmission belts" to solidify the relationship between the state and the party.[29] This relationship is reflected "in their [the mass organizations'] negligible autonomy evident in their public stances on a variety of issues."[30]

Theoretically, more than 80 percent of the Cuban population belongs to one or more of the youth and adult organizations, representing one of the state's objectives: the active participation of the entire population in social and state activities. The pedagogical and social importance of mass organizations in Cuba's social transformation cannot be underestimated. Revolutionary campaigns like the fight against illiteracy and the programs for reeducation and job training were influential in the construction of active, productive members of the communities. As studies of that era make clear, las masas were also inspired to devotion by Castro's almost messianic status.[31]

Descending from the mountains with peasants-turned-rebels at his side, Castro symbolized the battle to free Cuba from what revolutionary pedagogy defined as the three evils of the Batista government: hunger, misery, and exploitation. As Damián Fernández notes, "Charisma, popular religiosity, and political religion . . . are keys to understanding the emotional force of the revolution in the early years and the issues of legitimacy, authority, political strategies, and violence. The revolution evoked feelings and also relied on those feelings to muster support and, in no small measure, to survive in power."[32] Narratives like that of a man named Rivera reflect these commitments: "I have always favored the Revolution and hated *gusanos* [worms]. . . . Those gusanos forget the miserable poverty in Machado's time. . . . People complain we're not free because we have no elections and are under Fidel's dictatorship. But there's more freedom now in every way. . . . And it was Fidel who gave the country back to the people! I feel patriotic for the first time, because now Cuba is *our* country."[33] The state's various mass organizations were an important mechanism that fed on this early revolutionary fervor and rallied support around revolutionary objectives and projects, in particular the project of building an egalitarian communist state.[34]

Shortly after the Cuban revolution, a plethora of state institutions, sup-ported by an elaborate network of mass organizations, managed to exercise an unparalleled degree of authority in promoting various public health initiatives, such as decreasing infant mortality and detecting and containing infectious diseases. These initiatives, which reinforced the state's commit-ment to health care as a constitutional right and repudiated the evils associ-ated with class-stratified, capitalist societies, were rooted in the underlying principles of the revolution. These principles suggested that attempts to restore the health of individuals, in the broadest sense, are also attempts to restore the health of the society as a whole. Consequently, the health, wel-fare, and accomplishments of the revolutionary government are "at heart, political; they are contingent on state priorities, on types of programs gov-ernments choose to finance, and the groups targeted."[35]

On January 1, 1959, when the Cuban rebel army marched victoriously into Havana, the emphasis of the new government was on dismantling discriminatory practices and making universal provisions for basic needs and health care.[36] Like other developing nations with socialist ideologies of that era, Cuba embraced a vision of modernity that entailed not only taking advantage of the scientific and technical revolution but also being part of it.[37] Incorporating science as an element of their strategy for the overall socioeconomic development of the island, the revolutionary government embraced the socialist vision of science as a means for achieving a rational and planned social transformation.[38] Public health and medicine were key areas in which considerable investments were made: research facilities, tech-nology, research and development strategies, and human resources were amply funded. In the revolutionary context, health became an important index of the larger social transformations associated with the socioeconomic development of Cuba, including the elimination of hunger, inadequate housing, discrimination, and the reduction of exploitative labor practices.

At the onset of the revolution in 1960 influential figures like the Argentine-born doctor-turned-revolutionary Che Guevara assisted Castro in outlining a system of social medicine. Seeking to cure the social ills of society, Guevara believed disease prevention consisted not only of a detailed compilation and analysis of diseases, but also of a history of "what their [Cubans'] sufferings are . . . including their chronic miseries for years, and what has been the inheritance of centuries of repression and total submission."[39] Under Guevara's plan for "the creation of a robust body with the work of the entire collectivity upon the entire social collectivity," the revolutionary government invested considerable amounts of attention to expanding and democratizing access to the public health system.[40] The government created a model of health care that was informed by the revolutionaries' vision of a new social order, which in turn would help to create the hombre nuevo.

During the early 1960s roughly half of the country's doctors fled the island when the revolutionary government began expropriating and nationalizing all foreign-owned enterprises. As a result, the first priority in reforming public health care was to begin training an entirely new medical corps under the philosophy of the hombre nuevo. Moving against the trend occurring in other developing countries, the state focused on training fully qualified physicians to handle every level and aspect of curative medicine. The medical responsibilities given to paramedics and community health workers diminished. Drawing heavily on revolutionary metaphors, Guevara proclaimed, "Now the conditions are different, and the new armies which are being formed to defend the country must be armed with different tactics. The doctor will have an enormous importance within the plan of the new army."[41] Instead of the Hippocratic oath, medical graduates promised to abide by revolutionary principles: "They were asked to agree to serve the rural areas, not engage in private practice, promote preventive medicine and human welfare, strive for scientific excellence and political devotion, encourage proletarian internationalism, and to defend the revolution."[42] The first priority of the revolutionary government was the organization and development of an integrated national health system that would govern the health of the entire population, making it the full responsibility of the state.

Of the 6,300 physicians in Cuba in 1959, only 3,433 remained in 1967 after their exodus en masse, principally to the United States and Spain.[43] In addition, in 1960 only sixteen professors remained at the only medical school in the country, in Havana. Severely hampered by the paucity of medical professionals, the government initially encountered difficulties in extending health care to marginalized groups in urban and rural locations and in maintaining the existing state-run health services in Havana. However, Cuba's newfound relationship with the Soviet Union in 1961 was influential. The Soviet Union helped Cuba to enact its plan for a revolutionized health care system. For example, Soviet physicians and allied health professionals from other socialist countries compensated for the domestic shortage of doctors and professors. In 1964 the Havana Medical School graduated 394 physicians.[44] By 1971, 30 percent of all university students were studying medicine, and new medical schools were being built to accommodate the growing student body across the country.[45] In 1972, when the number of doctors reached 7,200, the quota was dropped to 20 percent.[46] To help address the shortage of physicians in marginalized areas, all new medical graduates were assigned to three years of rural service.[47]

In 1961 the first plan for a comprehensive national system of primary health service began to take form. After an initial purging of Batista supporters from the medical class (*la clase médica*), the administration of some hospitals and clinics was turned over to physicians who had served in the revolutionary army and to other physicians dedicated to revolutionary reform.[48] Following the Czechoslovakian model of health planning, which concentrated the administration of health care in one governing body with an administratively decentralized delivery system, Cuban public health officials formed the current Sistema Nacional de Salud (sns, national health system). The sns is organized at three levels: national, provincial, and municipal. The national level is represented by the minsap, which coordinates everything pertaining to health and health care and fulfills the methodological, regulatory, coordination, and control functions for the whole country.[49] Provincial and municipal levels are represented by public health offices, which are under the direct financial and administrative authority of their respective provincial and municipal councils. All levels integrate the basic functions of public health: treatment, health protection, long- and short-range planning, and scientific improvement of health workers.[50]

Under the direction of the sns, the existing state-run services fell under the control of the revolutionary government and were subsequently restructured. The two remaining systems, the mutualista program and private health care, were left intact temporarily to handle the severe shortage of medical personnel. However, a new law introduced in August 1961, known as Law Number 949, indicated that the minsap was in charge of all the health activities in the country, including the private health and mutualista systems. The latter two were phased out by 1970 and were either closed or changed into public facilities and integrated into the sns. In 1964 the integral polyclinic program (*policlínico integral*) was the first health services program that the new sns embarked on.

POLICLÍNICO INTEGRAL

Representing the earliest stage of establishing primary health care in postrevolutionary Cuba, the integral polyclinic program offered outpatient care that sought to decentralize the services traditionally supplied by hospitals by targeting medically marginalized groups in both rural and urban areas.[51] The four founding principles of the new revolutionary primary health care system were (1) The health of all people is the full responsibility of the state; (2) Universal coverage is guaranteed to all persons without discrimination; (3) The people must participate actively to assure and maintain high health levels; (4) Preventive care is the primary goal of health care. The polyclinic system was designed to instill, integrate, and address these founding principles through the provision of four basic services in a specifically defined area and population: clinical services (for example, curative-preventive care); environmental services (hygiene and sanitation); community health services (health promotion campaigns); and related social services (social workers).[52]

Between 1962 and 1970 the number of polyclinics in the country steadily rose from 161 to 308, and by 1976 there were 344 fully staffed polyclinics operating in the country and an additional 140 rural medical posts.[53] The polyclinic's health coverage was subdivided on a regional basis into sectors, each with about thirty thousand inhabitants served by health teams that included preventive and curative wings. Polyclinics typically offered primary care specialists, including several internists, a pediatrician, an obstetrician-gynecologist, a dentist, a nurse, and a social worker. Polyclinics also offered clinical outpatient services designed to prevent illness and to improve the quality of public health.

The foremost objective of the integral polyclinic was to reduce morbidity and mortality from communicable diseases, which were a major health problem in Cuba in the 1960s. MINSAP officials believed that continuous care by the same health team promotes a better understanding of the patients and their environments on the part of staff. Such an understanding, health officials thought, would be effective in addressing the physical and social causes of the patients' illness. By 1970 the following health programs were being implemented, in elementary form, in every municipal polyclinic: comprehensive attention to women, comprehensive attention to children, comprehensive attention to adults, hygiene and epidemiological surveillance, dental care, and postgraduate training programs for medical staff.[54]

The policlínicos relied heavily on the popular participation of state-promoted mass organizations in order to carry out various public health campaigns. During the October Missile Crisis in 1962, for example, the MINSAP needed to organize people to give blood so that the country would have a sufficient reserve in case of emergency. Within ten days the CDR had mobilized eight thousand Cubans to give blood.[55] Moreover, the mass organizations participated in health education, literacy training, and other social activities, all of which sought to incorporate the wider community in the state's various reform campaigns. These campaigns included mass immunization programs, blood donations, and disease-control campaigns such as hygiene and sanitation lessons.

A well-known example of widespread participation in disease control was the role played by mass organizations in the polio vaccination campaigns of the early 1960s (figure 4). These campaigns were carried out throughout the country in as little as seventy-two hours. As a result, polio was eliminated from Cuba by 1963, years before the United States succeeded in doing so. Campaigns were also carried out to vaccinate against tuberculosis (figure 5). These public campaigns were conducted in tandem with massive literacy campaigns and *brigadistas* (public health brigades) that explained the evolutionary cycle of parasitism and how poor sanitary conditions contributed to disease transmission. For instance, in an interview I conducted with Julio César Serra, born in 1955, he described his experience of several of these campaigns:

> When *la Revolución* arrived there was a great deal of ignorance. There were families that were afraid of the vaccines; there were people who thought they were diabolic things. You could hear any number of ridiculous theories and ideas about what was happening. The government immediately began educating the population, reading health education pamphlets on the television and the radio all over the country, trying to educate the population about boiling drinking water and about the importance of children using shoes to prevent parasites from entering through their feet. La Revolución informed families about all these problems and said, "Look, you can't have stagnant water because it can be a breeding ground for mosquitoes, and mosquitoes can transmit diseases."

Through the creation of mobile sanitary units that worked with mass organizations and traveled around the country to address environmental problems and implement health promotion and disease prevention, the

Socialist Governmentality and Risk

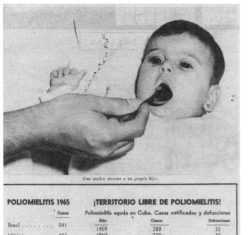

FIGURE 4. Elimination of poliomyelitis in Cuba. Source: *Bohemia*, 6 February 1970: 65.

FIGURE 5. Vaccinations against BCG tuberculosis. Source: *Bohemia*, 23 April 1965: 107.

population was encouraged to become more attuned to bodily functions and to adopt practices that linked health, hygiene, and the environment (figures 6–9). With catch phrases such as "Hagamos de Cuba el País Más Saludable del Mundo" (Let's make Cuba the healthiest country in the world) and "Higiene es Salud" (Hygiene is health), these campaigns aimed at transforming the social body by targeting individual bodily practices. In effect, these campaigns trained the population to increasingly view their bodies through a specific biomedical framework. For example, campaigns strongly advised the population to avoid ad hoc home remedies and self-medication of undiagnosed problems, especially among infants and children. Instead, the campaigns emphasized the importance of the physician as the *only* person authorized to determine the cause of unexplained ailments (figure 10). At the same time, campaigns educated the population about the symptoms and etiology of infectious diseases such as hepatitis (figure 11) and the biological functions of nutrition (figure 12).

In spite of these exhaustive campaigns and the optimistic efforts of the integral polyclinic, the program was not entirely successful in dealing with the burgeoning health needs of the population, which had been without basic health services for many years. Cuban public health officials found problems with the system. For instance, a shortage of medical personnel specializing in primary health care meant that a different physician treated the same patient from one visit to another.[56] This reduced the chances that a particular doctor would be familiar with a patient's life history. Second, physicians did not work in health teams, as originally planned, and as a result the interdisciplinary component believed necessary to address health issues was absent. Third, health care tended to be primarily curative, and physicians lacked the appropriate doctor-patient-community relationship required for the new socialist society. The poor training of primary health care workers led to an increased number of patient cases referred to secondary specialists and to the appearance of more people in hospital emergency rooms.

The shortage of physicians entering primary health care was a result of the lack of opportunities to engage in advanced teaching and training at the primary health level. There was little incentive, therefore, for professionals and technicians to enter this specialty. In an attempt to address these weaknesses, a general restructuring of the polyclinics' operations occurred in 1976 under the heading of Medicina en la Comunidad (Medicine in the Community).

Socialist Governmentality and Risk

FIGURE 6. Listen to this friend . . . ! The Sanitation Inspector will periodically knock on your door. This person is responsible for making sure that you follow the campaigns to exterminate the *Aedes aegypti* mosquito, which transmits Yellow Fever. We will eradicate the mosquito that transmits Yellow Fever! Source: *Bohemia*, 19 February 1964: 82.

FIGURE 7. Parasitism: Measures of control: Wash your hands; Boil water and milk; Wash fruits and vegetables; Cook meats thoroughly. Source: *Bohemia*, 23 April 1965: 107.

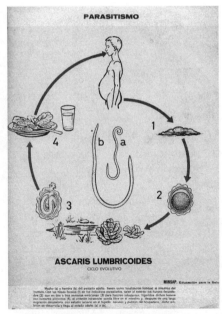

FIGURE 8. Parasitism: Life cycle of *Ascaris lumbricoides* (roundworm). Source: *Bohemia*, 26 February 1965: back cover.

FIGURE 9. Hygiene Is Health.
Let's Make Cuba the Healthiest
Country in the World. Source:
Bohemia, 5 February 1965: 80.

FIGURE 10. To a child with vomiting
and diarrhea . . . Giving them the
first home remedy recommended to
you IS DANGEROUS! Taking lightly the
use of informally procured medicine
has caused a great number of infant
deaths from GASTROENTERITIS. At the
first signs of vomiting and diarrhea,
GO TO THE DOCTOR! He is the only
person authorized to decide the
cause of those symptoms. Source:
Bohemia, 5 March 1965: 91.

FIGURE 11. What do you know about your
health? Infectious hepatitis. Source: *Bohemia*,
23 April 1965: 99.

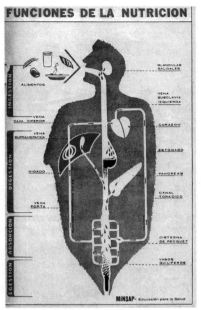

FIGURE 12. The functions of nutrition.
Source: *Bohemia*, 2 February 1965:
back cover.

This program was hailed as an improved model that viewed health as a function of the biological, environmental, and social well-being of individuals.

MEDICINA EN LA COMUNIDAD

The year 1970 marked a shift to a second, distinct stage in the development of
the public health system. In 1969 the Ten-Year Health Plan, which sought to
carry out various health initiatives from 1970 to 1980, was enacted. One of
the priorities of the plan was screening for asymptomatic diseases. Health-
related activities were directed at enriching and developing principles that
aimed not only to provide therapy, but also to investigate hidden morbidity.
The latter required the health teams to work on highlighting the social morbidity that contributed to nontransmissible chronic illnesses and their risk
factors. This meant giving priority to the treatment of healthy people who
exhibited risk factors for certain diseases or disorders over individuals who
were healthy but exhibited low risk factors. For example, the public health
campaigns of 1970, as evinced in health promotion advertisements, started
targeting smoking and lifestyle, such as unhealthy diets and sedentarism.

The Medicine in the Community program, also known as the *policlínicos comunitarios*, was first tested in the Policlínico Alamar in 1974. It incorporated existing health programs from the policlínico integral system. Polyclinic teams were assigned to a sector of the population, such as infants or the elderly, that was defined by its high-risk assessment. This allowed medical services to be dispensed through a system known as *dispensarización*, which provided continuous assessment and risk evaluation. Each municipality had a defined number of health areas, and each urban health area with twenty-four thousand to thirty thousand inhabitants had a polyclinic, while rural areas were served by rural hospitals.

Prior to Medicine in the Community, people went to the polyclinic in their area and saw the appropriate primary care physician. In the new program, the community-based model of primary care provided integrated health programs carried out by a health team that sought "to discover the health status of the population, to select the at-risk population groups for various health programs, to define the environmental, biological, social, and psychological factors that interrelate as determining variables in the health-illness process, and to analyze the needs and resources available."[57]

"The physician-nurse teams attend[ed] patients in the polyclinic [and] also visited patients in their everyday environment: the home, school, day-care centre, and workplace."[58] During the 1970s, in collaboration with the WHO and the Pan American Health Organization (PAHO), Cuba elaborated a strategy to advance medical science, health services, and the health status of the population to the highest international levels. Relying heavily on criteria such as the infant mortality rate that had been set out by the WHO as standard health indicators, Cuba created a number of national public health campaigns targeted at lowering infant mortality and increasing infant life expectancy at birth. Understanding Cuba's infant mortality rate as a reflection of the success of the country's health care system, the revolutionary government placed a strong emphasis on health care programs for women, with priority given to maternal and infant care programs.

The development of maternal and infant health care programs was carried out against a background of broad socioeconomic changes that affected women's lives, such as the redefining of traditional female roles in a revolutionary context. In the spirit of egalitarianism and arguably also out of a shortage of workers, the Castro government sought out women's participation in the newly designed workforce. The government made a concerted effort to facilitate this transformation, which Castro referred to as a "revolution within a revolution." In 1976 the constitution codified women's equal rights in marriage, employment, wage equity, and education. Sex discrimination was punishable by a withholding of rations or by imprisonment. Moreover, the famous family code of 1976 noted that men were to share household duties when women were gainfully employed. These measures were complemented by the massive extension of public day care facilities and, in 1974, a maternity law that guaranteed women paid maternity leave and the right to take time off from work to attend to their children's health care needs. Under the new revolutionary system many women had become actively involved in juggling the roles of working mother and good *revolucionaria*. Women were incorporated into mass organizations and participated in such revolutionary projects as seasonal agricultural labor and health education campaigns.

The FMC was an extension of the state apparatus that gave women a collective voice and ensured their full and equal participation in the revolutionary movement. A well-known indicator of women's changing role in postrevolutionary Cuba was the birth rate in the first two decades after the revolution, which has steadily declined since 1963 and represents one of the lowest in Latin American. For example, by 1979 the birth rate had dropped to 18.0 per 1,000 inhabitants from 28.3 per 1,000 before the revolution. While the revolutionary government always provided birth control methods at low cost to women who wanted them, it did not conduct public campaigns to promote family planning. Such a remarkable decline in the birth rate in the absence of any governmental effort to bring it about, while other countries like Mexico have used high-pressure tactics without success, indicates that the socioeconomic pressures for having many children had been mitigated, and women were beginning to assess on their own accord the advantages of having smaller families.[59]

In 1977 the MINSAP established a series of objectives to be met by primary health care centers nationwide: "Early detection of pregnancy (before the third month); early consultation with the obstetrical health team (also before the third month); provision of at least nine prenatal examinations and consultations for women in urban areas and six for women in rural areas; education about hygiene, health during pregnancy, childbirth, and child care; special prenatal attention to women considered to be high obstetrical risk; psychological counseling with regard to childbirth; instruction in birth exercises; and finally, a provision that all childbirth take place in hospitals."[60] Consistent with its objective to manage the country's infant mortality rate, the government also began targeting perinatal diseases and congenital problems, the main causes of infant death. Perinatal intensive care units were created in all maternal and infant hospitals, and therapeutic abortions were strongly advised for mothers found, through genetic screening, to be carrying babies with congenital abnormalities.[61]

Utilizing the extensive network of public organizations, specifically CDRs and the FMC, the MINSAP trained health brigade members (*brigadistas sanitarias*) to assist polyclinic staff in seeking out pregnant women. The aim was to target expectant mothers and discuss with them the need to go for medical consultation and to monitor those women who failed to appear for their scheduled appointments. This popular participation in health campaigns, which was described by PAHO as a critical strategy to achieve health for all by the year 2000, was crucial to the increased institutionalization of childbirth in Cuba in the early 1980s. In addition to basic health coverage, all women who were pregnant or breastfeeding were granted supplemental food rations and vitamins. Furthermore, measures were taken by the Cuban government to improve children's life expectancy from birth. For example, the use of such facilities as maternity homes guaranteed that nearly 100 percent of babies were born in hospitals with staffs trained to detect birth-related problems. Maternity homes, an integral part of the current primary health care system, are comprised of residential facilities with medical attendants where women go when they reached approximately thirty-seven weeks in their pregnancy. There, women await the birth in the company of other women and free of the responsibilities of maintaining a household. After delivery, new mothers and their babies generally go home on the first postpartum day and are seen in the home daily by a family doctor and nurse for the next ten days. Additionally, a doctor or nurse schedules a minimum of two monthly pediatric visits along with one home visit (figures 13, 14).

The successes of the Medicine in the Community health system, including the maternal and infant care health program, lent credence to MINSAP officials' claims that the individual could best be treated as a psychosocial being (that is, treated in both mind and body) in a specific environment. The new program was widely heralded by the government as an ideal social medicine program because it was designed to view health and medicine as integral to the overall socioeconomic development of Cuba. MINSAP officials

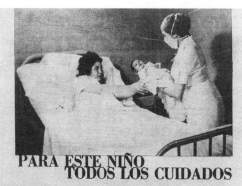

FIGURE 13. For this child, we are all caregivers: The pediatric identification card guarantees your child appropriate attention. Source: *Bohemia*, 15 January 1965: 71.

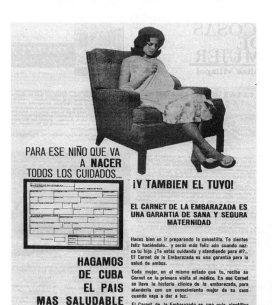

FIGURE 14. For this child who is to be born, we are all caregivers . . . and for you as well! Source: *Bohemia*, 8 January 1965: 91.

argued that the new health program would effectively provide health care to the country and reach the state's goal of making Cuba a world medical power (*potencia médica mundial*). Cuban leaders considered health indicators to be measures of the efficacy of the socialist revolutionary project. As a report from the MINSAP declared, "Infant mortality is one of the indicators internationally considered to be the greatest global measure for the health of a country. Before the triumph of the Revolution, infant mortality in Cuba was greater than 70 deaths per 1,000 live births, in 1987, we achieved a rate of 13.3. This rate is very similar to those exhibited in more developed countries, and the results of this and other indicators allow us to determine the state of health of our population."[62] The MINSAP's statements reflected the official public health discourse in Cuba, which cites the country's low infant mortality rate as a currency of symbolic exchange, whereby vital statistics index the success of socialist modernity. This increasing reliance on statistical fetishism, however, belies the increased role that women's reproductive labor plays in achieving these goals.

Despite Cuba's success in reaching a low infant mortality rate, the overall achievements of the primary health program quickly fell short of the objectives. Several studies have illustrated that the community health teams were not adequately trained to screen the population for certain ailments. Specifically, chronic illnesses like cancer and high blood pressure, along with related heart diseases, were not adequately detected and went untreated.[63] Cuban primary public health professionals commented that there were inequalities between the care offered at the training polyclinics—centers associated with teaching hospitals (less than 10 percent of those clinics in the country)—and that offered in nontraining polyclinics. In addition, health teams were unable to effectively address the behavioral determinants of ill health, including smoking, alcoholism, and promiscuity, that put people at risk. As a consequence, they failed to create health promotion campaigns aimed at high-risk groups and antismoking campaigns (figures 15 and 16). Some health care teams' lack of familiarity with the families and communities in which they worked meant that they were unable to identify other important social problems, which impeded a holistic, integrative approach to health care. The lack of personalized medical attention by the same health teams resulted in the persistence of symptomatic visits, which were treated as acute episodes, without an examination of the relationship between the illness and its broader biological, emotional, or social origins.

Socialist Governmentality and Risk

FIGURE 15. Why? You have a right to be healthy. Source: *Bohemia*, 13 November 1970: back cover.

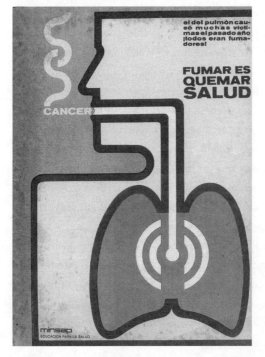

FIGURE 16. To smoke is to "burn" your health. (Lung cancer caused the death of many people in the past year. All were smokers!) Source: *Bohemia*, 16 January 1970: back cover.

In conclusion, public health officials determined that the community medicine program lacked the tools to provide an integrative evaluation that took into consideration all the factors affecting the well-being of patients. Doctors ended up having a passive role in the polyclinics and waiting for morbidity to arrive instead of seeking out, preventing, and controlling their patients' health problems after a careful analysis of the morbidity of the population. The excessive workload of the nontraining polyclinics contributed to the quality of care given, which was not the best in many instances. For example, many of the personnel at the polyclinics failed to make appropriate referrals to specialists at local hospitals. Often this resulted in patients preferring to go directly to the hospitals themselves (where the assistance was, at least, faster), bypassing the polyclinics altogether. As a result, the program did not achieve the objectives of an integrative, holistic medicine for the population and still had a technical-biological focus at the expense of attention to psychosocial and environmental variables.

Given the above conclusions, in the 1980s the Castro government became convinced that the structure of medical services and education in Cuba needed fundamental change. Castro formed the Carlos F. Finlay Medical Detachment in 1982 to restructure the profession of medicine. Given that the pattern of morbidity and mortality in Cuba had slowly changed from diseases of poverty, for example, parasitic and infectious diseases, to diseases of development, such as heart disease and cancer, Castro called for the training of better-equipped primary care family doctors to better address the changing populations' health needs. Under the newly formed detachment, Castro declared family medicine to be a new specialty in medical training, one that was subsequently designated as a new generalists' residency program termed Medicina General Integral (MGI), thereby eliminating the distinction between the practice of general medicine and specialization.

Medical education was extended from six to ten years when MINSAP instituted a new curriculum that required six years of undergraduate and predoctoral medical education and a four-year residency in MGI.[64] This new scheme meant that medical students would now graduate as *médicos generales básicos* (MGB). In order to integrate these new medical professionals into the SNS, the revolutionary government designated an interdisciplinary commission to "elaborate the conceptualization of community medicine within the Marxist–Leninist and socialist ideology and character of the health system."[65] Out of this process emerged the current primary health care system, MEF, created in 1984, that is central to it. As was evident shortly after the launch of the MEF program, Castro declared the participating physicians to be "symbols of the Revolution"[66] and focused on their roles as reinforcing the values of the revolution through their continual contact with the population.

4

CURING THE SOCIAL ILLS OF SOCIETY

In my community, and other similar rural communities, the doctor arrives like the *cacique* [chief] of the place. Everybody depends on the doctor to solve his or her problems. I remember one day in particular, the people called on me to decide if a person should be thrown out of the community. I said, "How is this possible?"

They said, "Doctor, you are the one who can decide who can stay or who can be removed from here. This man is a thief and a drunk." The *pueblo* depended on me to hand out justice as the *médico de la familia*. In these communities, the doctor is everything. Logically, the pueblo identifies with the doctor as a person that is more cultured than they are. The doctor is considered to have greater reasoning skills than the average person. In my capacity as a doctor, therefore, I may speak with greater authority about what the community's problems are, and so forth. In addition to everything else, the doctor works to identify the social problems or, we could say, the doctor manages the problems of the community. For example, I designed a project in my community that was not just about diseases, but also about fixing and cleaning up the streets. I knew that the community was in poor physical condition and full of weeds and trash. I also wanted to fix the communal water well and paint all the houses.

Of course, these activities were not directly associated with individual health. However, it is my belief that by improving the overall social environment, I was also improving the mental well-being of the pueblo. The individuals in the community felt that I was participating in bettering their social situation, and therefore they respected me more. They loved me more and saw me as kind of a leader.

Alberto Navarro, family physician, born in Cienfuegos in 1971

Alberto Navarro, a primary health care physician who worked for several years in a rural community, described his experiences as a family doctor in the rural outpost he was assigned to shortly after graduating from medical school. His sense of pride was linked to his ability to address the community's health and well-being by attempting to improve the social environment. What was not explicit in Navarro's narrative, but of equal importance, was the physician's political role in the community. For Navarro, community health and well-being were equally about managing dissent and reinforcing the state's sense of community. As he further noted, his work in the community was effective because he was able, in his own words, "to manipulate people into participating in their own health reform." By prompting citizens to work together toward a common goal—a healthy community—the physician was also promoting a specific orientation toward *la Revolución*: integrating individual notions of self into state objectives.

One of the clearest programmatic statements linking Cuba's family physicians to a political agenda is provided by the MINSAP, which declares family physicians should "abide by moral and ethical principles of deep human, ideological and patriotic content; such as, to dedicate [their] efforts and knowledge to the improvement of the health of humankind, to work constantly where society requires [them] and to always be available to offer the necessary medical attention where it is needed."[1] Furthermore, part of the honor code of Cuban health professionals is to pledge allegiance to *la patria* (homeland) and make an oath to maintain the socialist character of the health system, which the MINSAP declares as the moral and ethical basis for all of their actions. The physicians training manual states, "The practice of the health professional has in itself a profound ethical underpinning that is geared toward promoting the highest values in human beings in order to pay homage every day, and in every sphere, to the work of la Revolución, of which we are children."[2]

The nineteenth-century German physician Rudolf Virchow is considered by many to be the founder of social medicine. He is often linked to the now-famous aphorism that has become the mantra of public health movements: "Medicine is a social science, and politics is nothing but medicine writ large." Implicit in Virchow's argument was a demonstration of how social inequality was a root cause of ill health, and medicine therefore had to be a social science of alleviating suffering. Physicians, according to Virchow, should assume the role of statesmen because of their intimate knowledge of society's problems. In many ways, the role of physicians in local communities, whether urban or rural, is about curing what Guevara suggested are the social ills of society. Navarro's narrative is easy to read in that respect because of the self-aggrandizing tone, but it is also revealing, if in less obvious terms, of the disjuncture between Cuba's social health ideology and individual and governmental practices.

EL PROGRAMA DEL MÉDICO Y
LA ENFERMERA DE LA FAMILIA

In the 1980s, the MINSAP, instituting a measure considered to be the most ambitious phase of Cuba's SNS, initiated a proposal to train family physicians to participate in an innovative primary health care program called El Programa del Médico y la Enfermera de la Familia (MEF). Starting as a pilot project in the Policlínico Lawton in the municipality of 10th of October in 1984, with the incorporation of ten physicians and nurses, the program called for specially trained health teams to create a closer patient–physician relationship than had existed in the past and to provide extensive physician and support-staff care. Trained under the new medical school curriculum instituted by the MINSAP in the early 1980s, all new medical residents were to receive training in general medicine and then pursue a residency in comprehensive general medicine (MGI) (see chapter 3).[3] The MGI residency involves specialized training in primary health care, including a rotation in each of the primary care specialties—that is, internal medicine, pediatrics, obstetrics, and gynecology—as well as a rotation in neighborhood-based clinics, supervised by family physicians.

By the end of 1985 the MEF program had expanded to include 10,000 physicians, and by 2009 it included 34,261 physicians overseeing 100 percent of the population (table 1).[4] Physician-and-nurse health teams—*equipos básicos de salud*—are stationed in *consultorios del médico de la familia*, small clinics located throughout the country. Each clinic serves 120 families, approximately 600–700 persons, and is located in a designated health area (*área de salud*) that is attended to by the physician-and-nurse team. In organization, the MEF program calls for family physician-and-nurse teams to live and work on the city block or in the rural community in which they serve.[5] Moreover, physician-and-nurse teams are stationed in every factory and school. The role of the new family physicians, following the MEF work program issued by the MINSAP—Programa de Trabajo del Médico y Enfermera de la Familia, el Policlínico y el Hospital (1988)—was to carry out clinical and social-epidemiological vigilance of the population, promote

TABLE I. CUBA'S PUBLIC HEALTH STATISTICS, 2009

Human Resources

Total health service staff	582,538
Physician per 10,000 inhabitants ratio	66.6
Nursing staff per 10,000 habitants	94.7
Population covered by MEF program (%)	100

Service facilities

Hospitals	219
Consultorios MEF	12,068
Polyclinics	498
Health posts	127
Dental clinics	158
Maternity homes	338

SOURCES: Provisional data provided by MINSAP (2009).

health, and prevent disease by working in tandem with the community. As further stipulated in the MEF work program, the specific functions of the participating health professionals are (1) to promote health through education, lifestyle changes, and an improvement in hygienic and sanitary habits and conditions; (2) to prevent illness and conditions dangerous to health; (3) to guarantee early diagnosis and comprehensive outpatient and inpatient medical care over time; (4) to develop community-based rehabilitation for the physically or psychiatrically disabled; (5) to aid the social integration of families and communities; (6) to complete residency training in family practice with scientific excellence and a willingness to serve humanity; and (7) to do research that responds to the health needs of the population.[6]

According to the MINSAP, the design and structure of the MEF program allowed for greater accessibility to health care services and a closer relationship between health teams and their patients (figure 17). This tactic, the MINSAP proposed, would allow health teams an opportunity to obtain a more intimate knowledge of their patients and family members, enabling family physicians to better comprehend their patients' psychological and physical problems and to provide immediate, continuous care. Cuban leaders asserted the MEF program was the ultimate achievement in the field of health care. It went beyond the WHO's Alma Ata Declaration of 1978 on primary health care,[7] and made significant headway on a holistic approach

FIGURE 17. An MEF consultorio. Brotherton © 2001.

to health care that addresses biological factors in tandem with an individual's material and social environment, thereby providing a diagnosis on the social fabric that encompasses health and well-being.[8]

In the years after the launch of the MEF program, popular Cuban newspapers and journals like *Bohemia* and the Communist Party daily, *Granma*, and state-sponsored publications ran a number of feature articles on the MEF program. For instance, Marta Rojas, a widely read Cuban journalist, wrote a book titled *Doctors in the Sierra Maestra*, which chronicled the relentless sacrifice of physicians in the rural Sierra Maestra mountain ranges, a geographic region symbolically tied to the origins of the revolutionary guerrilla movement. Rojas's book draws on revolutionary metaphors such as heroic sacrifice and the importance of moral, as opposed to material, rewards in order to portray the doctors as versions of their revolutionary predecessors, like Castro and Guevara, only armed not with guns but with stethoscopes and compassion, which she suggests are products of Cuba's socialist ideology. Overall, the description of the MEF program in state-sponsored publications deftly integrated the trope of the valiant family physician as a revolutionary hero. In many ways, these publications emphasized the uniqueness of the MEF program and declared it an exemplary model in holistic primary health care delivery. Undoubtedly, these publications also serve as crucial media by which the government educates the population about the role of

Socialist Governmentality and Risk

the new physicians and, in no uncertain terms, explains why people should warmly accept them into their homes and communities.

Community participation in health care initiatives and the health care decision-making process are crucial to the MEF program. The creation of popular councils (*poderes populares*) in 1976 theoretically allowed citizens more grass-roots involvement in the government's decision-making process. For example, to allow citizens to play a greater role in what Castro referred to as the "defense of health," popular participation in health campaigns was to be facilitated by strategically placing consultorios in an area circumscribed by one or more mass organizations, such as CDRs or delegations of the FMC. As I noted in chapter 3, mass organizations historically worked in tandem with the primary health care system in disseminating health education and health promotion campaigns and actively took part in programs of hygiene and disease prevention.[9]

Going beyond the community primary health services provided in the past, the consultorios were supported by a massive expansion of secondary and tertiary health care institutions. In the 1980s, for example, in the drive to make the SNS comparable to those of other industrially developed countries, the revolutionary government made major financial investments in state-of-the-art tertiary care institutions, such as the Clinical Surgical Hospital Hermanos Ameijeiras and the Center for Medical Investigation and Surgery, and research facilities such as the Center for Genetic Engineering and Biotechnology.[10] These institutions offer a wide range of health care services, including organ transplants, in vitro fertilization, laser surgery, and magnetic resonance imaging; they have also been involved in the development of genetic engineering and biotechnology and in the production and research of vaccines and pharmaceuticals.[11]

Acting as an intermediary between the consultorios and tertiary institutions, a complex network of local polyclinics and municipal hospitals provides laboratory, ancillary, and emergency room services as well as supervision, teaching, and subspecialty consultation. To facilitate this organization, each polyclinic in every municipality oversees ten to fifteen consultorios that form a working group known as a Grupo Básico de Trabajo. Each polyclinic is staffed with a specialist in internal medicine, a pediatrician, an obstetric-gynecologist, a psychologist, a dentist, a supervising nurse, a social worker, a statistician, and an epidemiological-and-hygiene technician. All public health services are institutionally integrated, both horizontally and vertically. For example, under the MEF program a physician can refer a patient to the services in the polyclinics, which in turn can make referrals to a municipal hospital (that is, family medicine consultorio ⟺ polyclinic ⟺ hospital). The family physician is always the patient's primary provider and is consulted during diagnosis and treatment. Moreover, the family physician is required to follow up on patients who have been treated at other levels of the health system, such as at polyclinics and hospitals. In this way, the family physicians never lose contact with their patients, even if the patients are admitted to an intensive care unit. Physicians can also make suggestions on the treatment of their patients while they are in more specialized institutions.

A unique aspect of the MEF program is its consideration of the family as the basic unit of attention. This allows health teams to consider the repercussions of the problems of the individual on the family as a whole, and vice versa. Furthermore, ideally, the family is to be an integral part of all prevention, treatment, and rehabilitation of health problems. One of the hallmarks of the MEF program is the introduction of at-home treatment, based on the family physician's judgment, the patient's condition, and the family members' ability to care for the patient at home. Cuban health care administrators believed this approach would reduce the high expenses incurred by admitting and treating people unnecessarily in local hospitals, thereby freeing up the total number of beds available. Furthermore, as public health officials proposed, at-home treatment, when appropriate, encourages both patients and families to participate more fully in health care activities. Therefore, MINSAP officials argue, individuals and their families are also taking greater responsibility for their own health.

The local consultorio, according to the MINSAP, is the pillar of the primary health care system because it works at the level of a specifically defined community and acts as an intermediary between the community, the local polyclinic, the municipal and provincial hospitals, and the SNS. This organization permits all health initiatives to be specifically tailored to the needs of local communities (figure 18). Although the role of consultorios as specialized centers continues to be crucial, secondary and tertiary institutions have adjusted their structural and functional framework to meet the demands posed by the multilevel, comprehensive, integrated health care delivery approach: "Hospitals are no longer considered the mainstays of medical

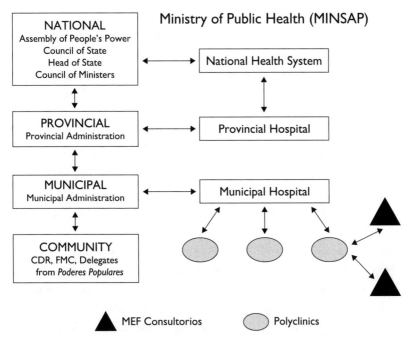

FIGURE 18. Organization of the SNS parallels politico administration.

attention in the Cuban health care system; rather, one of their principal duties is to contribute to solving local needs, when a solution requires more specialized services."[12]

The scheduling of physicians' hours, according to the MINSAP, is determined by patients' needs rather than by a predetermined structure. However, the typical day sees the family physician-nurse team conducting routine visits and checkups in the consultorio during morning office hours, usually from 8 A.M. to 1 P.M. In the afternoons, usually from 1:00 to 5:00, the health teams carry out home and field visits, known as *en el terreno* (in the field). Physician-and-nurse health teams follow a number of health programs set out by the MINSAP's guidelines for primary health care, or *atención primaria de salud*. In theory the family physician is required to see every patient in his or her área de salud at least twice a year. The physician is also required to maintain a *ficha familiar*, which is a record of preventive services and conditions for all patients in their area. This record is updated and reviewed at least monthly with a clinical supervisor who is an academically based family physician. Acute and chronic health problems are coordinated in a database at municipal, provincial, and national levels of the MINSAP. The monitored services and conditions include prenatal and natal care, immunizations, cancer screening by smear and mammography, risk factors such as smoking and hypertension, and follow-up for chronic conditions as well as psychosocial problems and sources of stress in the family or at work.

PRACTICING MEDICINE

The fundamental basis of MEF's primary health care philosophy, which health officials argue is a holistic-based approach to health, has historically proven to be an epistemological challenge for many health care systems the world over. The failure of much contemporary biomedicine to integrate the triad of mind–body–society, according to the anthropologists Margaret Lock and Nancy Scheper-Hughes, leaves people "suspended in hyphens, testifying to the disconnectedness of our thoughts."[13] This melding of hyphens in the MEF program has resulted in a kind of hybrid physician: clinician-epidemiologist-social worker-psychologist, and, importantly, revolutionary cheerleader. In practice, the physician's role in identifying risk, including chronic health problems, infectious diseases, antisocial behavior, wayward youth, sexually promiscuous adolescents, and elusive expectant mothers, is part of a larger project of corralling the population into the state's prescription for so-called normal behavior. Physicians in this program work on the individual and the social body, and this work constitutes a form of governance over both the individual and the community. In other words, the family physicians' actions constitute "a form of activity aiming to shape, guide or affect the conduct of some person or persons."[14]

In the following ethnographic case studies I address the *practice* of medicine in the MEF program as a unique form of governance. To do so, I juxtapose the physicians' narratives with those of their patients. Moreover, I address specific issues related to the municipal infrastructure in which the consultations were situated, and, where possible, I attempt to situate each consultorio within the wider communities.[15] My interviews with physicians and the general public revealed that experiences varied significantly from one consultorio to another. Given that the city of Havana, with an estimated population of 2.1 million and over 2,000 consultorios, is composed of a chaotic dispersion of sociodemographic pockets, it is impossible to make broad generalizations; however, I can address how physicians interact with their patients in their respective áreas de salud.[16]

CONSULTORIO LOS MOLINOS

I met Luis Pérez, a physician, at the birthday party of a mutual friend. He was, at first, reticent and shy. After I was formally introduced to him by the host of the party as a "good friend from Canada," he smiled and looked almost relieved. He had detected a foreign accent in my Spanish but could not place me geographically. My physical appearance had been deceptive, he later admitted. I did not look like the foreigners he was used to, much less like the stereotypical Nordic-looking, blue-eyed Canadian he would have expected. He took advantage of this chance meeting to practice his English, and we talked extensively about Canada and Cuba. During the conversation we agreed that I would visit his área de salud in order to carry out extensive interviews.

Several weeks later, when I visited Pérez's consultorio in Los Molinos, his neighbor Luisa caught sight of me from her front patio, where she sat painstakingly sifting through her ration of rice, separating the grains from the small pebbles and debris. "He is doing house visits in the neighborhood [en el terreno]," she cried out. When I scanned the scheduled hours posted on the front door of the consultorio, I noticed that, according to the schedule, Pérez should have been consulting patients. I returned to my apartment in the center of the city, about thirty minutes away by taxi. Pérez called me later that evening. He apologized for missing my visit, sounded exasperated, and quickly began describing the three pediatric cases he was treating. He had changed his normal schedule, he said, to accommodate his new "high-priority" infant patients. The infants, he stated, required antibiotic injections every four hours, which meant he was constantly trying to juggle his regular consulting duties with the scheduled visits to the infants' homes.

Pérez's consultorio was located in a house similar to many other residential houses in his neighborhood, with one exception: the two-story structure is built of prefabricated materials and towers over the surrounding bungalows. The bungalows were purely functional in design and contrast with the ornate Spanish- and French-colonial architecture of the city center. However, all the houses in the small subdivision (*reparto*) of Los Molinos, which is located in San Miguel del Padrón, a working-class municipality southeast of Havana, share one feature: they all are in various stages of disrepair. The narrow roads leading to Los Molinos were lined with gaping potholes, broken lampposts, and overgrown fruit trees that had engulfed many of the small houses. On one occasion I had mistakenly referred to Los Molinos as the countryside (*el campo*) because of the lush greenery and the rural atmosphere, but the doctor quickly corrected me, saying that the reparto was officially located in an urban municipality in the city of Havana. The residents of Los Molinos, he added, were proud to be *habaneros* (residents of Havana).[17]

The first floor of Pérez's two-story house consists of the consultorio: a simple multiroom complex with a small examining room complete with posters for health promotion campaigns, nutritional advice, and various health programs to be followed, all plastered on the painted but crumbling walls. The second floor of the house is the physician's apartment, a modest two-bedroom unit with little furniture, a borrowed black-and-white television set, a broken bed, a kerosene stove, and a small Russian refrigerator. Pérez apologized for the poor physical condition of his apartment. He indicated that the state had promised to improve his living conditions. He rolled his eyes and added half-heartedly, "At least, that is what the state has promised me, but you know how things are in Cuba. Currently, I am not a priority."

There was one luxury in Pérez's apartment: a phone, a rarity in this reparto. While still a scarce commodity, the phone is essential to a growing and complex social network of people. Pérez acts as a messenger, he stated, receiving calls from nearly all the provinces of Cuba, the United States, and Spain. He ends up relaying messages, he remarked, for about twenty to twenty-five people, some of whom live several blocks away. Many of his immediate neighbors are also reliant on his phone to place calls, and neighbors often knock on his door at all hours of the night. However, the doctor explained, he had recently devised a scheme to avoid these frequent interruptions. Louisa, whom I had encountered on my first visit to the consultorio is always on her front patio "to keep an eye on things" and had agreed to regulate any impromptu after-hours visitors. She would inform these people that "the doctor is not home" if Pérez so desired. This tactic, Pérez said, would allow him a reprieve from frequent visitors without causing conflict in the small community. As he also noted, after-hours medical emergencies, theoretically, should be attended to by the twenty-four-hour local polyclinic or in the *Cuerpo de Guardia* (emergency room) at the local municipal hospital.

Despite the availability of other health services, many of Pérez's patients did not have access to reliable transportation. In fact, most of the residents, the doctor noted, rely on him as a first line of defense for many of their medical emergencies. The doctor explained that this is what the state had intended by placing doctors in the community. But many residents hope the doctor can do more, "do them special favors." His amicable nature puts people at ease, and they feel comfortable requesting favors, he said. For example, one woman in his health area wanted to get her niece from another province checked into one of the popular tertiary institutions, Hermanos Ameijeiras, in Havana, for medical diagnostic tests. Pérez stressed that this was well beyond his capabilities. At the most, he noted, he could make strategic calls to the local polyclinic to organize ambulatory services in cases where people needed emergency transportation. Most people, he stated, cannot afford to splurge money on peso taxis, which charged anywhere from ten to twenty Cuban pesos per person (fifty cents to one U.S. dollar).

Pérez further stated that the community is less reliant on the nurse (*enfermera*), the other half of his health team, than on him. Historically, the government had placed so much emphasis on having fully trained family physicians that there was a point at which the number of nurses had lagged behind the number of doctors. When I asked Pérez if I could arrange an interview with the nurse on another day, he sarcastically remarked, "If she shows up." The nurse lives in another municipality and, the doctor commented, was often late or didn't show up at all. As it turned out, there were barely enough houses to accommodate the physicians and their families, much less the nurses. This was a common theme in all of the consultorios I visited. None of the nurses lived in the communities in which they worked. The nurse assigned to Pérez's consultorio is a recent graduate, he explained, although the consultorio had seen several nurses throughout his ten-month assignment. As he stated, many of the former nurses left because of "personality conflicts." He chose not to elaborate on this statement, although I suspected it had to do with what he later characterized as his "very demanding personality."

Returning to the consultorio on another day, I discovered that Pérez was again off en el terreno. I struck up a conversation with a man who was hanging around the front of his office. Holding two small bread rolls loosely wrapped in a nylon bag, the man, whose name, I learned, was Bernardo "Bení" Ortiz, was talkative and began to tell me about what a "wonderful guy" the physician was. In an unsolicited confessional style, Ortiz began to explain why he was bringing bread for Pérez. The physician, who had recently moved from the eastern province of Santiago de Cuba to take on the position of the médico de la familia in this neighborhood, was still awaiting authorization from the appropriate municipal authorities to provide him with a ration book (*libreta*). Without a libreta, Pérez was unable to collect his designated ration of subsidized foods, including rice, beans, bread, sugar, and so forth. *El pueblo*, Ortiz proudly informed me, were pitching in to make sure the physician wasn't left without sustenance. Ortiz's wife, Mariella, had recently sent over her specialty, *papas rellenas* (stuffed potatoes), because the physician had worked late the previous night attending to sick infants. She wanted to make sure that Pérez at least had something to eat.

As I explained my reason for being in Los Molinos, Ortiz listened attentively. "I can tell you a great deal about the médico," he offered. He invited me to his house, located no more than three minutes away from the consultorio. He told me he was fifty-three years old, but he looked years beyond his age. When we reached his house Ortiz quickly searched around for a glass to offer me some rum, a practice common among the majority of the men I had interviewed (women generally offered me coffee). After I politely declined, Ortiz insisted he would not take no for an answer. Watching Ortiz quickly down a glass of the acrid-smelling liquid, I reluctantly sipped at the small shot glass of unrefined white rum he gave me and tried to stifle the burning sensation as I swallowed less than a teaspoon. "You won't get this stuff in Canada," he beamed, prodding me to shoot back the glass, as he had just done. "This is my first drink in sixteen days," he pronounced solemnly. Bení, as he later asked me to call him, said he had "a little drinking problem." Pérez was working with him to provide a cure, Ortiz stated. "Louisito, the médico, comes by the house every so often and sits down with me and watches TV and talks about my problem. He gave me some pills [*pastillas*], which I think are some kind of vitamin because I need to get my appetite and strength back," he described.

When Ortiz's wife, Mariella, appeared at the door without notice, he quickly became agitated. "Where did you get the rum?" she demanded. "It's just a little," he whimpered. I introduced myself to Mariella, and she sat down and apologized that her husband was drinking again. As she explained, Pérez was trying to cure her husband's drinking problem. She didn't have much hope, though. "The médico said we all have to work together like a family to support him. The médico said it is not Bení's fault that he suffers from this illness, but I can't take it anymore," she declared. Looking upset,

Ortiz offered his defense: "I am working with the médico and making progress." Immediately, he started to enumerate the various changes and ongoing projects of social reform he was involved in: painting the window frames, cleaning up the yard and surrounding streets, and trying to be more actively involved in the community. He emphatically stated he was trying to become integrated into the community and take responsibility for his drinking and the effect his drinking had on others. With the encouragement of the médico, Ortiz had recently joined a volunteer microbrigade to help with various revolutionary initiatives. The latest plan, he told me, was Castro's project to fix up all the schools nationwide before the opening of the new school year in September.

Mariella, hearing her husband's long list of projects, sighed in frustration. In a matter of hours he would be drunk again, she said. She contradicted Ortiz's claim that he was cutting back on his drinking and reminded him that only the day before he was drunk. "Louisito works with him and has made so much progress, but Bení is surrounded by so much temptation," Mariella sighed. Pointing to her neighbor's house, she described what the problem was. The neighbors in the crumbling house next door had built a patio on their roof that resembled a bar with large speakers and umbrellas emblazoned with the brand name of one of the national beers of Cuba, Cristal. As Mariella pointed out, her neighbors ran an informal bar and club from their house, and her husband was a frequent visitor. Mariella apologized for Bení's behavior and asked if I would come back again to interview her about her opinions on the health care system. She accompanied me back to Pérez's office, where I left a note for the doctor, and she emphasized how she regarded the médico as one of her sons. "Louisito is all alone in Los Molinos, and we try to take good care of him," she said as she smiled. On Mariella's back patio, as she had pointed out, several of Pérez's white lab coats (*batas*) were on her clothesline swaying in the breeze. She also washed the médico's clothes as if he were one of her children—"just to help out," she said.

Later that evening Pérez visited my apartment, which was an hour and half away by multiple local buses, and apologized for missing my visit again. Mariella had informed him of my meeting with her husband. Pérez proudly stated that he was personally working with Ortiz to treat him. "He is a good man and needs specialized attention, but I cannot do it alone," he said. The área de salud for which he is responsible is quite difficult, the doctor noted. Charged with servicing more than eight hundred people spread over a wide geographical area, Pérez and the nurse have to deal with serious social and health problems. According to Pérez's records, a little over 40 percent of the people in his área de salud were under thirty-five years of age. In addition, 45 percent of the residents were women. Surprisingly, Pérez also was able to recite, without looking over any notes, the exact number of people in his health area who were hypertensive, diabetic, over the age of sixty-five, of child-bearing age, and so on. As he stated, he had memorized his *fiche familiar* because he dealt with it on a daily basis. He could also recite, he noted, a social history of each of the households in which he worked. The doctor explained that he made a point of visiting all of the households in his community on a regular basis.

Los Molinos was a housing settlement built in the 1940s as rental accommodation for service staff and agricultural workers from other provinces. Many of its residents used to make the daily trek to various large plantations located nearby. According to Mariella, whose mother (now deceased) was a former servant in the house of one of the previous landowners, the house Mariella currently occupied was awarded to her mother through the agrarian reform laws after la Revolución. This history was similar to that of other residents of Los Molinos. The agrarian reform nationalized large segments of private land and property for redistribution to the population. The former landowners, Mariella indicated, fled to the United States, but rumor had it, she noted, they were waiting to return to Cuba "after Fidel" to reclaim their property. Many current residents of Los Molinos traced their family history, usually through their parents, back to a working-class background on the former plantations.

In addition, however, a growing population of illegal migrants from rural eastern provinces, often derogatorily labeled as *palestinos* (Palestinians)— had now settled in Los Molinos. The recent arrivals to the city, often related, if only tangentially, to somebody in the neighborhood, had built what Pérez described as abominable makeshift houses on vacant property. He said these houses were reminiscent of the overcrowded tenement housing in the congested city center, projects known as *solares*. He named these parts of his health area Oriente because the majority of the occupants were illegal migrants from the eastern provinces. The growing population of unregistered residents in Pérez's área de salud made his task of risk evaluation and treatment more difficult. The general problems in both populations, the recent arrivals and the longtime residents, including teenage pregnancy, infant and adult malnutrition, and alcoholism, were matched by an increasing number of chronic health problems such as diabetes, asthma, and high blood pressure. All of these problems, Pérez added, sighing resignedly, were compounded by a critical lack of material resources.

Working anywhere from sixty to seventy hours a week, Pérez was paid four hundred Cuban pesos a month (in 2002 approximately nineteen U.S. dollars). Although he complained of being poor in comparison to Cuba's new U.S.-dollar economy, his salary was actually on the high end of the scale for state employees. While Pérez did not have to pay rent or utilities where he lived, he informed me that his salary did not allow him to meet his basic expenses.[18] In addition to his regular duties, which included a certain number of night shifts (*guardia*) at the local *policlínico*, he covered several other physicians' night shifts to earn extra money. The other physicians made informal agreements with Pérez to pay him a hundred pesos per night shift, approximately five dollars, under the table so they could avoid the undesirable red-eye shifts. The extra money, Pérez added, provided few luxuries.

Pérez had to send money to support his two sons from a previous marriage. His two children, both in their teens, lived with their mother in Oriente. Pérez was also responsible for sending money to his parents, both of whom were living on state pensions that between the two of them totaled no more than 220 pesos a month (11 dollars). As the doctor ironically stated, he left the countryside in the hope of becoming a "big-city doctor," so his parents, former unskilled laborers, had high expectations for him. Pérez told me he had three siblings who lived in the United States, but who almost never called and rarely sent money. His siblings had become "Americanized," he concluded. "You know the saying, 'Drink Coca-Cola and forget about everything.'" He smiled because in Spanish the words form a rhyming jingle in the style of a commercial: "Toma Coca-Cola y olvídate de todo."

One day, looking physically exhausted and still dressed in his white bata, Pérez visited my apartment. He stated that his current medical post was one of the hardest assignments he had held since he graduated from medical school in 1987. Born in the Province of Santiago de Cuba in 1963, Pérez had worked in various rural medical posts in his home province and throughout Oriente before requesting a transfer to the City of Havana Province. He had hoped to leave the country lifestyle behind and receive a posting in one of the fashionable municipalities of Havana, such as the Plaza of the Revolution or Old Havana. But when he had arrived ten months earlier, Pérez was disappointed to find he was assigned to one of the outlying municipalities of Havana. Los Molinos resembles a small rural town rather than part of a large city. As Pérez noted, his move to the city was not motivated by money. The pay for a physician was fairly standard across Cuba. Rather, he was looking for more satisfying work and life experience, something he described as working with the cultured city dwellers rather than with what he termed "ignorant rural peasants."

The residents of Los Molinos, the physician said as he sighed, were unfortunately no better than the people in the countryside. They were functionally literate, he claimed, and for the most part worked, if at all, as laborers in local factories. The socioeconomic conditions of Los Molinos were deteriorating. The community had gone through several médicos in quick succession, each one requesting a transfer after only a brief stint. "I too want to transfer to another area," he told me. However, the community had responded well to him and treated him with respect and generosity, perhaps, he added, in hopes of convincing him to stay.

CONSULTORIO SANTA MARÍA

I met a doctor named Andrea Ochoa through a friend of a friend, which I found was the most common way to get access to the usually tight-lipped family physicians. Ochoa, a forty-two-year-old family physician, agreed to have several interviews with me, but only after she had a chance to meet with me informally on various occasions. Previously, Ochoa had been a family physician in a high school for several years. Her work in the school consisted primarily of health promotion campaigns on issues such as sexual health and healthy lifestyle choices, for example, not smoking, eating nutritional foods, getting exercise, and so on. As she commented, community-based medicine was a complete change from what she was used to. Two years earlier she had been assigned as a replacement physician at Consultorio Santa María, when the original physician became an *internacionalista*—a Cuban health professional who provided voluntary medical services in developing countries. Despite being told the post would only be temporary, Ochoa had been at Santa María ever since.

Consultorio Santa María is located in the municipality of Central Havana at the border of the municipality of Plaza of the Revolution. The área de salud comprises a burgeoning population scattered throughout an intricate network of dilapidated buildings. The apartment buildings, collectively

known as Edificios Santa María, are a striking contrast to Havana's postrevolutionary social order. They had been prime real estate in the prerevolutionary era. Each building is approximately seven to eight floors high and over-
shadowed by several high-rise hotels located nearby. As seen from the street,
the grand, ornate balconies and large picture windows of Edificios Santa
María speak volumes about their former grandeur. In one of the buildings a
majestic foyer with crumbling marble floors surrounds a small bust of the
independence fighter José Martí, symbolizing Cuba's postrevolutionary
mantra: la Revolución is independence.

The majority of the apartments in Edificios Santa María have decorative
wrought-iron front doors—recently added for security reasons, I was told—
giving the place the eerie atmosphere of a jail. Behind the barred front doors,
the majority of the apartments in the buildings, originally large three- and
four-bedroom suites with en suite bathrooms and maid's quarters at the
back, have undergone multiple transformations. Several of the residents in
the Santa María buildings, in the prerevolutionary era wealthy urbanites,
have remained in their apartments until the present day. The decorations
and furnishing in their houses, from what I surmised from the apartments I
entered, were testaments to the wealth they once held. However, other
wealthy residents fled Cuba in the early 1960s, and now many of their former
servant staff and their extended families are the legal occupants of the apartments. In Edificios Santa María the prerevolutionary past and revolutionary
present are seemingly intertwined, if unevenly, in a complex fusion of rich
and poor, old and new. However, these categories do not necessarily overlap
in predictable ways.

At the first floor of the buildings the insignia "MF" is written in white
block capital letters on one of the outside doors, signifying the consultorio
del médico de la familia. This sets it apart from the other, nondescript
residential doors. Ochoa's consultorio is literally an ad hoc space. It was built
into the base of one of the buildings in the mid-1980s, and it is obvious that
it had previously been a residential apartment. Ochoa's small, three-room
clinic is neatly laid out: waiting room, office, and examination and treatment room. Throughout the consultorio, health promotion posters on infant and maternal health, sexually transmitted diseases, and nutritional advice formed a colorful collage on the walls. Ochoa smiled when I asked her
how many people she was responsible for. "Officially about 700, but I
suspect there are well over 850, if not more," she stated. She was generally

upbeat and gregarious and seemed unfazed by the maze of rundown build-ings that literally engulfed her consultorio.

Ochoa lived in the neighboring municipality of Plaza, located about fifteen minutes away from her consultorio by bus. However, as she ex-plained, she often rode her large, old-fashioned "Chinese bicycle"—one of the many bicycles sent by the Republic of China to Cuba in the early 1990s during the height of the petroleum shortage—to work. Her área de salud is rather typical, Ochoa indicated, of the generally overcrowded city center. The area is such a compact mass of humanity that various Cuban scholars have reported that the temperature in central Havana is often one to two degrees Celsius hotter than the daily average temperatures in other parts of Havana.[19] The MINSAP, Ochoa noted, is well aware of the health problems posed by the densely overcrowded pockets in the city. The government, however, did not currently have the financial or material resources to address the problem. The scarcity, Ochoa noted, was partially owing to the U.S. embargo (el bloqueo). However, another problem, she remarked, was the sheer magnitude of rebuilding a city that had gone without basic mainte-nance for over forty years.

Currently, all the restoration and construction activities in the city center are in prime tourist areas and, for the most part, are undertaken with the help of significant foreign investments through joint ventures, for example, financial aid from Spain, Italy, and other countries, or special programs, such as UNESCO, under which Old Havana was declared a World Heritage site. According to several residents of neighboring areas, Santa María, de-spite its close proximity to hotels, is still in a relatively undesirable area. It is thought to be dangerous, especially at night, to walk down the side streets in the vicinity of Santa María. A police officer is located on every major city corner in the heart of the city, so I found this characterization surprising. However, the dangerous element, as I found out, was a growing number of prostitutes and young hustlers (all considered jineteros) peddling illegal boxes of Cuba's famous cigars and other wares on the street. The jineteros apparently lure unsuspecting tourists away from their hotels to complete their illicit transactions away from the watchful eyes of the army of police that surround the hotel areas.

When I asked Ochoa about the rumors of Santa María being considered a dangerous place by nightfall, she attempted to delicately skirt the issue. The reality was, as several of Ochoa's patients pointed out, that she left Santa

María by five o'clock every day to return to the relatively affluent suburb where she lived with her parents, her husband, and her two children. Ochoa stated, however, that Santa María, while far from the worst area in the city, had serious problems with illicit activities that made health care in her area difficult.

Ochoa was born in 1958, shortly before the revolutionary government came to power, and she graduated from medical school in 1984, coincidentally, the year the MEF program was inaugurated. She grew up in a middle-class family in the neighboring province of Matanzas. In the 1970s her family had moved to Havana, where her father worked in a high-level position in the Ministry of Sugar. Ochoa had completed all of her schooling under the revolutionary pedagogy and, as she stated, firmly believed in the underlying principles of la Revolución. However, she noted that in practice, the recent economic changes were affecting everyday life, making it difficult to fulfill her revolutionary commitments.

Health education, Ochoa stressed, was key to her job. She stated that her health area included several professionals who made her job easier in many respects. However, a large number of the residents in Santa María arrived from the countryside shortly after the revolution. Ochoa remarked that people from the countryside (*campesinos*) were much harder to "reform" than city dwellers, but they also had greater respect for the revolution and for doctors in general than the city dwellers: "The campesinos are people who, before the la Revolución, never saw a doctor. They tend to treat you with a great deal of respect and are *extremely* grateful." As several other doctors I interviewed pointed out, it was not uncommon for campesinos to show up at consultorios, polyclinics, and hospitals with presents for the attending physician as a sign of their gratitude. Most of the time the presents were food items that were highly desired and expensive in Havana, such as roasted pork legs, lobster, shrimp, vegetables, and certain fruits. While the gifts were not necessary, the doctor noted that they were always welcome.

Ochoa organized several meetings on a regular basis to discuss specific themes with state-defined demographic groups. She scheduled informal chats (*charlas*) with adolescents to discuss sexuality and contraception, especially with women over the age of fourteen. She also met with the elderly club (*círculo de abuelos*) to discuss the importance of exercise to combat sedentarism. One of the major problems in Ochoa's área de salud, she reported, is the increasing socioeconomic stratification within the local population and the severe problems with hygiene and housing maintenance. These conditions are matched by a rise in chronic health problems and, as Ochoa noted, "unhealthy lifestyle choices and entrenched cultural habits." As she made clear, many people simply do not heed her advice.

For example, she explained to me, lack of money plays a significant part in why many people consume unhealthy foods, foods high in animal fat, for instance, and shy away from purchasing more costly fruits and vegetables, thereby causing hypertension and heart problems. Entrenched cultural attitudes, she said, "are also difficult to change. Cubans like fatty and salty foods." Many individuals smoke and drink heavily because they feel these are among the few luxuries they can still afford, especially given the recent shortages in rationed food items. "The younger ones are easier to deal with because they listen—at least, in my experience they do," she said. Despite her continued efforts to keep her ficha familiar updated, Ochoa felt overworked, and this was compounded by the obligation to regularly attend postgraduate courses and to keep abreast of current developments in primary health care.

Her área de salud had become more complex because of the recent influx of tourists in the building complex. Several of the residents in Santa María rented their apartments or rooms in their apartments to foreigners, legally or illegally. One day, for example, I was interviewing an unmarried elderly woman, Lydia Morales, in a large, beautifully decorated three-bedroom apartment she had inherited from her parents. She had never married and had no children, so Morales began illegally renting rooms to supplement her state pension. When I interviewed her several young German tourists were taking the sun on her front terrace and drinking beer. Morales was not bothered by the fact that she didn't have a state license to rent to foreigners. What she was worried about, however, was that the young men might bring jineteras into her house. She did not want "strange Cubans" in her home, she emphatically stated.

Ochoa was well aware of the problem of illegal renters, but the complex infrastructure of the building, she stated, made it difficult to pinpoint where exactly the foreigners were staying. Most of the building's residents were tight-lipped about the illicit activities. I suspected that Ochoa, seeing that the residents were not complaining about the matter, did not want to get involved: "I try to build a sense of community," she stated. Ochoa's consultorio was located in close proximity to the CDR headquarters. On several occasions problems had arisen between foreigners and Cubans or between building residents, for example, because of loud parties or disputes and fights over money. Ochoa, who did not live in the community, was informed of these events when she arrived at work, and she would then meet with the local CDR representative to discuss the matter. She made notes of the various problems and officially documented them. As in all community health matters, the municipal authorities regularly reviewed her ficha familiar.

Several residents of Santa María recounted how the state housing authorities had arrived unannounced one day, apparently for no reason, to check people's housing registrations. In addition, the Cuban Ministry of the Interior, which controls immigration, visited the building the same day to verify that the foreigners staying in various apartments were legally registered. News spread quickly in the building, and, as Ochoa noted, people started acting suspiciously around her. Unlike the local CDR representative, who lived in the building complex, Ochoa was an outsider. It was evident that Ochoa worked in a social environment that was very distinct from that of Pérez's consultorio. Several of the residents in Ochoa's área de salud had regular access to U.S. dollars from formal and informal work in the local tourist industry and from friends and relatives abroad. The local socioeconomic stratification was visibly noticeable to me.

One of the residents in the building complex, Julio César Serra, best illustrates some of the contrasts in the Santa María complex. Following a long, narrow corridor between two adjacent buildings, I entered the heart of the building, which formed a narrow, L-shaped core. This winding corridor, once the former service entrance for the building, is now home to twenty or more families. As one climbs a narrow, crumbling staircase that hugs the inner wall of the building, another life emerges. A myriad of brightly colored clothes and sheets hang off back patios, and pervading the air was the stench of garbage, including everything from soiled diapers to egg shells and orange peels, that people had thrown from their windows onto their neighbors' space below. The doors of small studio apartments line the inner artery of the building; these were formerly quarters of the maids who served the wealthy apartment dwellers whose ornate balconies face the front. After negotiating six flights of stairs, I arrived at Serra's tiny one-room apartment. This is where his neighbor's former maid had slept, cooked, and bathed. "We were, and I think I can still speak in the present tense, are, the ass [*culo*] of the rich," Serra remarked.

Serra, a forty-five-year-old man, is an eloquent and poised speaker, and he was not shy about expressing his disdain for the MEF program. His complaints, however, tackled head-on some of the problems raised by over 50 percent of the general population that I interviewed in connection with various health issues. From our first meeting I was convinced that Serra was an ardent counterrevolutionary (*gusano*, literally "worm"), and in the course of several interviews it became apparent that, for the most part, he is anti-Castro. But while the distinction between counterrevolutionary and anti-Castro may appear blurred, it speaks to the contradictions that are inherent in the way people make distinctions between ideology (socialism as a theory) and practice (the actions of the government represented by Castro).

Serra moved into the Santa María buildings when his partner, José de Jesús, a designer for a state-run clothing company, traveled to Spain on business in the late 1980s and decided to stay. When the state became aware that Jesús had defected, they confiscated his house and all of his property. Serra, who was originally from another province, had no legal claim to the property. A year later, after much bureaucratic wrangling, Serra decided to follow his partner to Spain, but shortly after his arrival in the Canary Islands they broke up, and he was unable to get a resident permit. He decided to return to Cuba, where he rented a small studio apartment from a woman in the Santa María building. After many years he managed to illegally buy the title of the property for fifteen hundred dollars from the maid and has lived there ever since with his current partner, Carlos Alberto Ramos.

Serra has had various encounters with state security, he claims, for openly expressing his negative views of Castro. In 1993 he was arrested and detained for several days for screaming anti-Castro obscenities from the building stairwell. He states that the *período especial* had created an untenable situation, and he wanted to let people know that "Fidel Castro and his minions in the Party" were living the high life at the expense of the people. Given Serra's history of conflict and his vocal stance against the government, I anticipated he would paint a negative picture of the health care system. Yet his comments fit neatly within other people's narratives. In many respects, Serra, a former physiotherapist who now worked as a self-employed beautician, is a firm supporter of the basic tenets of the socialized health care system. Implicit in his narrative is the underlying premise that access to health care is a basic human right. After over forty years of socialism, Serra had internalized the socialist government's position on health care. He was, as he stated, not concerned with critiquing what he believed were Cubans' fundamental rights, defined as basic access to health services free of charge.

When I asked Serra about his experiences with the MEF program, he gave the following account:

In my opinion, I don't like the médico de la familia program. No doctor can know every specialty. For me, this idea of family doctors with a specialty in general internal medicine is very limiting. Scientifically speaking, I have my doubts about these family doctors. At least, I don't have confidence that they know what they are doing. I mean, if I have a dermatological problem, I want to see a dermatologist. Before, in the polyclinics or community medicine programs, we could go directly to the specialist we needed to treat our specific problems. Now, the objective of the family doctors is to work within a defined area and work with people first to help eliminate unnecessarily going to specialists directly. To me, it is another form of bureaucracy.

At this point in Cuba, and I know this is an elitist thing to say, the majority of the population has been inundated with basic medical knowledge thanks to la Revolución. Generally speaking, most people are sufficiently educated to know, for instance, that if you get a blow to your arm or leg, you don't want to see a family doctor. You know you want to see an orthopedic doctor, because you know that he is a specialist in this area. You want X-rays and stuff. You go to the family doctor when you have a high fever or need to be vaccinated. If nothing else, la Revolución has raised the level of medical awareness in Cuba to a surprisingly sophisticated level.

Serra raised some important points that were recurring themes in interviews, most notably the problem of local family doctors being considered "unethical" or "state informers":

This whole idea about living together with your personal family doctor as your neighbor is a farce. I don't want any doctor interfering in my personal life. Personally, I don't want the doctor to know anything about me. Nobody knows what these doctors do with this information they collect on you. I am not sure these doctors are very ethical. I know of very serious cases, for example, of people who went to the family doctor for a sexually transmitted disease or something. These things are supposed to be kept strictly confidential; that is, between the doctor and the patient. However, very quickly the neighbors were gossiping about it. This is the kind of lack of professionalism and breach of ethics I am talking about. I think this is typical of Latinos. Above all, we have characteristics typical of our Spanish heritage. We Cubans often refer to Spaniards as *chismoso* [gossips]. Unfortunately, and I don't know why, I think Cubans have inherited a lot of this behavior.

The mixture between neighbor, doctors, nurses, and patients is very intimate. It becomes hard to separate personal conversations from medical conversations. This is obvious. Of course, you cannot ignore the importance of having a doctor right there at your convenience, close by. However, I think the divisions between médico and neighbor need to be clearly defined. These doctors work closely with the government, and so you have to think, how much do I want this doctor to know about me?

Ultimately, the physicians work for the state, and some people viewed them with skepticism. Several of these same individuals commented that family physicians are, in practical terms, of little use. As Serra and other interviewees remarked, it is more advantageous to have a friend who is a physician in secondary and tertiary institutions because, at the very least, they have more resources available to them than local family physicians. The case of Serra's neighbor, Dulce Frances, is an excellent example of the latter.

Frances scoffed when I asked her about the family physician. "She is useless," she stressed. Frances's mother had undergone chemotherapy recently and was severely ill. Her brother, she added, had sent all the medications and equipment her mother needed from the United States. Opening a drawer in her kitchen, Frances pulled out a stethoscope, needles, medicine vials, pills, and various bandages and gauze. She stressed that her brother had sent almost everything her mother's condition demanded. She maintained a close friendship with doctors who worked in local hospitals and called on them if she needed medical advice. Frances was convinced that the family physician was a state informer (*chivato*). "Clearly," Frances remarked, "el médico is unable to solve the majority of the most basic medical problems." As she stated, on the rare occasions she needed Ochoa to write prescriptions for the local pharmacy, the doctor did not even have the correct forms to do so. Moreover, Frances resented the doctor's wanting to visit her apartment and check up on her mother. She remarked that the doctor was absent throughout the treatment of her mother's cancer, which the doctor must have been well aware was taking place, so she does not see any reasons for the doctor to become involved at such a late stage. Ochoa, Frances declared, was simply being nosy.

When I asked Ochoa if she would comment on her role in the community, she stressed that she had her work cut out for her. Some of the patients she treated were receptive and grateful, but others, she admitted, were outright resentful. The majority of the residents I interviewed in Santa María saw the doctor as being rather ineffectual. While several of her patients characterized Ochoa as a nice person, most people in Santa María could not recall the last time they had seen the family physician. Ochoa admitted that, despite her attempts, she was not familiar with all of the residents in her health area, as is stipulated by the program. In her defense, Ochoa argued that many of the residents of Santa María went directly to one of the major hospitals within walking distance. In the emergency rooms, as Serra noted, one can seek out the help of the relevant specialist directly. Having visited the emergency room several times myself, I was surprised to see that emergency room specialists were not too concerned about whether a patient had visited the local consultorio first or not. In addition, the local hospitals can carry out medical tests that are not possible in the local consultorio, and as a result many patients bypassed the consultorio altogether.

CUBA'S MEDICAL IMAGINARY

The development of a primary health program that focuses on clinical and social-epidemiological vigilance of the population, health promotion, and disease prevention by working in tandem with the community is a strategy that has led Cuba to international prominence. The island now boasts one of the highest physician-per-inhabitant ratios in the world. What this has translated to on the ground, from the 1960s until the present, is the gradual building up of an unprecedented cadre of physicians attending to increasingly smaller sections of the population. This system has worked to disseminate biomedical knowledge across the population and in a highly personalized fashion through intimate physician–patient interaction and health-promotion and disease-prevention campaigns.[20] Ironically, such campaigns strongly advise individuals against engaging in self-medication and autodiagnosis. Various international health policy analysts suggest that Cuba mystifies the power of professional centralized medical expertise by delegating almost every level of curative and preventive health measure to an army of fully trained physicians.[21]

Yet, contrary to these claims, the practices of individual Cubans indicate that years of massive health education and disease-prevention campaigns have, in fact, created a medically literate population.

The very concept of the primary health care physician as one's neighbor creates a novel circumstance through which individuals not only integrate the health professionals into their communities, but also view them as reservoirs of accessible specialized knowledge. Family physicians, more often than not, are seen as *socios* in a complex therapeutic itinerary, an itinerary in which individuals are driven by what Mary Jo DelVecchio Good (2007) refers to as the "medical imaginary" and the "political economy of hope," pursuing different avenues, through informal activities and state institutions, to desired health outcomes. Increasingly, biomedical innovation and intervention have taken on affective and imaginative dimensions that envelop physicians, patients, and the public in a "biotechnical embrace." That is to say, physicians and their patients, as well as the general public, become much more invested in a biomedical imaginary. Such an imaginary valorizes biomedical intervention and, in some ways, has created desires among the population that are rooted in the promise of biomedicine's ability to "cure" the individual and social body. The MEF physicians presented in this chapter must straddle this uncomfortable divide. On the one hand, "curing the social ills of society" through recommending healthy doses of "social integration" or charlas aimed at modifying risky lifestyles are tangible therapeutic options in an economy of scarcity. On the other, Cuba's highly medicalized population, constantly bombarded with state media campaigns on the country's role as a world "medical power," has now come to expect and demand "biomedical interventions" that are increasingly ineffectual in addressing people's everyday needs and desires.

Socialist Governmentality and Risk

5

PREVENTIVE STRATEGIES AND PRODUCTIVE BODIES

For this task of organization, as for all revolutionary tasks, fundamentally it is the individual who is needed. The revolution does not, as some claim, standardize the collective will and the collective initiative. On the contrary, it liberates one's individual talent. What the revolution does is orient that talent. And our task now is to orient the creative abilities of all medical professionals towards the tasks of social medicine.

Ernesto "Che" Guevara, "On Revolutionary Medicine"

In his famous speech "On Revolutionary Medicine" Che Guevara argued that the role of the Cuban revolution, through the practice of social medicine, was to liberate and direct one's individual talent. In this way, the revolution was envisaged as an agent capable of shaping behavior, particularly in redefining an individual's notions of the self in relation to the demands of the new socialist society. For instance, the gradual emergence of Cuba's primary health care system was intimately tied to the construction of the state's socialist apparatuses and in turn to a particular form of subjectivity: the revolutionary *hombre nuevo*.[1] This new man was to be egalitarian in outlook, selfless, cooperative, nonmaterialistic, hardworking at both manual and nonmanual tasks, and morally pure. This new model of citizenship set the precedent for defining what constituted a good revolutionary (*buen revolucionario*) and, by extension, an individual integrated with the objectives of revolutionary reform. This effectively shaped a new model of citizenship that was attached to a particular notion of health and also defined a system of socialist values and ideals.

For Cuban health officials, the MEF program represented the institutionalization and bureaucratization of the prized bio-psycho-social model of health care delivery. In this transformation, however, it also created an anxious slippage between the physician as caregiver and as political agent of the state. This has led to accusations by international health policy analysts that the country's current program of health care is not solely social medicine, but a form of social control. For example, it has been noted that "the reorganization of medical care in Cuba reflects the Cuban regime's attempt to harness the medical profession in the service of social control well beyond that necessary to meet acceptable standards of individual health."[2]

I argue, though, that all medical systems contain some form of social-control apparatus that exists side by side with something more subtle and dynamic. Medical policies and practices are always thoroughly moral and political in what they perform.[3] This begs the question of what defines a normal or acceptable level of social control vis-à-vis different medical and sociopolitical systems?[4] One system may work effectively for some people in very specific contexts but necessarily come with certain sacrifices, for example, putting the collective interests over individual rights. On the other hand, the same system may be more controlling for others if they are labeled, for example, as noncompliant or antisocial.

While risk strategies and health promotion campaigns can work to enumerate, classify, and regulate subjects who passively take up government imperatives, of equal concern is how they operate and may become internalized, resisted, modified, ignored, or adapted to as part of people's everyday lives.[5] Power, in this context, is both constructive and oppressive. One needs, therefore, to be more sensitive to the subtle operations of power, not strictly as a coherent or coercive force exercised only through control and discipline, but also as "an all-pervasive, normative and positive presence, internalized by, and thus creating, the subject."[6] Through an examination of the diverse applications of epidemiological risk, I interpret several of Cuba's public health programs within the framework of a productive notion of state power that includes strategies for self-development that both constrain, by means of objectifying techniques, and enable, by means of subjectifying techniques, individual agency.[7]

DISPENSARIZACIÓN: ANALYZING THE COMMUNITY HEALTH SITUATION

Over the past twenty-five years Cuba's epidemiological profile, which is similar to the profiles of other economically developed countries, has come to reflect high levels of urbanization and low levels of fecundity and mortality. Mortality from infectious diseases and parasites steadily decreased, from 45.4 per 100,000 in 1970 to 6.8 in 2009.[8] This transition in Cuba's epidemiological profile is, in part, a reflection of the massive social welfare program the country has so effectively institutionalized since 1959. For the past two decades the principal causes of death in Cuba for people of all ages were cardiovascular illness, cancer, and accidents as well as chronic health problems such as diabetes. A report authored by the MINSAP in 1996 contends that trends in Cuba's epidemiological profile were directly linked to the "factors of risk such as smoking, the drinking of alcohol, cultural attitudes toward the consumption of unhealthy foods, and unsafe sexual behavior, all leading to illnesses whose prevention and control are dependent on changes to lifestyle."[9]

Whereas previous public health efforts had focused on transforming the social body through social and political change, lifestyle as a risk factor received considerably less attention. In the late 1970s and early 1980s, with the launch of the MEF program, causal variables, including factors of risk such as the link between smoking and chronic heart and lung disease became crucial to the project of individuals' taking responsibility for their health. The epidemiological concept of risk created a complex picture of "webs of causation" and presented disease incidence in populations as the sum of the individual cases, thus thinning the social context of disease to measurable attributes of individuals.[10] The implementation of the MEF program represented an epidemiological and epistemological approach to handling health problems. As a result, the creation of enumeration technologies and interventions used to identify risk factors took diverse forms. The MEF program stresses the importance of relative associations between variables, including those defined as socioeconomic and cultural, and between clusters of variables and diseases. The concept of risk factor, from this perspective, took on an ambiguous meaning: for instance, that risk could be used to denote association with, cause of, predisposition to, or responsibility for disease.[11] This led to shifts in public health practices, specifically, the way in which the focus on epidemiological risk factors resulted in a far greater emphasis on individuals' lifestyle choices in relation to the health status of the population.

In 1991 the MINSAP drafted a document entitled "Objetivos, propósitos y directrices para incrementar la salud de la población cubana 1992–2000" (Objectives, aims, and guidelines for improving the health of the Cuban population 1992–2000). In 1996 the document was revised to stress four priority health programs: maternal and child health, chronic noncommunicable diseases, communicable diseases, and the care of the elderly.[12] These programs were to be integrated into the daily functions of the MEF program. The MEF physicians follow ten basic primary health care programs: five for treating people, three for improving the health environment, and two for health administration.

In my research I was primarily concerned with examining three of the five programs addressing the care of individuals. These programs include the integral care of women aged fifteen and above, the integral care of adults over fifteen, and the epidemiology program.[13] The program for the integral care for women gives priority to maternal and infant care education, while the integral care of adults focuses on educating people to recognize, manage, and prevent chronic and contagious diseases. Last, through the epidemiology program, all health education campaigns run by the MINSAP are monitored to survey their overall effectiveness in communities in detecting, registering, treating, and following up on persons who fall within their designated target categories or on patients targeted through a health initiative called dispensarización, first developed in the former Soviet Union.

Under the patient classification surveillance system of dispensarización, the physician-and-nurse health teams evaluate the health situation in a specific area and define the at-risk populations by patient, for example, hypertensive, diabetic, expectant mother, and so on. Each patient then receives an assigned priority and differentiated treatment in accordance with nationally prescribed procedures and programs appropriate for their age, gender, and risk factors.[14] For instance, the dispensarización program, under the auspices of MEF physicians, is tailored to provide continuous care for specific populations. In the case of the maternal and infant health program, for example, the program stipulates mandatory prenatal care and the daily monitoring of newly born infants and is designed to follow life histories: the development of a woman's pregnancy and the period after delivery; the growth of the child, his or her psychomotor development and behavior at school, and his or her maturation and entry into the workforce; and finally, his or her actions at work and in the family. The program, therefore, aims not only to identify and target risk, but also to monitor the overall development of individuals in their family unit, environment, and, ultimately, their involvement in the wider society.[15]

Socialist Governmentality and Risk

After the MEF health teams conduct an extensive risk evaluation in their respective *áreas de salud,* a *ficha familiar* is formulated. As I mentioned in the previous chapter, this document is a record of preventive services and conditions for all patients as a family unit, with a list of each of its members, in a region and is updated at least every three months. In principle, the ficha familiar divides the health area into four basic risk categories. The physician Alberto Navarro summarized these risk categories as follows:

> The ficha familiar allows physicians to categorize the population into four fundamental groups. Group One is the "healthy group," that is, "supposedly healthy." Group Two is the group with risky behavior. Group Three are individuals who have illnesses that need to be monitored and kept in check. Group Four are people with illnesses that have specific consequences, for example, disabilities or specific impairments. As you can see, in each group, we assess the risk and what needs to be done. Group One, the healthy group, we do not monitor; at the minimum, we must do an evaluation of an individual's health status at least two times a year. We monitor Group Two depending on the nature and severity of their risks. We have to assess the health status of individuals in this group at least three times a year. Group Three, the group with illnesses, we have to monitor as much as is necessary, depending on their illness, in order to be able to effectively control it. Group Four is similar to Group Three, but the population in this group is often very small.

(See table 2 for a detailed description of risk categories as summarized by MINSAP.)

The ficha familiar is used as a template to record and assess the health situation of any given community. Moreover, it serves as primary material for the derivation of local, municipal, and national epidemiological data, which provide the base from which MINSAP health officials construct appropriate health education and disease prevention campaigns in response to the health needs of a specific community (see figure 19 for the flowchart of epidemiological data). For each identified risk group or illness, for example, there are national health education and disease prevention programs with a clearly outlined criterion to be followed, including the number of times an individual or family unit is to be monitored in a year. In addition to assigning a risk group, health teams, as stipulated by the MEF methodological manual, qualitatively assess the socioeconomic factors of each household in three categories—cultural hygiene, psychosocial characteristics, and the pro-

TABLE 2. DETAILED DESCRIPTION OF RISK GROUPS FOR ANALYZING THE HEALTH
SITUATION OF A COMMUNITY

Risk Group[a]	Analysis
One	Supposedly healthy. Person in whom no illness has been detected after being examined and does not have risks to his or her health.
Two	Exhibits risk factors. Person who, after examination, does not have any illness but is subject to determined risk factors, including biological, psychological, or social factors that can make her or him ill.
	The risk factors that are the object of dispensarización are the following: 1. Infants (less than one year old) 2. Lactating (less than one year) 3. Maternal-perinatal risk 4. Pregnancy 5. Smoking 6. Risk due to contact with certain illnesses (for example, tuberculosis) 7. Antisocial risks (for example, desertion, failure to attend school, lack of integration in family unit or community) 8. Other risk factors (for example, frequent international travel)
Three	Person who suffers from one or more diagnosed debilitating illnesses: 1. High blood pressure 2. Cancer 3. Cerebrovascular illnesses 4. Diabetes mellitus 5. Alcoholism 6. Parkinson's disease 7. Bronchial asthma 8. Epilepsy 9. Chronic diarrhea 10. Malnourished child 11. Tuberculosis 12. Obesity (adult) 13. Syphilis 14. Hepatitis 15. Other Illnesses
Four	Person who, as a result of an illness or an accident, shows changes that are either temporary or indefinite and that affect sensory-motor or psychological abilities or both.

SOURCE: I have merged the two tables and given examples from MINSAP (2001): 44–47.

[a] MEF physicians use the same four risk categories, with different examples and methods of evaluation, for children under five years of age and for the rest of the population.

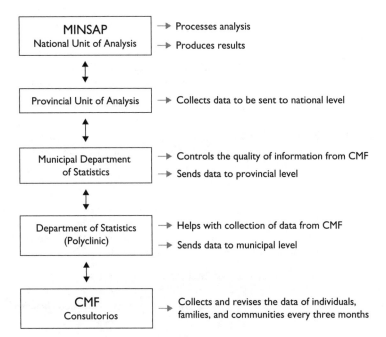

| MINSAP | → Processes analysis |
| National Unit of Analysis | → Produces results |

| Provincial Unit of Analysis | → Collects data to be sent to national level |

| Municipal Department of Statistics | → Controls the quality of information from CMF |
| | → Sends data to provincial level |

| Department of Statistics (Polyclinic) | → Helps with collection of data from CMF |
| | → Sends data to municipal level |

| CMF Consultorios | → Collects and revises the data of individuals, families, and communities every three months |

FIGURE 19. Flowchart of basic health statistics.

vision of basic necessities—by assigning a letter of rating of *G* for good, *R* for regular, and *B* for bad (table 3).

The role of family physicians extends beyond the stereotypical doctor in the clinic to one of active engagement and assessment of the social and material condition of patients. Since the launch of the MEF program, family physicians have moved away from the state objectives that were quantitatively defined, for example, mortality and morbidity rates, toward a qualitative assessment of specific community health needs. Health teams, as stipulated in the program, record the assessments of socioeconomic factors (see table 3) in addition to extensively reviewing each of the occupants in every household and recording their full names, age, date of birth, gender, profession, and level of formal education; identifying at-risk groups (smoking, excessive drinking, and so on); and describing each household and its surrounding environment: for example, a house may have poor ventilation or lighting, low maintenance of hygiene, or the presence of animals. As is evident from the qualitative descriptions in table 3, the assessment of socioeconomic factors by family physicians includes a host of factors—among them, psychosocial characteristics such as revolutionary involvement, that

TABLE 3. MEF GUIDELINES FOR ASSESSING SOCIOECONOMIC FACTORS IN
HEALTH AREAS

Cultural Hygiene

G [Good]	Follows physician's advice and is familiar with appropriate orientation toward health promotion and practices. Has good personal hygiene and collective well-being.
R [Regular]	Partially follows the physician's advice for health promotion but does not practice it. Personal hygiene and collective well-being not the best.
B [Bad]	Does not accept the physician's advice.

Psychosocial Characteristics

G	All the members of household of working age are working; those of studying age, study; maintain harmonious relations in the family and with neighbors; and regularly participate in mass organization initiatives.
R	At least one individual does not study or work in accordance with his or her age for reasons beyond control; has conflicts with neighbors for inappropriate behavioral patterns; and participates infrequently in mass organization initiatives.
B	At least one individual does not work or study in accordance with her or his age for reasons of her or his own choosing; has conflicts with neighbors based on inappropriate behavioral patterns including unlawful activity; and almost never participates in the initiatives of mass organizations.

Satisfaction of Basic Necessities

G	Provides basic necessities, including nutrition and recreation, and maintains good personal and community hygiene.
R	Provides some of the basic necessities or partially satisfies them.
B	Presents serious difficulties in provision of nutritional, recreation, and educational needs and lacks the necessary means to guarantee personal and environmental health.

SOURCE: MINSAP (2001): 143–44.

is, participation in mass organizations, and community and familial relations—that significantly extend the scope of the physician's primary health care assessment. A clear reference to the additional role of physicians as medical social workers can be found in Castro's speech at the launch of the MEF program:

These family physicians have a special professional code, especially a code of ethics, which is rigorous. Why is this? For the access these physicians have to families, and for the trust that these families offer them. The new family physician needs knowledge of psychology and psychiatry. In certain ways, many of the families these physicians will serve will ask them for advice about problems that will make them professionals of significant influence with great prestige. These physicians will be of substantial help in providing the health welfare of our people. Furthermore, I think these physicians will contribute to prolonging the average life expectancy of our population. Cuba will be among the leaders in the world in the field of public health. The family physician will play a fundamental role in this task.[16]

CONSULTORIO LOS MOLINOS

Referring in general terms to the patients in his área de salud, Luis Pérez discussed the various cases he was currently treating. Home visits, he made clear, were the only way he could get an adequate diagnosis on the chronic and acute problems in each household. While shortages had affected his daily practice, Pérez emphasized that with certain health programs, such as that of infants and pregnant women, absolutely no risks were taken. He would personally and immediately notify the local polyclinic or municipal hospitals of any shortages or required medicines or supplies. The death of an infant in one's área de salud, he cautioned, was subject to serious investigations by the municipal authorities. Pérez had to meet once a month with a clinical supervisor, an obstetrician-gynecologist from the polyclinic, to review all of his pediatric cases and prenatal appointments. The maternal and infant care programs were the most important of his daily activities. He spent hours reviewing his notes and getting them in order before the supervising obstetrician-gynecologist made her monthly rounds in his área de salud. Not having a computer, Pérez assembled the majority of his files and notes in a binder. For the most part, as stipulated by the MEF program, adult patients kept their own clinical history as well as that of their underage children and were required to bring their file with them on visits to the family physician, *policlínico*, or local hospitals.

Two cases were particularly troubling, he noted. He was treating two children with pneumonia who lived in separate households, and nobody in either home was employed, at least, not legally. "They live on air [*el aire*]," he said, sniffing ironically. In these houses there were more mouths to feed than were registered in the *libreta*. He claimed that the children, three and four years old, suffered as a result of poor household management.

"The children are malnourished," he said. He added that he had already called a social worker in to help him work with the families. The local government, Pérez said, was not to blame for the plight of the young children. He suspected that the children's food, already heavily subsidized by the state and rationed out to the families, was being bartered on the black market in exchange for cigarettes, rum, and money.

The physician's suspicions were later confirmed when a concerned community member informed the doctor of black market dealings by the two families. On the basis of this information, Pérez spent several days with the families involved, explaining the importance of infant nutrition. He told me he had handled the matter of the illicit black market trading delicately and stressed to the families that the infants must come first. He let the families know he would be making regular house calls to ensure his orders were being followed. He also strongly recommended that several of the family members of working age, who were not gainfully employed, become more involved in the community. The doctor also informed them that the CDR would be keeping an eye on the family for aberrant behavior. Pérez concluded, "I don't involve the police, because most times these things can be handled diplomatically. This is a community, and to create tension and distrust among residents is dangerous. Most people respect what I say. Cubans are gossips [*chismosos*] by nature, so word usually gets around on who is doing what." Many people viewed Pérez as a local authority, someone occupying a position similar to that of other state officials. He dealt with various complaints and was often called upon to tactfully handle disputes between neighbors.

The latest scandal, the doctor said, was that his patient, Bení Ortiz, drunk again, had recently exposed himself in front of a group of neighbors where small children were present. The doctor, annoyed by the lack of involvement of Ortiz's sons, contacted one of them immediately to inform him of what was going on. Ortiz, whom I had interviewed on several occasions, had agreed that I could speak with Pérez about his case. Ortiz was a lonely man who used alcohol as an escape, Pérez said. He was a former *militante* (Communist Party member) but voluntarily turned in his membership to the party over ten years ago because of his alcoholism. He now worked as a general laborer in a local factory, earning 156 Cuban pesos a month (6 U.S. dollars). When the factory was low on primary materials, which Ortiz claimed was becoming a regular occurrence in recent years, he was temporarily laid off. He made a little extra money on the side by fixing Russian radios, which were distributed to the population in the 1960s and 1970s. However, this specialized skill was becoming increasingly obsolete with the fall of the Soviet bloc and the resulting decreased use of Soviet technology in everyday life. Nowadays, Ortiz said, people had their hopes set on Sony and Panasonic mini-stereos sold in the U.S.-dollar stores; the lucky ones received money from relatives abroad, and others usually worked at informal jobs to earn extra cash to make such large purchases.

Ortiz's two sons, who were in their late twenties, had left home several years earlier and rarely spoke with him. On the occasions when the sons did visit, Ortiz asked the *médico* if he would speak with them about his progress. He wanted his sons to know he was trying to get better. Ortiz's wife, Mariella, in her early fifties, revealed in an interview that she was prone to depression and "nervous attacks." She solved this problem by taking a cocktail of sedatives she bought on the black market—mostly sedatives such as diazepam, a generic version of Valium, or mepbromate, a muscle relaxant and precursor of Valium—but the pills (*pastillas*) often caused her to doze off quickly when she got home from work. She had worked as an accountant for over twenty years in the same factory as her husband. Unlike many of the other residents I interviewed in Los Molinos, Mariella had completed a technical college degree and was paid the reasonably high salary of 300 Cuban pesos a month (15 U.S. dollars). However, she admitted that she spent at least half of her salary on coffee, cigarettes, and the cocktail of pastillas that she bought on the street or managed to buy with prescriptions she got from doctors.[17]

Pérez explained that he was working with Mariella to stop her dangerous habit of abusing sedatives. "All of these factors are part of the same problem," he said, and "depression and alienation" were the root causes of many of the problems he encountered, such as Ortiz's alcoholism and Mariella's addiction to prescription tranquillizers.[18] Aware of the challenges he faced, the doctor, with a touch of pride and a cadence reminiscent of Castro, offered this: "I live in the community, and like anybody else here, I know intimately what people's domestic problems are. The solutions for many of these people's problems lie outside of the *consultorio* and in the environments they live in. This is what makes the *médico de la familia* program so unique. I do not simply diagnose the individual; rather, I diagnose the family, and the community, as a whole."

Pérez argued that from his experience he would venture to diagnose the problems of his community and, by extension, of the nation: "We live an enigma in Cuba. . . . What we are building in Cuban society is a great thing." But he went on to say that the growing economic problems were creating insurmountable barriers in everyday life. He was adamant about one thing, however; like the other physicians I interviewed, he stated that to stop working because of financial hardships would be immoral. "People have a right to health care," he asserted bluntly. Unlike the countless physicians who, at the beginning of the revolution and in more recent years, had fled Cuba in search of a better economic life, mainly in the United States and Spain, Pérez was still committed to the underlying principles of the Cuban revolution, which he described as committed to humanity. He laughed when I asked if he considered himself a revolucionario. "Don't think I am a saint," he said. "I skip work some days because I'm exhausted. I'm not perfect. I would love to have what we Cubans refer to as the holy trilogy: a color Sony TV, a VCR, and a new stereo. I do not agree with all of the policies of *El Señor* [Fidel Castro] either. However, health care is fundamental to our society. The right to health must be protected. I know I am a role model in my community in many ways. It is obvious that my job in the community as a physician is not only to tell people what to do, but to show them that it can be done. I guess you can say I lead by example."

Pérez's effectiveness in his community, he argued, stemmed from his ability to seamlessly integrate himself into people's households. For instance, in the case of his patient Bení Ortiz, it is evident that a cure in part includes his participation in public mass organizations, which, on a theoretical level, were presumed to be an effective means by which to encourage people to embrace socialist values and ideas. The MEF program relies heavily on the underlying tenets of Cuba's socialist ideology, such as treating people as an integral part of their specific social and material environment. Given the restricted resources available to physicians participating in the MEF program, it is evident that their activities are limited in many ways to disease prevention and health promotion rather than treatment. The importance of the former approach, however, cannot be underestimated; in particular, the role of physicians in buffering the effects of macroeconomic changes brought about by the *período especial.*

As Pérez noted, "alienation and depression" are at the root of many people's health problems. A reported survey of 121 Cuban family physicians, 17 health leaders, and 26 administrative personnel leaders suggested that, following direct biological problems, socioeconomic factors were among the major contributors to health problems. Two other areas were also identified as following in relative importance: lifestyle choices that presumably put individuals at risk and personal and community hygiene.[19] The results of this study are not surprising given that, up until the 1980s, the revolutionary government had been effective in combating the so-called diseases of poverty that typically fit within the one agent–one disease model of causation. However, the rise of chronic noncommunicable diseases that became major health problems in the 1980s severely challenged the MINSAP's approach to social medicine. In practice, highly trained physicians with little equipment are better suited to managing noncommunicable chronic health problems than to addressing complex health problems.

The physician's role is limited to promoting healthy habits in communities and to screening community members for referrals to secondary and tertiary institutions. In this respect, then, Pérez's prescription of healthy doses of "social integration" in his consultorio appears to be, in part, a response to the new epidemiological profile of urban residents, where biomedical intervention plays a less significant role. An example from Pérez's consultorio illustrates this latter point. After going through his ficha familiar, noting the various illnesses people suffered from, and listing major risk behaviors, I asked Pérez how many people were "supposedly healthy" (*supuestamente sanos*), or in Group One, in his área de salud. "Not many," he replied. Between chronic and infectious illnesses, expectant mothers, illegal migrants, smokers, sexually promiscuous youth, alcoholism, criminality, and general antisocial behavior, Pérez's área de salud was an epidemiological nightmare of risks waiting to unravel into health problems.

The concept of risk has, as Sandra Gifford notes, two dimensions: a technical, objective, or scientific dimension and a socially experienced or lived dimension.[20] A problem arises, however, when epidemiological statements about risk, which are statements about groups of people, are translated into clinical practice. Contemporary concepts of epidemiological risk describe relationships between uncertain knowledge and unwanted outcomes, and thus the problem for medical practitioners becomes one of how to apply this knowledge in the clinical context.[21] Eliana Gutiérrez's experience with a physician who was posted in the Consultorio Los Molinos in the early 1990s illustrates this point:

> During my last pregnancy, when I was expecting my son José, I had this young médico de familia who was a complete nuisance. He told me that at my age—I was only thirty-six years old—I should not have become pregnant a second time. But at that point my financial condition enabled me to have another child, and I wanted to have another child. It was clear, however, that the doctor was not in agreement with me. For example, when I asked the doctor to give me a medical certificate so that I did not have to work one day because I was physically exhausted, which is quite normal during a pregnancy, he told me there was absolutely nothing wrong me and that if I could get pregnant at my age, then I could work. I am a strong-willed person, so of course I was not going to go to work if I felt that I was weak, so I went directly to the pediatrician who attended my first child and he signed the medical certificate without any problem. The other médico acted the way he did out of spite because he was convinced that as a thirty-six-year-old woman, I should not have become pregnant. I gave that young médico a piece of my mind the next time I saw him. I told him, "It is my body, and I will do whatever the hell I want with it." This imaginary age when you cannot have kids is rubbish. Just go to the countryside [*el campo*]. The women there are giving birth at forty and still having more kids, and they are born perfectly fine, without all this bureaucracy [*mucho papeleo*] around them! If I have a choice, I avoid the young médicos because they are too eager and try to do everything by the book, but without enough practical knowledge. In real life, no médico, much less those young ones, can do all the stuff the state wants them to. If I need any kind of medical attention for my kids or myself, I go directly to the pediatrician, who is an older, knowledgeable man. The médicos de familia are all talk, but what can they really do?

In Cuba, the dispensarización of the population into an exhaustive listing of risk groups has left the majority of individuals in the categories of prepathology. This is not to suggest that such hypersurveillance has drastically affected the practices of individual citizens. As Gutiérrez's experience indicates, individual citizens are not disciplined subjects who passively incorporate the state's primary health care objectives into their everyday practices. Rather, individuals can and do critically respond to their daily bombardment of health education and risk campaigns that address their everyday lives: the

Socialist Governmentality and Risk

consultorios, family physician home visits (*en el terreno*), and health campaigns carried out through mass organizations and the popular media.

While certain aspects of the dispensarización program may be interpreted as intrusive and objectionable, other parts are embraced. For example, most expectant mothers or mothers with children expressed few complaints when responding to my questions about MINSAP's maternal and infant care programs, including the mandatory prenatal exams, institutional childbirth, or the daily visits from the family physician for newborn infants. "Why wouldn't you want them to?" women often responded with puzzled expressions. "Who wouldn't want to have a healthy baby?" Theoretical discussions of the control and surveillance of women's bodies could not be easily mapped onto individual's narratives.[22]

"FOR YOUR OWN GOOD": POPULAR
PARTICIPATION AND HEALTH EDUCATION

One day I answered a knock at the door to my apartment. "Good morning, *compañero*," said the young woman standing outside. She was dressed rather shabbily in a faded gray uniform, with a small, official-looking badge on her front pocket and a folder in her hand.

"Your apartment will be fumigated in fifteen minutes," she said. "Please remove your sheets and store any open food in the refrigerator."

"Why?" I asked. "I don't want the place to be fumigated." Judging from my last experience with the fumigation brigade, when they sprayed pungent black smoke into my quarters and told me to wait on the street with my neighbors for half an hour, I was in no mood to spend half the day cleaning the smelly residue from my apartment. Now, the fumigation was becoming nearly a daily event.

"I'm sorry, but you have no choice in the matter," she insisted. "Where is the foreigner [*extranjero*] who lives here?" She had obviously observed the bright-blue triangular logo on my door that indicated my apartment was "rented to foreigners." She looked past me to address my Cuban friend, whose white skin caught her attention, and addressed him directly.

"Please, Señor, *España* [Spain] right? Can I speak with you?" she inquired, her tone becoming soft as she shifted to formal Spanish upon assuming that it was he who was the foreigner.[23]

"*Soy cubano* [I am Cuban]," he replied.

"Why are you making my job so hard then?" she barked at me, reverting to her original unfriendly manner. "You both know we must fumigate. We are fumigating against the mosquito, the transmitting agent of dengue fever.[24] It is a very dangerous illness." She huffed, frustrated by my questioning: "Can you please show me where you have tanks of water."

"What kinds of chemicals are you spraying?" I persisted.

"I don't know exactly. It is some kind of insecticide to kill mosquitoes," she replied. Oddly enough, in my two years in the same apartment I had never once seen or been bitten by a mosquito, although the rumor of people coming down with dengue fever was always present around the time of these fumigation campaigns.

After entering the apartment, the young woman checked each of the storage water tanks and then initialed and dated a small white MINSAP card behind the door to indicate that an inspection of the premises had been conducted.[25] No hygiene violations were found, meaning there were no areas in which mosquitoes could breed (*focos*) in the apartment. Less than ten minutes later a young man with a tank strapped on his back and equipment that looked like a leaf blower entered the apartment, closed all the windows, and started spraying clouds of black smoke.

One of the MINSAP's stated objectives under the MEF program is the containment and eradication of contagious diseases. Under the epidemiology program, MEF health teams carry out surveys in communities to "detect, register, treat and follow up persons with acute respiratory or diarrheal diseases, tuberculosis, venereal diseases, leprosy, malaria, and other communicable diseases. Diseases that are prevented through vaccination are managed in this manner."[26] Moreover, the sources of all infections are investigated to determine if there are other ill persons or carriers of disease who, when located, must be treated as well. The above account of my experiences with the "mini-brigades against dengue" was an oddity for several of my neighbors, who questioned why I would not welcome the regular fumigations and household inspections. "It is for your own good," several of them said to me on several occasions in a chastising tone of voice. "Why inspect our homes when the filth and stagnant water are all over the city?" I inquired. I pointed out the garbage strewn in the alleyways on either side of our building and the rotting piles of household refuse, now home to a family of aggressive stray cats who were in plain view. One of my neighbors, who often took advantage of the time we spent waiting on the street while the building was being fumigated to gossip with everybody, turned to me: "Oh, my dear," she laughed, "don't let it get to you [*no cogas lucha*]. When Fidel wants to kill mosquitoes, let him kill mosquitoes! You should know better than anybody else, as a foreigner, that things in this country do not have any logic! Look at the broken pipes over there, oozing sewage down the streets and people throwing garbage everywhere. If mosquitoes were going to eat us alive, they would have done so years ago. Now, at least we can attempt to get people, as a community, to participate and clean up the streets. Of course, after the scare goes away, things will return to normal and people will continue to litter filth everywhere without any regard for anybody." Several of my neighbors nodded their heads. "This is politics," she concluded.

My passive-aggressive resistance to participating in the fumigation campaigns quickly dissipated when one morning, very early, I refused to leave my apartment. Although I was being difficult, my rationale at the time was that I did not want to languish for thirty minutes on the street at eight o'clock in the morning. Asserting that I was indeed the "resident foreigner," I told the brigade to come back later. Shortly thereafter, a middle-aged man dressed in typical military garb appeared at my door and firmly told me I had no choice in the matter.

"Fumigation is the law," he stated.

He left with no discussion. When the fumigation brigade triumphantly arrived at my door, I asked if the pungent smelling chemicals they were spraying could at least kill cockroaches. Cockroaches the size of dollar coins had recently begun to have a field day in my apartment in the late evenings and early mornings. They were causing me much grief. Based on the fumigation staff's assurances that the larvicide and pesticide sprays would rid me not only of the offending mosquitoes, but of the roaches as well, I eagerly opened the door for the nearly daily onslaught during the weeks of the campaign. Despite the repeated intrusion of the "mini-brigades against dengue," the cockroaches continued to haunt my apartment, and I learned, thankfully, to ignore them.

In September 2002 the MINSAP broadcast an alert about an increase of *Aedes aegypti* mosquito breeding grounds in the city of Havana. Immediately after the announcement, consultorios, polyclinics, and hospitals in each municipality were on high alert, working with their respective Municipal Centers for Hygiene and Epidemiology and with various health professionals to carry out house-by-house fumigations and inspections. The consultorios coordinated local organizations to help with massive community cleanup programs and education campaigns. These stressed the importance of eliminating potential breeding areas for the offending mosquito.

The presence of dengue in Cuba is not a new phenomenon. The revolutionary government reported the first case of dengue-1 in 1977.[27] In 1981 the appearance of a dangerous serotype, dengue-2, "spread rapidly, reaching epidemic proportions within a month; 344,203 cases were recorded during the four-month period (June-September) that the epidemic lasted."[28] A total of 159 people died as a result of the epidemic.

The Castro government, weary from the last battle with dengue-1, contended that Cuba's exposure to dengue-2 was no accident.[29] As Castro pointed out in his "26th of July" address to the nation in 1981, he suspected the involvement of U.S.-based counterrevolutionaries, that is, Cubans in exile, in the use of biological operations against Cuba. He also indirectly accused the U.S. government of fostering these bandits of biological terrorism against the small island nation. Castro's speech, infused with recurring tropes of anti-imperialism, heroic sacrifice, and Cuba's struggle for communism, provided an ideological framework in which to situate the battle against dengue, which then took on a symbolic and political fervor. Shortly after Castro's speech, "a 'health army' [*ejército de la salud*] was established comprising 13,061 trained men and women rigorously selected by People's Power, the municipal health administrations, the FMC, and the Union of Young Communists, with the assistance of the party. The health army was charged with continuous inspection and the elimination of real and possible breeding places and equipped with back-pack larvicide sprayers. This group of trained volunteers would remain available to carry out vector elimination in the future."[30]

The health army organized to eradicate the *Aedes aegypti* mosquito is a crucial part of the socialist government's primary health care philosophy: the popular participation of the community in health initiatives. On a brief visit to Cuba in February 2002 I was staying once again in the apartment building I had previously rented, and this time the citywide fumigations were being carried out by small mini-brigades of students. These small groups of students were from the state's Social Workers Program, which incorporates wayward youth into various community projects. A group leader, usually a recent university graduate completing his or her required year of *servicio social* to the government, oversees a group of students known as a mini-brigade (*microbrigada*).[31] Each microbrigada is responsible for a specific area of the city.

One of the group leaders I interviewed told me that in this recent campaign against dengue, many of the students in the microbrigadas were from other provinces, thereby making their work efforts in the capital city an enjoyable excursion.[32] As he further stated, the socialist government was hoping to channel the negative tendencies of these problematic youth into productive endeavors of social transformation that would form part of their social reform. In cleaning up the city and specifically targeting areas that could be potential mosquito-breeding sites, the microbrigadas coordinate all of their efforts with the local, municipal, and national health education and prevention campaigns. The students are trained to provide detailed explanations to the population on the reproduction of the *Aedes aegypti* mosquito and the importance of eliminating stagnant water and trash in order to eradicate the problem.

As is true of every accomplishment of the revolutionary government, Castro best summarizes its success in one of his speeches. In the case of the microbrigadas against dengue he said,

> The enormous wealth of human resources that has been created and the traditional spirit of sacrifice and heroism demonstrated by our professionals, technicians, and workers in the health-care sector, . . . the immediate and crushing offensive that wiped out the latest outbreak of dengue in just 70 days at the beginning of this year; all of these things demonstrate and will continue to demonstrate the immense power achieved by our people, their health-care workers, and our medical-science sector.[33]

Like the dengue campaigns carried out in the early 1980s, this recent mass mobilization of the population can be interpreted as reflecting the symbolic importance of Cuba's battle against the United States.[34] In this fight (*lucha*), Cubans are asked to give of themselves selflessly and follow the state in achieving collective goals against a common enemy. But what was the opinion of the citizenry regarding the dengue campaigns?

Many of the citizens I interviewed were well aware that the dengue campaigns were one part public health safety measure and two parts political propaganda. During the regular fumigations throughout the height of the campaign, I heard repeated rumors that the actual epidemic was more pronounced, while the MINSAP was not using the word *outbreak* but was speaking of fumigations as the control and prevention of limited breeding areas of the offending mosquito. For example, a physician I interviewed intimated that the epidemic was a little more severe than what was being admitted. When I asked him to elaborate, he stated almost in a hushed voice, "Well, we are not supposed to say this, but I know there were quite a number of fatal cases." However, this supposedly hushed revelation was already widely known and circulated among individual citizens on the streets, many of whom often prodded other people to safeguard their houses against what was now being described as the deadly mosquito. When I asked individuals in private if they actually believed these rumors many simply stated, "No."

While I was walking through central Havana with a family physician during the height of the dengue campaign, patients from his área de salud, known as Consultorio Sierra Maestra, complained to him that he was not doing enough because the fumigation brigades still had not come to their homes.

"Miguelito!" a woman shouted, affectionately addressing the physician by his first name, "what about us? Why haven't the brigades come to our houses? Look at this place! I know there must be mosquitoes everywhere!" Her arms were flailing in the air.

The physician firmly admonished her and the small group of dissatisfied residents who were adding their own commentary on the failure of the brigades to include them: "*Señora*, the fumigation is not going to work if you still have filth on the street." He pointed to the crushed cans and garbage that were strewn about. Why, he wondered, because she was so concerned about her well-being, had she not taken the initiative to organize a street cleanup campaign with her local CDR?

"*La Revolución*," the physician proclaimed, "helps those who help themselves!"

As we were leaving, the same woman started to yell at her surrounding neighbors for being pigs (*cochinos*) and for allowing the neighborhood to become littered with trash.

Having met the physician on various occasions, I was relatively sure these actions were not being staged for my benefit but reflected his general approach to dealing with patients, whom he normally described as apathetic and belligerent.[35] When I asked the physician about the rumors, he expressed serious reservations about the validity of such claims.[36] Instead, he

Socialist Governmentality and Risk

argued that, in his opinion, the rumors were a way to get people to actively take part in the campaigns. In many of the mass mobilization campaigns in Cuba, including those directly related to public health, the use of slogans, matching clothing, and microbrigadas organized into separate but competing units is a form of collectivization.[37] In these collectives, people are strategically rallied around particular causes. As Richard Fagen notes, "A primary aim of political socialization in Cuba is to produce a participating citizen, not just one who can recite the revolutionary catechism perfectly. The test of the new Cuban man is how he behaves."[38]

In the campaigns against dengue, *risk* stresses a threat to the collective, that is, a concern for everybody. Therefore, the socialist government politically mobilizes communities in a battle against a common enemy—in this case, a viral-borne illness symbolically linked to U.S. imperialism—and attempts to draw individuals into the revolutionary ideology. On another level, however, one can look to the previous work of David Armstrong (1983), who points out, for example, that the medical dispensary in nineteenth-century England was concerned with disease as a social phenomenon and that this led to an increasing practice of community surveillance. However, community surveillance was a self-fulfilling prophecy: the discovery of disease in the community necessitated further surveillance.

Health brigade members (*brigadistas sanitarias*) have served a crucial role in Cuba's public heath campaigns since the early 1960s. The health education messages at that time urged the population to "Listen to This Friend: The Sanitation Inspector," who was on the hunt for the *Aedes aegypti* mosquito, then linked to yellow fever. The discourse of risk in the case of yellow fever also served as a powerful motivator to create a closer relationship with state authorities who ostensibly worked to keep the population healthy.[39]

After the período especial, the state's ability to motivate people to participate in other mass campaigns, like voluntary agricultural labor, has become increasingly compromised. According to Andrea Ochoa, differential access to material resources changed the interpersonal dynamics of her consultorio in Edificios Santa María. Throughout her two years there Ochoa had noticed a visible decrease in community participation in mass organizations, although a recent outbreak of dengue fever in the city had brought the building's residents closer together. Ochoa had helped coordinate a massive hygiene and cleanup campaign. Residents of the building worked together in the revolutionary spirit, she said, to eradicate potential breeding grounds for mosquitoes. This was a sign, she suggested, that there is still hope for Santa María, but more resources are definitely required to better equip family physicians and local consultorios.

Despite the government's widely televised reports of mass participation in various rallies and marches, the general public was well aware that the participants, for the most part state employees, were bussed into the city for the occasion. Many individuals were clearly aware of the subtleties of the socialist government's hybrid public-health-cum-political programs, and rather than protest by not getting involved they participated in the hope of improving their immediate circumstances. As the physician walking with me through central Havana noted, "Whether politics or a public health crisis, the end result is good for everybody: a cleaner city free of a potential threat." This is not to suggest, however, that the threat of dengue is a fiction of politics, but to show how the notion of collective risk, in this context, can be interpreted to reinforce political ends.

The reoccurrence of dengue in Cuba, however, also speaks volumes to the disintegrating infrastructure; for example, in the city of Havana, widespread broken pipes, garbage-strewn vacant lots, and a host of housing issues, including overcrowding, all contribute to putting individuals at risk. While fumigation serves as a quick fix to eradicate the troubling mosquitoes, the location of the focos is as diverse as the causes of their very existence. Selectively defining risk as something that can be addressed through chemical intervention shifts attention away from the institutional changes that are equally needed to address such problems, which nevertheless far exceed the state's material resources. By increasingly focusing on changes to individual bodily practices, that is, eradicating stagnant water in individual households, the larger macroinstitutional and infrastructural changes are shrouded, remaining out of focus and unaddressed.

AN EPIDEMIC OF SIGNIFICATION: HIV/AIDS EDUCATION AND PREVENTION PROGRAMS

I knew I was HIV positive long before the doctor gave me the results. I remember the day I went to pick up my results and the doctor handed them to me on a slip. He was a little taken aback because I did a little pirouette and extended my arm out to pluck the slip from his hand. I was trying to be lighthearted about the whole thing, you know, sort of like a ballerina from *Swan Lake*. At least the other people in the waiting room laughed. When I went in for counseling the doctor informed me that I would have to spend eight weeks in the HIV/AIDS education "resort" to learn about my illness. I am joking, of course. I know it is not a "resort," but for any Cuban, not just an HIV positive one, it is quite luxurious. You get three meals a day, and I mean real meals with meat and vegetables, not this rice and beans shit. You have an air-conditioned room and TV. Also, there are doctors, psychologists, and heaven knows who else there to help you adjust to your illness. I am being playful here, but seriously, I did not go out and get HIV on purpose; I was stupid and reckless. However, I get upset when foreigners come to Cuba and make it sound like the government is locking us up and throwing away the key.

Javier Sánchez, unemployed, born in Havana in 1970

Since the identification of HIV/AIDS in the early 1980s, AIDS has become a heavily politicized disease and in many ways has helped to expose the delicate infrastructure of how bodies have become the site of regulation. HIV/AIDS has been called an "epidemic of signification,"[40] which means in part that it is ultimately interwoven within the politics of language. The ever-changing discourses surrounding HIV/AIDS inform discussions concerning economic inequalities, political agency, and forms of resistance. It is within these discussions that various acts of rebellion against traditional politics of exclusion and privilege are concomitantly expressed. HIV/AIDS, in other words, has been firmly situated in political action. An examination of HIV/AIDS produces a political arena of contestation and complexity in which an array of discursive sites converge.

In the mid-1980s, when HIV/AIDS appeared as a potential threat, Cuba's response was similar to the one they deployed with other infectious diseases it had faced, such as dengue and African swine fever: to take measures to rapidly isolate, confine, and treat those who were infected. Throughout the course of my research, I conducted several interviews with individuals who were HIV-positive. In addition, I discussed the HIV education and prevention campaigns with the MEF primary health care physicians who participated in my research and carried out several interviews with health professionals working at the National Center for HIV/AIDS Education and Prevention, the Cuban Society for Family Planning, and the National Center for Sexual Education.

In 1985 the first case of HIV was detected in Cuba. Shortly thereafter, the MINSAP made a national announcement in 1987 that they would test the entire population over the age of fifteen for the HIV virus, which, if left untreated, leads to full-blown AIDS (in Spanish, SIDA). By the end of 1990 the

Cuban government had carried out over eight million HIV tests, detecting 449 positive cases, of which 325 were male and 124 female. Of this group, 63 people had shown symptoms of AIDS, and 32 of them had died. According to an article entitled "Hablemos Francamente" (Let's talk frankly) in the popular Cuban magazine *Bohemia*, the majority of new HIV cases in 1995, 53.7 percent, were from heterosexual transmission, while 44.8 percent were attributed to homosexual transmission. The remaining cases, health officials believed, were attributable to maternal HIV transmission and blood transfusion recipients.

As of 31 October 2007 a total of 9,304 persons had been diagnosed as HIV-positive in Cuba, this being the cumulative number of total cases since the first detected case in 1985. Of this total, 81 percent were men. The highest rates of transmission exist between people twenty to twenty-four years old, followed by the twenty-four to twenty-nine group. Eighty percent of the cases involve people between fifteen and twenty-nine years of age.[41] While open to more critical discussion, these recent figures of transmission and prevalence of HIV/AIDS in Cuba represent one of the lowest internationally: according to WHO 2008, a 0.1 percent prevalence rate.[42] However, although Cuba's HIV/AIDS transmission rates are low, this should not draw attention away from the source of the international debate, namely, the highly controversial nature of Cuba's HIV/AIDS-prevention program, which implemented an initial policy of quarantining all people who had tested positive in sanitariums, also known as *sidatoriums* (AIDS sanitariums).

The government's implementation of a quarantine policy in the first sanitarium, popularly known as Los Cocos, established eleven kilometers outside of Havana in 1986 and administered by the Ministry of Defense (MINFAR), was severely criticized from its inception.[43] The MINFAR stated that quarantining was voluntary, although they later admitted that considerable pressure was brought to bear on those who resisted. Many international critics interpreted the actions by the Cuban government regarding the AIDS sanitariums as a form of "imprisonment"[44] or "repressive discrimination against homosexuals."[45] The quarantine program was seen to reflect the *machista* (macho) assumptions underpinning the approach to the AIDS-prevention programs, especially the belief that homosexuality, similar to "male sexuality, is uncontrollable and unchangeable."[46] Such criticism assumed that all the individuals quarantined were male, which was not the case as close to 40 percent of the residents of Los Cocos were heterosexual women.

Despite the socialist government's attempts to defuse the issue, some international commentators were quick to draw on remarks made by Castro in his earlier revolutionary years, remarks such as "Nothing prevents a homosexual from professing revolutionary ideology and, consequently, exhibiting a correct political position. But I will be frank and say that homosexuals should not be allowed in positions where they are able to exert influence upon young people. In the conditions under which we live, because of the problems which our country is facing, we must inculcate our youth with the spirit of discipline, of struggle, of work."[47] Castro's remarks were problematic, especially given that in the seventies and eighties the socialist government had embodied the Stalinist–Maoist notion that homosexuality was a manifestation of capitalist decadence.

While Castro's statements during the height of la Revolución fueled the fire of many of his opponents and rallied international gay and lesbian rights groups against Cuba's human rights record, these international critics neglected to situate Castro's remarks, which he has publicly retracted, within the context of the equally volatile political positions many of their own governments, especially those of the United States, Canada, and Great Britain, had pursued toward homosexuality in the early 1960s. For example, homosexuality was classified in North America and Great Britain as a psychological disorder that required treatment.[48] While by no means a justification of the socialist government's action, before 1959 homosexuals in Cuba were subject to extreme isolation and repression, a bias enforced by civil law and augmented by Catholic dogma.[49] In light of his subsequent AIDS-prevention policies, Castro's earlier remarks should be criticized primarily for their general hypocrisy and ignorance in matters of sexuality.

While AIDS was presented, at least in the North American context, as a "gay disease" during the initial responses to the epidemic, there has been no evidence to support claims that the quarantine program in Cuba was motivated by a homophobic agenda. In the HIV/AIDS educational campaigns, though rife with heterosexist language and assumptions, the emphasis has always been on the number of sexual partners and on the sex acts performed rather than on the sexual orientation of those involved.[50] For example, several health promotion campaigns for condom use that were posted in local pharmacies had cartoon figures that represent heterosexual pairings with headings such as "Use a Condom. The couple's best friend" and "Use a Condom. If Not, No! Protect Yourself!" However, in health education pamphlets produced by the Ministry of Public Health, such as ¿Qué es el SIDA? (What is AIDS?) and Hombres . . . hablando entre nosotros (Men . . . talking among ourselves), the focus is on unsafe sexual actions rather than on identifying, as many North American campaigns did in the 1980s, "unsafe sexual orientations." In more recent years there have been several outreach programs throughout the city that target, among other areas, popular gay hangouts at the beach and in the city center.

This is not to suggest that repression of homosexuality has not or does not occur in Cuba, but it is to suggest that the debate should be redirected away from sexuality and identity politics to the more salient question: Is Cuba's AIDS-prevention program, as critics of the MEF assert, really a means of social control?[51] To answer this question requires an examination of the most controversial aspect of Cuba's AIDS-prevention program, namely, the initial decision to quarantine all HIV-positive people, regardless of whether they manifested any signs of illness, and to physically separate them from the rest of society.

Although health officials described the luxurious living conditions, especially by Cuban standards—the abundance of food, necessary medicines, and on-site, around-the-clock medical care—many international critics viewed the quarantine as expressing a disregard for the human rights of people with HIV/AIDS. Cubans, in general, were subject to increased mass screening (for the most part voluntary), especially those who had been abroad and those with a history of sexually transmitted diseases. Additionally, those individuals who tested positive were compelled to disclose their sexual contacts. Many Western observers argued that these tactics were not necessary and, in fact, produced mass hysteria rather than effective management of the epidemic.[52]

Very few social scientists have carried out a critical, systematic study of HIV/AIDS-prevention in Cuba.[53] Julie Feinsilver, for example, describes the Cuban quarantine system in the 1980s in which those interned in sanitariums "have unlimited controlled contact with their families and friends, are allowed to go out for various social purposes, and get weekend passes to go home . . . only under the watchful eye of a relative or a designated medical student."[54] While Cuba did employ these practices in the late 1980s and early 1990s, by the end of 1993 the HIV/AIDS treatment program had undergone drastic changes. As my direct observation and interviews show, the quarantine system is much more liberal and open than many scholars' depictions of it.

In 1993 the MINSAP implemented an Ambulatory Care Program similar to the MEF program that stresses home care and states that, when possible, HIV-positive individuals are to be incorporated into the community, thereby reducing the stigma associated with HIV as an illness that should be hidden. All new MEF physicians receive extensive education on the treatment and the special arrangements that need to be made for HIV-positive patients in their respective áreas de salud.[55] According to MEDICC Review (with the support of Oxfam International), as of April 2008 there were 220 people living at Havana's Comprehensive Care Center for People with HIV/AIDS (formerly known as the Santiago de Las Vegas Sanitarium). Cuba currently has twelve sanitariums around the country. The five individuals I interviewed for this book, who self-identified as being HIV-positive, openly discussed the fact that they were provided with a good life, a life, many of them added, that was slowly disappearing in Cuba's present economic crisis, which is characterized by massive food and medicine shortages. After an eight-week HIV/AIDS education course, all of the individuals I interviewed returned to their homes and were in regular contact with their friends and family.

While the above information is in and of itself cursory, the popular perception of HIV and AIDS among members of the Cuban public I interviewed was that the government's program of using sanitariums was effective. However, several people and some physicians did voice concerns that, given the recent economic changes in Cuba, the "epidemic was no longer under control." Many people questioned whether the government was capable of monitoring and containing the undetected number of HIV cases due to jineterismo (prostitution). While governmental policies under Castro sought to limit Cuban–foreigner interactions, a noticeable exception was workers in the growing sex industry, which reestablished itself in Cuba with the influx of tourism in the 1990s. Increasing numbers of tourists, particularly in Havana, come to Cuba not merely for the rum, tobacco, and salsa music, but also to find sexual partners who are racially and culturally different.[56]

Several citizens argued that HIV, like several other viral illnesses, including dengue, originated abroad, specifically, in the U.S. government's supposed armory of biological weapons to be used against Cuba. Many individuals repeated conspiracy rumors that HIV-positive Cuban-Americans were "on the loose," having sexual relations with Cubans without protection in order to knowingly infect them. Surprisingly, several primary health care physicians I interviewed repeated this rumor, firmly believing the Cuban exile community was behind the new cases of HIV transmission. Physicians also remarked that owing to the low incidence of the virus in Cuba, the population, especially young people, had become complacent. According to a study carried out in 1995 by Cuban physicians in one polyclinic in Havana, among the 669 patients identified as being at risk (*dispenzarizados*) the leading "risky behavior" was adolescent sexual activity (17.3 percent), followed by social risks (12.6 percent), which were well ahead of problems like asthma (9.6 percent) and hypertension (8.2 percent).[57] Another study, led in 2000 by a group of Cuban physicians, surveyed 2,703 adolescent students in the city of Havana regarding their attitudes toward HIV/AIDS education and prevention.[58] The researchers determined that 69.5 percent of those who were sexually active did not use condoms,[59] 43.1 percent had several sexual partners that year, and 24.9 percent had more than one sexual partner simultaneously.[60] The adolescents began having sexual relations at an early age, with a mean age of 13.84 for males and 14.83 for females.

Several of the physicians I interviewed, such as Luis Pérez, complained that despite regular *charlas* (chats) on sexual health, the adolescents in his área de salud repeatedly arrived at the consultorio with sexually transmitted illnesses and, increasingly, unwanted pregnancies. As many of the physicians complained, especially those in the city center, they were so busy that there was no way they could identify the long list of risks outlined in the MINSAP's requirements. As Andrea Ochoa at the Consultorio Santa María noted, it was impossible to monitor the behavior of so many people, and neighbors are not as willing as in the past to report each other's activities. The very notion of community surveillance and the role of individual citizens in alerting authorities, including physicians, about risky behavior, for example, a woman trying to conceal her pregnancy or people involved in illegal activities, have changed in recent times.

REDEFINING COMMUNITY SURVEILLANCE

On the outskirts of Old Havana is an area known as Los Pocitos. Most *habaneros*, however, refer to it as *la candela* (literally, the fire) because of the boisterous behavior of the occupants of its formerly grand colonial houses, now converted into *solares* (tenement housing). In a cramped two-room apartment I interviewed Norma Herrera. Almost seventy years old and a chain smoker, she was eager to talk about her experiences with the local médico de la familia. She began the interview with a startling revelation: "I am not a communist, you know, nor have I ever been one, although I respect communists and my children are communists." Laughing apprehensively, she explained to me why this clarification was necessary. Having worked as a former secretary to a high-ranking minister throughout the Batista administration, she explained that she was afforded many opportunities to leave Cuba after la Revolución but for personal reasons decided to stay. Now, as an elderly woman suffering from a number of medical complications due to a recent stroke, she made clear that la lucha that has characterized contemporary Cuban life cannot be separated from issues of health and, in general, the collective well-being of *el pueblo*.

Herrera was a lapsed Catholic; she said she left the church in the late 1950s because it was out of touch with people's everyday realities and was rife with hypocrisy. Drawing a comparison between the church and the contemporary Cuban state, Herrera explained that the contemporary socialist government was slowly moving away from meeting the needs of the people, which, in theory, worked against the notion of Cuba as a "state of the people." Born into a poor family in the province of Cienfuegos in 1930, Herrera won a scholarship to attend a Catholic private school, where she was eventually trained to become a high school Spanish-language teacher. She worked only briefly in this career before getting married to her first husband, with whom she had two children, and moving to Havana in the early 1950s to seek out better employment opportunities. After a brief stint as a secretary in a lawyer's office, she was recommended, through friends of friends, to take on a secretarial post in El Capitolio, the parliamentary building. Her husband, however, found it very difficult to find a permanent position and was growing increasingly frustrated. Shortly after la Revolución, he fled Cuba, leaving his wife and children behind. To date, Herrera has had no contact with him, although he does communicate with his two children directly.

Although unwilling to describe herself as a *revolucionaria*, Herrera, who now lives alone, was previously an active member of various mass organizations, such as the CDR and FMC; however, she now finds these institutions increasingly obsolete. As she made clear, her initial integration into la Revolución was shaped by her lived experience:

Before la Revolución I had never had any consciousness of class. I was very poor and I was never involved in a union because in reality there was no union I could join at the time, especially given my profession as a secretary. I did not really feel anything toward politics. When the Batista government started to commit all of the crimes against el pueblo, I was right there in Capitolio, but I was the kind of person that kept to myself. I knew I was in an environment of criminality, but at least my boss was not part of the crime rings that were operating in the government in those days. It became clear that things were going downhill when the government officials started openly stealing from the state coffers. Those who spoke up ended up as cadavers or, worse, people were found burned alive. Horrors! For this reason, I would say I became more political when la Revolución took power, because Fidel exposed these atrocities and condemned them. Although I never formally considered myself part of Fidel's movement, I had great respect for it from the beginning. In those days, the FMC and CDR had a common goal, and we worked toward building a new society. In those days we could become involved and actually see the changes you were involved in. Now, what you have is *El Bobo* [Castro, literally, the fool] making a bad situation even worse. The days of revolutionary fervor are long gone; now people need to know how to get food on the table.

As Herrera remarked, the recent increase in corruption is directly linked to changes in the relationships between the state, related institutions, and individuals in the community. For example, Herrera indicated, as did several other individuals I interviewed, that it was not uncommon before the período especial for people working with mass organizations in local neighborhoods to report on other community members for being promiscuous, drunk, or shirking their work duties. Such behaviors, Herrera asserted, were deemed antisocial or seen as possible signs of counterrevolutionary attitudes. These networks of community surveillance closely linked the state to individual activities. In this manner, the state had, up until very recently, managed to effectively keep counterrevolutionary discourses at bay, muffle internal political dissent, and monitor lifestyles deemed risky or unhealthy. The período especial, however, has changed this relationship. Concepción Hernández, a young family physician working close to Herrera's área de salud, summarizes this point:

Nowadays, the president of the CDR needs to feed his family as well, which means he too is going to be doing things to get dollars to be able to buy stuff.

Socialist Governmentality and Risk

So, he isn't going to be too concerned about looking at what other people are doing. I mean in Cuba now, there is lots of jealousy and envy of what other people have or don't have. Things are not like before, when people cared about their neighbors. Now, everybody wants the dollar to live well. Doesn't matter if you are a physician or a taxi driver. There is no reward in Cuba anymore for being a good worker. I mean if you are a doorman at a hotel you make more than a heart surgeon. Can you believe that? I mean there is no justice in that. I am a revolucionaria, and like anybody I too want access to good things. You hear people saying, look, to be a revolucionario means to be a *come mierda* [shit-eater]. To be dedicated to la Revolución doesn't matter anymore.

Herrera commented that before the período especial she could rely on her neighbors to check up on her once in a while because she was an elderly woman who lived by herself. In recent years, she remarked, helping out your neighbor is practiced less and less. One evening Herrera invited me to her apartment to talk and, as she said, "keep an old lady company." As she was a wonderful storyteller, I accepted her offer, despite the difficulties in finding reliable transportation to her municipality, which was prone to frequent power outrages that left the densely populated area in darkness for hours at a time. Arriving a little after eight o'clock in the evening, I found Herrera in good spirits, and we sat on her front terrace overlooking the street. Almost as if planned, Herrera started pointing out her various neighbors who came into view throughout the evening: the CDR president, who was at the time illegally renting out his apartment to foreigners; two younger women, dressed provocatively, both with older male foreigners on their arms, and who, according to Herrera, were *jineteras* who hosted new foreigners nearly every night; her immediate neighbor to the right, who sold rice and milk powder from her door, all stolen from her job at the local *bodega*; and, finally, her immediate neighbor to the left, who had a car that he drove for a state company but also used on the side to run an illegal taxi operation.

Summarizing all of the illegal activities, Herrera inquired, "Who is going to report whom?" As she stated, she saw her neighbors' involvements in *lo informal* as being endemic in the community, if not the country as a whole: "It is part of life, now." The explanation for this apparent contradiction was related to the widespread dual moral code or duplicity (*la doble moral*) of contemporary Cuban life. In this system, there is a contradiction between two normative frameworks, the public and the private, in which one outwardly accepts the state's moral code of conduct but rejects it in practice.[61] Beyond the simple linear opposition between public and private, or *en la calle* (in the street) and *en la casa* (in the house), la doble moral is much more complex and endemic in everyday interactions, both political and nonpolitical.[62] For example, while many people preach the revolutionary principles, denouncing jineterismo and lo informal as a regression in the moral standards of contemporary Cuban society, many of these same individuals (for example, policemen and other state officials) turn a blind eye to its existence or economically benefit from the practice (private restaurant owners, rental property owners, and ordinary citizens) by establishing mutual agreements with jineteros to bring foreigners who will rent apartments, buy goods or services, or purchase medications or consumer goods abroad.

A clear example of the doble moral was a local CDR meeting I attended in the neighborhood where Consultorio Las Vegas was located.[63] The area was centrally situated in a tourist area and was also frequented by what one CDR delegate (*cederista*) referred to as "marginal individuals: gays, transvestites, jineteras, and that sort." At the meeting, apartment renters and neighbors alike were asked to be vigilant about the types of people they allowed to rent their homes. Seeking to crack down on rooms and apartments that were rented to foreigners and Cubans without legal declarations, an official announcement from the Ministry of Housing proclaimed that houses found to be engaging in the promotion of illegal activities would be confiscated by the state. The majority of the people at the meeting were in wholehearted agreement on what needed to be done: report aberrant activities immediately to the relevant authorities.

Much later that same evening, sitting on the front steps of my building, many of my neighbors laughed and discussed the uselessness of the earlier CDR meeting. Despite their previous agreement and earnest nodding of heads, they explained that it was only to "show face" and that they had no intention of reporting anything. The reality was that jineteros, male and female, along with foreigners were the vast majority of their clientele. In addition, there existed a general agreement that the renters would pay the jineteros a commission of five U.S. dollars per day to bring customers to their apartments. On a different note, a usually timid, older woman who attended the CDR meeting, frail and dressed in a faded white nightgown, grabbed her breasts and shook them at us playfully, declaring, "I would be a

Socialist Governmentality and Risk

jinetera too if I could, but I don't have what I used to." Laughing, most of my neighbors agreed that people needed to luchar—engage in the complex web of associations in lo informal—and that the jineteros, like everybody else in Cuba, were no different. They just wanted a good life. I encountered several families that supported this opinion; often one or more of the family members were dating foreigners, often several foreigners within a span of two weeks, which seemingly did not arouse attention.[64]

This state of affairs signals a breakdown in the state's network of mutual vigilance: "The existence of strategies of power does not necessarily correspond with the successful exertion of power, and . . . intended outcomes often fail to materialize because disciplinary strategies break down or fail."[65] What does this mean for Cuba's primary health care system? For example, the concerned citizens of Consultorio Los Molinos reported on their neighbors for bartering their infants' rations on the black market. The roles of the CDRs are optimally to stimulate these kinds of behavior: mutual vigilance that guards against antisocial and counterrevolutionary actions. From an epidemiological point of view, this unprecedented level of surveillance, which amounted to a kind of panopticon gone awry, with people watching and being watched, was an ideal model, theoretically speaking, for the control and prevention of communicable illnesses. Nevertheless, over the course of the past forty years the role of the CDRs in the city of Havana has lessened in many respects, with a greater percentage of the people paying only lip service to its existence and objectives; that is, to its commitment to mutual watching.[66] Some of the recent changes within community surveillance ultimately change the ability of health professionals' efforts to identify risk.

As was evident from the interviews I conducted in Ochoa's consultorio, physicians must negotiate a fine line between their role as health providers and as perceived state officials. The ability of physicians to integrate themselves effectively into local communities is key to their success in completing their mandates. Historically, la Revolución diminished the class stratification that was apparent in the prerevolutionary era. The state's sense of community, defined by a strong feeling of social cohesion, was easier to enforce because individuals, theoretically, were provided with equal opportunities and equal rewards. In an environment of egalitarianism, the work of physicians was facilitated by the strong presence of the state, which, in response to community health matters, reinforced the ideology of various institutions, such as the control and distribution of resources, the media (for example, health education campaigns), and a willingness to participate in mutual vigilance.

The período especial has challenged the state's construction of community. The current MEF family physicians' ideological tools are increasingly poorly adept in combating the ever-increasing socioeconomic stratification and the practices that were once seen as working against the health of the community and, more broadly, against revolutionary principles: lo informal, antisocial behavior, and engaging in high-risk sexual activities.

In Cuba there will be no
shift toward capitalism.
Brotherton © 2001.

I believe that, in the future, it will never be necessary again to ban the possession of dollars or other foreign currencies, but its free circulation for the payment of many goods and services will last only as long as the interests of *la Revolución* make it advisable. Therefore, we are not concerned about the famous phrase "the dollarization of the economy." We know very well what we are doing.

Fidel Castro, June 2000

Shortly after the fall of the Soviet bloc, Cuba's socialist project underwent relentless changes, many of which seemed to contradict its underlying revolutionary principles. For instance, the government introduced reforms that sought to increase the economy's responsiveness to the world market through the legalization of the circulation of hard currency and the search for foreign capital and technology, among other key changes that were consistent with capitalist values.[1] Many of these changes reflected the clashing of the small island nation and the capitalist world economy and heralded a new beginning in the country's revolutionary historiography; Cuban socialism entered what Stefan Sullivan terms the "post-communist era."[2]

In 1991 MINSAP drafted a document titled "Objectives, Aims, and Guidelines for Improving the Health of the Cuban Population 1992–2000" to define the state's health goals and objectives to be achieved by the year 2000. In this document MINSAP designated biotechnology and high-technology medicine as priority sectors for continued investment, despite the general program of economic austerity measures that characterized the SNS. These strategies, the government argued, were part of the greater plan to build Cuba's economy and ultimately make the island more self-sufficient. First, they were a means to address the local shortage of pharmaceutical products created by the cessation of Soviet aid and the U.S. embargo. Second, it was to capitalize on their newly acquired high-technology medical capabilities. Nowhere were changes to Cuban socialism more evident than in the strategic expansion of the country's "health tourism" industry, Turismo y Salud S.A., in the mid-1990s.[3] This signaled the emergence of what I refer to as socialist entrepreneurs offering health services on a treatment-for-pay basis, theoretically to the foreigners on the island.

Within this changing socioeconomic context individual bodily practices in the health sector—manifested through individuals' interactions with and around institutions of the state—began to thrive on transnational capital in the form of a flourishing economy of remittances and joint-venture socialist corporations selling health care and medical supplies in hard currency. Whereas the state was once the arbiter of health policy, care, and knowledge, a role its citizens were inculcated to accept via la Revolución, it now relies on transformed bodily practices that match new health agendas and new capital mobility.

STATECRAFT: TURISMO Y SALUD S.A.

An advertisement by the state-run agency Cubanacán (figure 20), which markets Cuba's health care services, reads as follows:

> An ideal destination for your health: Cubanacán Turismo y Salud, S.A. is the latest development in Cuban medicine. Cubanacán offers you specialized medical attention supported by an extensive network of institutions outfitted with modern equipment and staffed by prestigious, internationally renowned scientists. Now you can enjoy your vacation without worrying about your health. Cubanacán "Health and Tourism" provides you with specialized attention and even guarantees your hotel room. You can find our international clinics, pharmacies, and optical stores in every important tourist destination throughout the country. We are your medical resource in Cuba, with the most modern medical technology for your health-care needs.[4]

During Cuba's period of economic hardship the socialist government began pursuing a variety of strategic programs, one of which was Cubanacán. The programs included the rapid expansion of a domestic pharmaceutical and biotechnology industry and a health tourism industry, coordinated by Servimed, a subsidiary of Cubanacán.[5] Pivotal to the unbridled development of Cuba's health tourism sector were the liberal economic reforms instituted

We Have to Think Like Capitalists

TURISMO Y SALUD

Ave.43 No. 1418, esquina a 18, Miramar, Playa, Ciudad de La Habana, Cuba.
Telef: (537) 24 4811 al 13. Fax: (537) 24 1330 y 24 0119
E-mail: servimed@tursal.cha.cyt.cu

un destino ideal para su salud

Cubanacán Turismo y Salud S.A. es el reflejo del desarrollo de la medicina cubana, ya que brinda la atención médica más especializada, a través de una amplia red de instalaciones dotadas con un moderno equipamiento y prestigio internacional de consagrados científicos. La posibilidad de disfrutar de unas vacaciones sin preocuparse por su salud.

Con Cubanacán Turismo y Salud la atención primaria al turista está garantizada desde el propio hotel. También podrá contar con Clínicas, Farmacias y Opticas en los destinos turísticos más importantes del país. Somos el aseguramiento médico con el más moderno soporte tecnológico para la salud en Cuba.

tratamientos y servicios especializados

- Retinosis Pigmentaria
- Vitiligo
- Psoriasis
- Adicción a las drogas
- Parkinson
- Ortopedia
- Pediatría
- Cardiología
- Oncología
- Oftalmología
- Rehabilitación en restauración neurológica
- Transplantología
- Programas de calidad de vida
- Opticas Miramar
- Red de farmacias

La mejor forma de conocer Cuba
www.cubanacan.cu

FIGURE 20. Cubanacán Turismo y Salud. Source: *Avances Médicos de Cuba* 7(23) (2000), back cover.

in the 1990s, particularly the search for foreign capital and technology. Of critical importance was the Cuban Foreign Investment Act (5 September 1995), popularly known as Act No. 77.[6] This law sought to "broaden [foreign investment] and facilitate foreign participation in the nation's economy . . . for the fundamental purpose of achieving sustainable development in the country and a recovery of the national economy."[7] Act No. 77 states,

> In today's world, without the existence of the socialist bloc, with a globalizing world economy and strong hegemonistic [*sic*] tendencies in the economic, political and military fields, Cuba, in order to preserve its accomplishments despite the fierce blockade to which it is subjected; lacking capital, certain kinds of technology and often markets; and in need of restructuring its industry, can benefit from foreign investment, on the basis of the strictest respect for national independence and sovereignty, given that such investment can usher in the introduction of innovative and advanced technology, the modernization of its industries, greater efficiency in production, the creation of new jobs, improvement in the quality of the products and services it offers, cost reduction, greater competitiveness abroad, and access to certain markets, which as a whole would boost the efforts the country must undertake in its economic and social development.[8]

Foreign investment was authorized in all sectors of Cuban society, according to Article 10 of this act, "excluding health and education services for the population and the armed forces institutions, with the exception of the latter's commercial system."[9] One of the outcomes of Act No. 77 was the institutionalization of the *sociedad anónima*, or S.A. (literally "anonymous company" or share company, the equivalent of "Inc." in the United States), a "Cuban commercial company [that] adopts the form of a nominal share corporation in which one or more national investors and one or more foreign investors participate."[10] In the 1970s the Cuban government established several corporations abroad, mainly in Western Europe and Panama, under the legal umbrella of sociedades anónimas to facilitate foreign trade and circumvent the U.S. economic embargo.[11]

In 1979 the Cuban government established the first domestic sociedad anónima, Corporación de Importación y Exportación S.A., also known as CIMEX S.A., which, among other things, now operates the country's dollar stores, Tiendas para la Recaudación de Divisas (Stores for the recuperation of hard currency). Popularly referred to as shops (*chopins*), these stores sell a

We Have to Think Like Capitalists

FIGURE 21. The return of Western Union to Cuba. Brotherton © 2005.

host of basic goods and food items as well as luxury items such as televisions, refrigerators, stereos, and so on, at significantly marked-up prices. In 1999, several years after the legalized circulation of the U.S. dollar, the money transaction agency Western Union returned to Cuba. Western Union had left the island in the early 1960s in response to the country's nationalization and socialization of private property under the agrarian reforms laws adopted in 1959. Ironically, Cuba's Western Union branches are currently operated under the umbrella of the CIMEX, S.A. (figure 21). With changes to the remittance laws under various U.S. administrations, the return of Western Union to Cuba represented an easy and steady flow of hard currency into the country from relatives of Cubans who were living abroad. Before 1999 Cuban immigrants in the United States were reliant on a network of agencies with links to businesses in Cuba to get money to friends and relatives on the island.

More generally, however, Act No. 77 was influential in attracting foreign investors to participate in domestic sociedades anónimas, making them more widespread in the country's economy. As Andrew Zimbalist notes, "For most purposes [sociedades anónimas] are allowed to operate independently of the central state apparatus. They behave as profit-maximizing entities and engage in joint ventures inside and outside of Cuba. In part to facilitate trade insurance and to diminish the perceived foreign exchange risk to trading partners, the Cuban state has arranged for most of these corporations to be owned privately by individual Cubans."[12]

Cubanacán's Turismo y Salud S.A., falling within the sphere of Cuba's burgeoning tourist industry rather than its health industry, has been able to capitalize on these foreign investment laws by offering medical care to foreigners under state promotional campaigns like "Sun and Surgery," which advertise packages that include specific health services, travel to and from Cuba, and accommodations. For example, during the 1990s tourism became a priority sector for Cuba's economic development and evolved from a peripheral activity to become the most dynamic sector of the economy, earning more hard currency than sugar. With increased foreign investment in joint ventures in the tourist industry, both hotel room occupancy and the number of airlines serving the island rose exponentially to accommodate the burgeoning number of people choosing Cuba as a tourist destination that could now include health services.[13]

For example, in 2006, on a flight on Cuba's national airline, Cubana, I saw several in-flight promotional commercials for the Cira García International Clinic, the most popular health tourism institution in Cuba. The Cira García provides state-of-the-art medical and dental facilities, offering services ranging from plastic surgery to arterial grafts to neural transplants for treating Parkinson's disease (figure 22). The glossy Cuban magazine *Avances Médicos de Cuba* (Medical advances in Cuba), sold only in U.S. dollars, bombards readers, presumably foreign subscribers, with full-page color advertisements for Cuba's prized international clinics, among them, Hermanos Ameijeiras, featured in Michael Moore's documentary *Sicko* (figures 23 and 24). The clinics' services include everything from organ transplants and drug rehabilitation to stress management, psoriasis treatment, cardiac surgery, and oncology. One of the advertisements (see figure 20) promises readers "the possibility of enjoying your vacation without worrying about your health," alongside Cubanacán's Turismo y Salud motto, "Honestidad, Calidad Científica y Profundo Contenido Humano" (Honesty, scientific quality and dedication to humanity).

The irony of this form of marketing is highlighted by various foreign critics and local citizens, who question the underlying politics behind the investment of hard currency in high-technology medicine in the face of massive shortages in the primary health care sector. For example, in stark contrast to the well-equipped, ultramodern health centers cropping up across the city, the average *consultorio* consists of a simple multiroom complex with a small examining room, complete with health promotion campaigns, nutritional advice, and various health programs to be followed. Far more troubling than

CLINICA CENTRAL CIRA GARCIA

Honestidad, Calidad Científica y Profundo Contenido Humano.

Servicios / Services

Consulta externa y hospitalización
en todas las especialidades.
*Out patient clinic and hospitalization
in all medical specialties.*

Medios diagnósticos y terapéuticos
de alta tecnología.
*High technology diagnostic and
therapeutical media.*

Servicio de urgencias médicas y estomatológicas
las 24 horas del día.
*Medical and dental emergency services,
24 hours daily.*

Visitas a domicilio por especialistas y enfermeras
altamente calificados.
*Home visits by highly qualified
specialists and nurses*

Farmacia abierta las 24 horas.
Servicio de mensajería.
*Drugstore, open 24 hours daily.
Messenger service.*

Servicio de ambulancia con moderno
equipamiento.
*Ambulance service with up-date
equipment.*

Acompañamiento médico al extranjero.
*Medical accompaniment service
to other countries.*

Calle 20 # 4101 esq. Ave 41, Playa, C. Habana, Cuba.

Teléfonos: (53-7) 24 2811 al 14
Telefax: (53-7) 24 2640, 24 2660 - Fax: (53-7) 24 1633
E-mail:ciragcu@infomed.sld.cu // E-mail:faculta@cirag.sld.cu
www.cira.cubanacan.cu // www.infomed.sld.cu/cira

cubanacan
TURISMO Y SALUD

FIGURE 22. Cira García International Clinic. Source: *Avances Médicos de Cuba* 7(23) (2000), 23.

FIGURE 23. Hospital Hermanos Ameijeiras. Source: *Avances Médicos de Cuba* 7(23) (2000), 9.

FIGURE 24. Advertisements for some of Cuba's international clinics and research centers. Source: *Avances Médicos de Cuba* 7(23) (2000), 32.

the aesthetic differences, however, was the lack of basic medical supplies and equipment essential to primary health care delivery, such as stethoscopes, basic surgical instruments, thermometers, and antiseptics.

In 1997 Servimed earned twenty million U.S. dollars by serving six thousand patients in thirty-eight facilities. As was obvious from my visits to local *consultorios*, where the availability of essential drugs and vaccines was intermittent at best, the sale of drugs and high-technology services for U.S. dollars to foreigners is paradoxical. The Cuban government contends that foreign medical services represent a small percentage of Cuba's universal health care system. By MINSAP's account, only 400 to 500 of Cuba's 66,263 hospital beds are used by foreigners. In addition, Cuba's vice minister of economic affairs reports that 98.5 percent of the gross income from foreign patients remains within the health care system. The hard currency earned from treating and selling medications to foreign patients, official reports claim, is used to purchase medicines for Cuban patients, who receive them free in hospitals and at subsidized prices in pharmacies.[14]

Official claims by government representatives notwithstanding, most of the individuals I interviewed for this book were outraged that a two-tiered health care system existed. This opinion was held also by several primary health care physicians who pointed out acidly that the health professionals who work with foreigners often receive a portion of their salary in foreign currency as a material incentive. Several of these primary health care physicians further complained that, although they were celebrated in the state media campaigns as selfless individuals dedicated to la Revolución, they were generally expected to work for moral incentives rather than for monetary compensation; that is, to be good *revolucionarios*.

Once one of the main pillars of la Revolución, Cuba's health care system is an apt example through which to interrogate the broader social, political, and economic changes that characterize contemporary Cuban life. As the following ethnographic vignettes illustrate, the Turismo y Salud S.A. industry is not limited to foreigners alone but has "unofficially" opened its back door to individual Cubans who have foreign currency. The trend signals the reemergence of a parallel, profitable, private sector health care system operating within Cuba's socialist economy. The rise of socialist entrepreneurs in Cuba's health sector should be viewed less as a marketing ploy for tourists than as a form of state income generation, especially in areas in which the domestic social welfare system is faltering.

We Have to Think Like Capitalists

LIVING IN CUBA WITH DOLLARS IS LIKE
NOT LIVING IN CUBA AT ALL!

On a blistering August night, while dancing at a party until the wee hours of the morning, Dimitri Martínez lost one of his contact lenses. He had neither eyeglasses nor replacement contacts. Suffering from severe myopia, the twenty-eight-year-old state employee had been on a waiting list for months to buy a pair of subsidized eyeglasses from the optometrist in his designated *área de salud*. He was frustrated, he stated, especially because in his job as an editor for a state-run newspaper he was required to read and write for eight to ten hours a day. Walking into the emergency room at a local hospital in the Plaza de la Revolución, he was quickly attended by an ophthalmologist. Although sympathetic to his plight, the specialist indicated that if paid for in Cuban pesos, it would take a minimum of six months to replace the lenses, if they could be replaced at all. Examining his vision, she concluded that, given his poor eyesight, perhaps he should consider joining the growing number of people on a waiting list for eye surgery.

The doctor stated that MINSAP was considering incorporating laser technology for eye surgery in the upcoming months, but she was not sure whether it would be available for payment in Cuban pesos. Martínez pointed out that even if the laser technology became available in Cuban pesos, access would depend on one's strategic connections or on *socios* who worked in centers that had the technology. This was the case for a growing range of high-technology medical equipment in Cuba, such as computed axial tomography scanners and magnetic resonance imaging scanners. Not having connections, Martínez noted, one's chances of getting off the waiting list were slim to none. A close friend of Martínez confirmed his concerns. On hearing of his plight, this man offered to put Martínez in contact with the chief ophthalmologist at a local medical center to help resolve his problem, whether through eye surgery or getting lenses quickly. As his friend stated, however, Martínez would be expected to give the doctor a *regalito*, a gift. Martínez declined, arguing that his money would be better spent at an international optometry clinic, Ópticas Miramar, operated by the Turismo y Salud S.A. program, where at least he could be assured of getting what he was paying for (figure 25).

I accompanied Martínez on his visit to the optical store, located in the diplomatic center, Miramar. After briefly speaking with the receptionist, Martínez paid five dollars for an optometrist's consultation. We sat in a beautifully decorated, air-conditioned salon, where we were entertained by

Sus ojos: uno de sus mayores tesoros
Your eyes: one of your greatest treasures

OPTICAS
MIRAMAR

Una amplia gama de armaduras y gafas de sol,
lentes bifocales, multifocales, transicionales en color
natural y fotosencibles, lentes de contacto graduados
y cosméticos, consultas de optometría y contactología,
entre otros, son los servicios que ofrece Ópticas Miramar.

A su disposición de lunes a viernes de 10:00 a.m. a 6:00 p.m. y los sábados de 9:00 a.m. a 1:00 p.m.

Casa Matriz
Calle 7ma. esq. a 24, Miramar, La Habana. Telfs: 24 2269 y 24 2990
Fax: 24 0289

FIGURE 25. Ópticas Miramar. Source: *Avances Médicos de Cuba* 7(23) (2000), 33.

the Discovery Channel (in Spanish) via satellite TV, and we browsed through the store, which sold, among other things, the latest U.S. and European designer eyewear. When Martínez's name was called out, a neatly uniformed optometrist accompanied us into the examining room and began her routine examination using what she said was the latest in computerized diagnostic equipment. The technology used in the optical store made the hospital appear, in Martínez's words, like a "stone age" facility. The optometrist, drawing elaborate diagrams of his eye and explaining each test she conducted and what the results meant, spent a little over twenty minutes informing Martínez why his eyesight had been slowly deteriorating over the past several years.

The optometrist concluded that eyeglasses would be of little use to him because his peripheral vision was poor. In addition, the hard contact lenses he had been wearing for over six years without replacing and that were made from an impermeable glass that he cleaned and stored in boiled tap water, had prevented his corneas from breathing. What he needed, she concluded, were gas-permeable contact lenses, available only for U.S. dollars in Cuba. They were made on-site within three business days for seventy-six dollars. Surprised by the high price, Martínez once again considered waiting several months for state-subsidized lenses that cost a mere fifteen Cuban pesos (equivalent to less than one U.S. dollar), especially in view of his monthly salary of two hundred pesos (approximately ten dollars), which, in 2001, was higher than the average Cuban salary of eight to ten dollars a month. The optometrist, sensing his hesitation, quickly explained the various benefits of

We Have to Think Like Capitalists

immediately ordering the lenses from Ópticas Miramar: the three-year warranty, which included the periodic on-site maintenance and cleaning and the health benefits of wearing breathable lenses for a person whose sight was so poor. After five minutes of thinking and attempting to gauge whether such lenses were worth the price, Martínez decided the lenses in Ópticas Miramar were his best option.

The optometrist, pleased by the sale, turned to me and asked in English if I would be making the payment in cash or by credit card. As she indicated, Ópticas Miramar accepted all major credit cards except those sponsored by U.S. banks. As she smiled at me, it was obvious that she dealt with Cubans accompanied by foreigners regularly. Martínez paid for the lenses in cash, and the staff gave him a date on which he could pick them up. Martínez confided that he found the price of the lenses a bit high. He was further shocked to discover that the new lenses required a specialized cleaning solution and that boiled tap water would be insufficient to sanitize them. Thankfully, Martínez conceded, he had intermittent access to dollars from his brother, who lived in Venezuela and sent money from time to time. However, later that afternoon, clearly upset, he pondered why, when the state has the equipment to make the lenses in Cuba, it takes over six months to obtain them if one pays in Cuban pesos. The answer, as he knew, was that the peso and dollar economies are, for the most part, mutually exclusive, one operating for the welfare of the people and the other as a savvy, profit-making enterprise. For many Cubans, including Martínez, the contrast between the state as provider and the state as a corporation was a bitter pill to swallow. The very government that for many years had preached nurturance and access to health care as a right was now participating in and promoting an economy of haves and have-nots. As we left the diplomatic quarter and made our way back to the city center, Martínez reflected on his experience and exclaimed, "¡Vivir con dólares en Cuba, es como si no estuvieras viviendo en Cuba!" (Living in Cuba with dollars is like not living in Cuba at all!). The other customers in the Ópticas Miramar waiting room, a well-heeled group of Cubans, several of whom were accompanied by foreigners, reinforced this view. Other individuals corroborated Martínez's experiences in other spheres of Cuba's health sector.

NAVIGATING THE TWO-TIERED HEALTH CARE SYSTEM

Consultorio Las Vegas was often a nodal point along Maria Menéndez's patients' therapeutic itineraries. Armed with prescriptions obtained from various physicians, an increasing number of her patients convinced friends and relatives abroad to send them medications or medical supplies and equipment. For example, despite the long list of restrictions on items that travelers can bring into Cuba, one notable exception is up to ten kilograms of medicine in the original packaging, which is exempt from duties and taxes.[15] In addition, some agencies send medicine and medical supplies to friends and families in Cuba. Several such agencies have their offices conveniently located in Canada to avoid limitations imposed by the U.S. embargo.[16]

While many individuals revealed that the various ailments they claimed to suffer from were not clinically diagnosed, they were adamant that their medications were essential (and, I may add, desired). Alternatively, I interviewed some patients who, flush with foreign currency, regularly frequented the international clinic pharmacies cropping up across the city, such as the Cira García International Clinic, to buy prescription drugs, ranging from medicines for chronic health problems to chemotherapy, and basic medical supplies such as gauze, antibiotic ointments, and vitamins. As numerous individuals I interviewed caustically pointed out, many of the drugs sold in international pharmacies were "hecho en Cuba" (made in Cuba) yet were unavailable at any of the pharmacies in the peso-based economy.

On several occasions I accompanied Cuban friends who had prescriptions from their local family physicians to international pharmacies at certain hospitals and clinics to buy prescription drugs and other medical supplies. The only requirement to make purchases at these locations was a foreign passport. As I soon found out, Cubans who were eager to make purchases but did not know any foreigners would often linger outside the pharmacy, waiting for foreigners to help them facilitate their transactions. On one occasion, as I was making purchases for a friend of mine, two individuals I did not know approached me and asked if I would help them purchase their prescription drugs as well. The pharmacy staff, aware of what was transpiring, went about their business courteously. When I inquired why the foreign-passport rule was in effect, the staff informed me that the international pharmacy, run by Cubanacán, was not geared toward Cubans. Rather, the pharmacist stated, Cubans had the option of going to their local pharmacies and paying in Cuban pesos.

We Have to Think Like Capitalists

One of the strangers I helped on that occasion, a middle-aged woman, became visibly upset and roared, "You know damn well there is nothing in those pharmacies. In this country, *los extranjeros* [foreigners] come first. *El pueblo* [locals], on the other hand, we eat shit." The pharmacy staff ignored her comments. As we left, the irate woman held her receipt up in the air, shaking it violently, and stated, "Look, eighty-six dollars, and for what?" She cursed the woman in the pharmacy for being *doble cara* (two-faced) and said her medications, which she remarked were for treating her heart condition, had been unavailable in her local pharmacy for months, despite, she added, their having been hecho en Cuba. Her daughter, who lived in Spain, had sent her money to buy the drugs she needed. The scene that played out in the pharmacy was not uncommon in the two-tiered health care system that was slowly emerging in Cuba, as several individuals I later interviewed pointed out. Although this particular pharmacy required a foreign passport to complete a purchase, the reality was that many others would make sales without a foreigner present; several people I interviewed purchased items at international pharmacies in hotels without the assistance of a foreigner, and others merely offered hospital pharmacists regalitos, which customers considered material incentives rather than bribes.

Angela Torres Jiménez, a woman I interviewed over the course of several years, was regularly in contact with me about securing a supply of Dilatrend (generic carvedilol). This drug belongs to a group of medicines called beta blockers, used mainly to treat heart disease and angina. Jiménez's husband, diagnosed with coronary heart disease at the Instituto Nacional de Cardiología in Havana in 2006, was required to take one twenty-five-milligram carvedilol tablet a day. However, because of the irregular availability of the medication in the peso pharmacies, Angela Jiménez would often be counting the days until she ran out. When left with no other options, she was forced to purchase the needed medications at the international pharmacy in the Hotel Sevilla, located in Old Havana. With my passport, Jiménez was able to buy several packages of Dilatrend, which is made by a foreign company. The drug sold for twenty-eight *pesos convertibles*, or the equivalent of about thirty U.S. dollars for a package of thirty tablets.

Most of the foreign-made drugs enter Cuba through mediCuba, a Cuban company dedicated to the importation and exportation of medical products (figure 26). The Cuban Industria Médico-Farmacéutica oversees nineteen companies and research institutions, as well as forty-one manufacturers

FIGURE 26. mediCuba. Source: *Avances Médicos de Cuba* 7(23) (2000), 3.

that locally produce 87 percent of the drugs that are consumed on the island.[17] Most of the drugs that are manufactured in Cuba require the use of imported raw materials, some from the former Soviet-bloc nations. This fact has forced the Cuban pharmaceutical industry to focus on the lines of production that can be sustained by Cuban research and materials. It may

We Have to Think Like Capitalists

also feed the rationale for the sale of certain classes of drugs made in Cuba to the domestic population in foreign currency. It is seen as a cost-recovery program, especially as the cost of producing certain classes of drugs is increasingly reliant on the import of expensive raw materials.

Most of the money Jiménez managed to save to make these purchases was from remittances sent by her relatives in Miami as well as by her son, who lived in England. He had left Cuba the year before to complete a master's degree in education, but once the scholarship ended he never returned; in the Cuban government's official terms, *desertó*, that is, he deserted or defected.[18] While the physicians at the Instituto de Cardiología often worked diligently through church donations to secure medicine and medical supplies for Jiménez, they were also willing to write prescriptions for her to take to the international pharmacies. Rather than see the peso-based health care system and the emergent dollar-based sectors as working against each other, one should regard the private, informal economy in the health sector as being dependent on infrastructures and medical knowledge that are products of the socialist system, for example, the army of well-trained physicians and auxiliary health professionals and the expansive network of consultorios, clinics, hospitals, and pharmacies. In fact, in many ways, one reinforces the existence of the other.

The Cuban government argues that the health institutions operating under the banner of Turismo y Salud S.A. are structured for foreigners only. The Cubans who use these services are assumed to do so of their own free will and not because of shortages in the heavily subsidized peso-based health care institutions. Yet many citizens remain skeptical of the state selling domestically produced pharmaceutical products and offering health care services to foreigners in hard currency, while simultaneously preaching sacrifice for the common goal of socialism. The latest slogan to take precedence— "Cuba is and always will be a socialist country"—seeks to reconfirm what is increasingly being called into question: How many capitalist strategies can one incorporate into the local economy and still maintain a veneer of socialism? Likewise, the internal contradictions of a state that increasingly responds to external pressures by resorting to forms of pragmatism in its day-to-day operations are also reflected in the practices of individuals, who have incorporated, both willingly and begrudgingly, a form of pragmatic capitalism into their everyday lives. The socialist state has perpetuated a dual moral code, or *doble moral,* by which the state has shifted its position on well-established policies by, for instance, the very creation of the dual economy in U.S. dollars and Cuban pesos.

Having regular access to U.S. dollars, many of the people in various consultorios join a growing number of other Cubans who are able to navigate the two-tiered health system: one in U.S. dollars and the other in Cuban pesos. Several individuals made no bones about their informal use of the dollar health care services and facilities. They stated their unwillingness to wait with *las masas* (the masses) for basic services; others made clear their willingness to pay physicians on the side to provide everything from aesthetic plastic surgery to Cuba's renowned experimental therapies, often touted in foreign publications, to which the local population rarely has access. In addition, some individuals are increasingly reliant on prescription drugs to treat chronic and acute ailments and wish to avoid having to contend with the regular shortages in the peso economy or having to pay intermediaries to get subsidized drugs or privileged access to health services. The reality is that, as basic services in the Cuban peso economy shift to the dollar economy, many individual health care needs are being met through dollars. It would be difficult to argue that the Cuban state is unaware that individual Cubans are increasingly turning to the U.S.-dollar health sector to meet their everyday needs. Rather, I suggest that these trends reflect the pragmatic capitalism that has clashed with socialist discourse on the provision of basic human needs.

As Akhil Gupta similarly argues in his recent work on the technology industry's outsourcing of labor to call centers in India, the current labor pool of India's "technical excellence" is the direct result of at least two generations of state-sponsored investment in scientific and technical education, and most of those with technical expertise are graduates of heavily subsidized public institutions.[19] In Cuba, if a specialist at one of the state hospitals requires an X-ray but the machine at the hospital is broken, the patient can access the privatized informal sector, including backdoor access to well-equipped *clínicas internacionales* S.A.s. Or the patient can get access to X-ray equipment from a socio at another hospital for a fee and then return to the original state hospital with the X-rays needed to diagnose the case.

New forms of capital in Cuba's post-Soviet economy are equally dependent on the socialist system for their circulation and use value. In recent years this hybrid economy has become more conspicuous, especially as the state attempts to contend with the capitalist longings of a population that is increasingly exposed to the influence of widespread consumerism through tourism, the international media, and, now, the state's own campaigns and policies. Almost as if embodying the comment by García I cited in the introduction, "We have to think like capitalists but continue being socialists," Turismo y Salud S.A. challenges the moral legitimacy of the socialist project, yet is necessary, on the ground, for the maintenance of the country's crumbling health and welfare system.

MACHINATIONS OF THE STATE

Sociedades anónimas, also known as *empresas mixtas* (joint ventures), embody the very spirit of citizenship in twenty-first-century Cuba; this entails hybrid or fragmented subjectivities that bear traces of the competing politico-economic realities that encompass people's everyday lives. Cuba's recent economic reforms have transformed age-old state institutions, such as the media, from instruments of socialist, ideologically based education to flashy marketers designed to promote basic necessities like essential drugs, and certain luxury items. As a result, citizens, long accustomed to a steady diet of revolutionary pedagogy in the form of staid socialist slogans plastered on billboards, are now also being subjected to advertisements for goods produced in Cuba, such as beer, beauty items, and electronic equipment.[20] The state's return to certain capitalist strategies, albeit limited ones, has created two key concerns: first, the increasing economic disparities within the population; and, second, the state's desire to take advantage of these disparities by promoting the sale of Cuban products—and thus earning much-needed hard currency—over those imported products increasingly made available through astute foreign companies operating in Cuba. Socialism has literally repackaged itself; Ariana Hernández-Reguant astutely describes the recent transformation as "socialism with commercials."[21] An anecdotal point speaks volumes to this issue: products made in Cuba, such as coffee, juices, beer, rum, and soft drinks, often carry the slogan *"Lo Mío Primero"*(Mine first, meaning Cuban products first), yet they are sold only in U.S. dollars and are well beyond the economic reach of the majority of the population. Consequently, many Cubans have informally suggested that the slogan should read, "Cuban products first, and Cuban people last!" This

FIGURE 27. An advertisement for a vitamin made from seaweed and manufactured in Cuba. In Cuba it can be found only in U.S.-dollar stores and on the black market. The advertisement reads, "Spirulina, 100% Natural, Made in Cuba. For businessmen, athletes, and the kind of people who use a lot of energy and are under a great deal of stress: One of the natural wonders." Source: *Avances Médicos de Cuba* 7(20) (2000), 55.

FIGURE 28.
Cubita coffee:
Lo Mío Primero.
Brotherton
© 2004.

irony is also commonly applied to Cuba's burgeoning health institutions and international pharmacies developed for foreigners and people with access to U.S. dollars (figures 27 and 28).

The emergence of socialist entrepreneurs like Turismo y Salud S.A., marketing and selling basic, indeed, necessary, health services and supplies in Cuba's post-Soviet landscape, is testimony to the country's recent incorporation of what Kaushik Sunder Rajan refers to as "corporate regimes of governance."[22] These regimes, he argues, imply two things: "On the one hand, corporations themselves are taking on agential responsibility for dispensing services that, in the liberal ideology of the welfare state, were 'state' services.

On the other hand, the state itself is seen adopting corporate strategies or forms of governance." These recent shifts in state ideology in part reflect subtle responses to the island nation's participation, as a disadvantaged player, in the global economy. The emergence of selective pockets of transnational capital is part and parcel of the very socialist system that encompasses them; that is to say, the socialist state has provided key spaces, similar to incubators, within contemporary Cuban society in which a selective form of capitalism thrives. These incubators exist to take advantage of the differential access to foreign currency that is circulating in the hands of Cubans and, ultimately, to provide the state an opportunity to tap into individual wealth accumulation.

This argument speaks directly to what Aihwa Ong asserts is the "logic of exception," a form of selective governmentality whereby "new spaces [are] brought into being by techniques of calculative choice institutionalized in mechanisms and procedures that mark out special spaces of labor markets, investment opportunities, and relative administrative freedom."[23] Examining the coercive and noncoercive strategies that the state and other institutions urge on individuals, seemingly for their own benefit, Ong skillfully draws on examples of special economic zones in China to illustrate how the globalizing neoliberal logic of a free-market ideology becomes effectively "territorialized" to confined spaces that do not impinge on state sovereignty. This "exception," Ong argues, is central to understanding how globalizing politico-economic forces become localized and transformed, especially in non-Western contexts, in which neoliberal economic reforms do not always have to equate to state decentralization. Rather, the very presence of a so-called strong state, in the Weberian sense, is the catalyst that precipitates the controlled entry of different forms of capital.

It is necessary therefore to speak of another kind of governmentality, what Alexei Yurchak calls entrepreneurial governmentality.[24] Yurchak illustrates how former Soviet citizens acquired entrepreneurial knowledge by having to operate within the Soviet system itself, learning to exploit the socialist state and its resources through a pragmatic understanding of professional relations and particular hybrid understandings of the official plans, rules, laws, and institutions of the party state. The recent economic reforms in key areas of Cuba's socialist economy have meant that individual citizens must pragmatically navigate among state-sponsored health services, socios in the privatized economy, and access to foreign currency; and they must weigh their options at every juncture. Rather than being classified as *lo informal*, individual bodily practices are indeed an integral and necessary part of the therapeutic options available to many Cubans. These practices, for the most part, sustain the state's health care system by filling in the widening gaps between the socialist rhetoric of beneficence and the everyday lived experience of individual Cubans.

MY DOCTOR KEEPS
THE LIGHTS ON

Hoping to avoid the oppressive humidity of the late summer months, I arrived in Havana in May 2004 to carry out several weeks of research. As I systematically made my way through several *áreas de salud,* exchanging greetings with old friends, past interlocutors, and passing acquaintances, something was immediately obvious. Most of the *consultorios* I had previously worked in were now vacant. When I asked about the changes, people were quick to point out, with a sense of pride, that their respective physicians had been selected to participate as *internacionalistas* in medical brigades outside of the country. Despite the everyday lived experience of sacrifice, *lucha,* and material scarcity, most of the residents of the consultorios affected discussed the country's ongoing humanitarian aid programs in admiring terms. Although an economically disadvantaged player in the global sphere, Cuba had desirable resources in the form of human capital and medical expertise, many of them notable. The government's gifts of medical technology, aid, and health personnel to what many described as deserving recipients were a source of immense individual and national pride.

This humanitarian ethic has been part of the country's international solidarity campaigns since the early 1960s. For example, in 1960 Cuba sent its first medical team to Chile following an earthquake. Shortly thereafter, in 1963, Cuba launched its official program of "medical missions" by sending an international medical brigade to Algeria as part of its goal of supporting anticolonial struggles. In more recent memory, the medical brigades sent throughout Central America and the Caribbean after hurricanes George and Mitch in 1998 and the treatment of victims of the Chernobyl disaster in 1986 on the island reflected the country's ethos of humanitarianism and commitment to internationalism. This culture of caring was unquestioned in the various conversations that ensued in my interviews with officials, physicians, and average citizens. The message was clear: Cuba played a prominent role on the world stage as a medical power. On one hand, Cuba was selfless in providing much-needed medical aid in times of need. On the other, foreign countries often sought out Cuban medical advice, training, and personnel in the express hope of replicating the Cuban model of primary health care delivery. In doing so, these countries also hoped to produce comparable health outcomes.

Over the past few decades Cuba's medical internationalism programs have developed and incrementally expanded through the provision of free humanitarian medical treatment to citizens of various countries throughout the world.[1] Since the launch of the program, more than 113,585 Cuban health professionals and technicians have participated in health care collaborations in 103 countries. A total of 2,638 collaborators have already contributed their services by setting up Integral Health Programs, a variant of the domestic family doctor program, in foreign countries. Many of these medical missions, and the sheer empirical volume of what has been accomplished to date, have been prominently featured in Cuban media outlets inside the country and highlighted in public relations campaigns conducted by Cuban embassies abroad. The most striking figure, as Cuban officials note, is that these humanitarian programs have provided more medical personnel to developing countries than all the G8 countries combined.[2] In April 2008 it was reported that more than thirty thousand Cuban medical personnel were collaborating in seventy countries across the globe.[3]

As was evident in many of the interviews I conducted in the late 1990s and early 2000s, Cubans had, in many ways, participated in and helped propagate, relish, and circulate the state's narrative of "international solidarity" as a moral imperative of the country's socialist vision. Yet what was evident in the fieldwork I conducted years later, in 2007 and 2010, was a palpable shift in the popular discourse among everyday citizens on the rationale behind the increasing departure of physicians, nurses, pharmacists, and even teachers, on medical missions. The discourse of humanitarianism was no longer at the forefront of many of these discussions. Rather, the focus was now, without fail, on *los venezolanos* (the Venezuelans). In March 2003, for instance, Barrio Adentro (Inside the Neighborhood) emerged out of an agreement between the governments of Venezuelan president Hugo Chávez and Castro (figure 29). Under this program over twenty thousand Cuban

FIGURE 29. Mission Inside the Neighborhood. Source: http://www.barrioadentro.gov.ve/ (accessed 23 February 2011).

FIGURE 30. Operation Miracle. Source: http://www.barrioadentro.gov.ve/ (accessed 23 February 2011).

physicians and auxiliary health professionals would be stationed in primarily poor neighborhoods in Venezuela, providing medical care in exchange for highly subsidized petroleum—popularly dubbed the oil-for-aid deal. At the same time, the Cuban government also created an eye surgery program known as Operación Milagro, or Operation Miracle, which sought to treat over two hundred thousand patients in twenty-one countries with the aim of restoring sight lost to cataracts, glaucoma, diabetes, and other diseases. For the most part, the countries participating in this program had agreed to pay for these services with subsidized trade agreements with Cuba (figure 30).

As more Cuban physicians were earmarked to participate in strategic aid programs, many citizens were starting to ask, How were Venezuelans deserving recipients of the gifts of Cuba's medical aid programs? Why was it so hard to find a family physician in a country with an apparent surplus? In recent years the socialist government has been increasingly focusing on mobilizing biomedicine and medical expertise as a marketable commodity (rather than a gift) for international exchange. I want to look specifically at the domestic effects, both material and symbolic, of Cuba's massive mobilization and exportation of physicians. Historically, itinerant physicians on medical missions could be couched in the language of symbols of the revolution and be morally justified. As the state continues to preach the rhetoric of humanitarianism, citizens are beginning to critically question the government's move toward strategic aid programs, particularly as the material benefits of these programs fail to redress domestic shortages and lead to worsening material circumstances for citizens.

THE JANUS-FACED NATURE OF
MEDICAL INTERNATIONALISM

Scholarly attention on Cuba's medical internationalism programs has tended to focus on two distinct, yet not unrelated, themes. The first highlights how the missions operate as a form of medical diplomacy, or "soft power" politics, bartering medical aid as a means to strengthen diplomatic ties with other Third World countries. The country is able to harness a kind of political power, using gifts as a means to create social bonds, along with the recipient's obligation to reciprocate, either symbolically or materially.[4] For Cuba, in the face of an ongoing U.S. embargo, this is all the more important for establishing political allies that can help facilitate cooperation and aid agreements. Moreover, garnering supportive votes from countries in the United Nations and in other international governing bodies that are influential in dictating policy for or against the island is also a central goal of this ostensibly reciprocal exchange.

The second theme emphasizes the country's commitment to addressing global health inequity. The deteriorating health conditions among populations in the global South serve as a moral barometer to measure the failure of respective health infrastructures, existing aid programs, and the international response to these problems. In this fraught moral terrain, Cuban health professionals assume a prominent role, given that their medical education and training are "centered entirely [on] an ethical commitment to serve the destitute."[5] Benevolent Cuban physicians travel the world—"going where no doctor has gone before"—to treat individuals, many of whom have never been treated by a doctor in their lives.[6] A recent feature documentary, for example, titled ¡Salud! The Film (2006), chronicles the experiences of Cuban health professionals working "from the shores of Africa to the Americas."[7] ¡Salud! also collects personal testimonies from scholarship students studying medicine at Cuba's Latin American School of Medicine (also known by the Spanish acronym ELAM, or Escuela Latinoamericana de Medicina).[8] The goal of all medical school scholarships, health officials assert, is to support Cuba's dedication to internationalism and to train students from all over the world in social medicine so that they can return to their own countries to practice medicine.[9] Cuba's program for international solidarity is about producing physicians on an international scale, physicians who reflect the country's socialist values and ideals.

In both these portrayals, the moral parameter of the state's vision oscillates between savvy political actor and socialist humanitarianism. While seemingly oppositional, both characterizations speak to what I argue is the Janus-faced nature of medical internationalism. A former Cuban diplomat stationed in London who had worked in several Latin American countries cited an excellent example of the motives behind Cuba's medical missions. The diplomat claimed that despite the involvement of certain governments, for example, Nicaragua and Guatemala, in siding with the United States on various foreign policies against Cuba, the Cuban government was committed to providing free medical assistance to those countries. As the diplomat concluded, Cuba wanted to demonstrate that socialism was about promoting solidarity, not about forcing people to embrace a political agenda against their will. Cuba used actions, not words, to demonstrate the power of socialism, he asserted. Political will was the reason that Cuba accomplished its goals. Furthermore, individuals in various countries who benefited from free medical aid come to understand the extent of Cuba's generosity on their own terms.

Rodolfo Gómez, an MEF physician I interviewed, best sums up the diplomat's assertion. Gómez worked as an internacionalista in a remote region of Nicaragua for two years in the early 1990s, running the Integral Health Program. In the context of political changes in Nicaragua in the early 1990s and the popular backlash against the leftist-leaning Sandinista movement, the doctor explained that many of his patients disparagingly referred to him as a communist when he walked through the villages. Yet these same people lined up in droves for the free medical care provided by the Cuban government. As the doctor stressed, while treating the patients he reminded them that it was Fidel Castro and the Cuban people who had paid for their medical care, despite being communists. The doctor felt that by the end of his two-year posting in the village, the community had grown to respect him and the Cuban government's commitment to a humanitarian approach, which he noted was a product of Cuba's socialist orientation.

FROM GIFTS TO COMMODITIES

The marriage of humanitarianism and explicit or implicit (or both) political agendas is not unique or even limited to Cuba's medical internationalism programs. An emerging body of scholarship has highlighted the nexus among humanitarian aid, conditional trade agreements, militarism, and highly volatile flows of capital.[10] For example, throughout the 1970s and early 1980s Cuba, with the financial backing of the Soviet Union, was in a privileged position to export and also capitalize on marginalized but wealthier nations' desire to replicate Cuba's public health experience. While in the 1960s Cuba's focus was on humanitarian medical missions, this changed in the 1970s, when it began to charge oil-rich nations such as Libya and Iraq, which paid in hard currency, on an ability-to-pay basis. This became the foundation for early trade agreements.[11] In this respect, it is not my assertion that the commodification of humanitarianism is a radical departure from Cuba's foreign aid policies of the past. Rather, I argue that in the post–Cold War era the reconfiguration of global relations has meant that Cuba, as a result of its disadvantaged position, must increasingly forge these kinds of strategic relationships that are contingent on capitalizing on their medical know-how and personnel, in effect, making commodities out of the very things that have served as symbols of their success (figure 31). This strategy attempts to effectively translate the country's human capital, in the form of physicians, into material capital, thereby creating economic opportunities of preferential trade, credit, aid, and investment for the cash-strapped island.[12] This constitutes a form of transactional humanitarianism, that is, an assemblage of traveling actors, experts, practices, and specialized knowledge that are collectively marketed under the umbrella term *humanitarian* yet are ostensibly imbricated in market relations of economic and shifting moral values of exchange.

In 2007 one of my neighbors commented that Hugo Chávez had, in effect, become the country's Petro Papi; Venezuela's role was similar to that which the former USSR had played in providing highly specialized and dependent forms of trade and aid. Plan Barrio Adentro (later renamed Misión Barrio Adentro, or MBA) was established in Venezuela in 2003 as part of larger trade agreements; the first was signed in 2000 and the second in 2005:[13] "As of December 2006, MBA included 23,789 Cuban doctors, dental specialists, optometrists, nurses, and other personnel and more than 6,500 sites where patients were seen. By July 2007, 2,804 primary-care stations were being staffed by physicians, community health workers, and health promoters."[14] These agreements allowed for preferential pricing of Cuba's exportation of professional services in return for a steady supply of Venezuelan oil, joint investments in strategically important sectors for both countries, and the

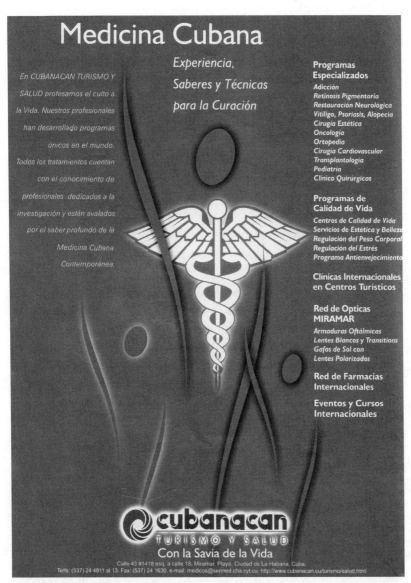

Medicina Cubana

Experiencia, Saberes y Técnicas para la Curación

En CUBANACAN TURISMO Y SALUD profesamos el culto a la Vida. Nuestros profesionales han desarrollado programas únicos en el mundo. Todos los tratamientos cuentan con el conocimiento de profesionales dedicados a la investigación y están avalados por el saber profundo de la Medicina Cubana Contemporánea.

Programas Especializados
Adicción
Retinosis Pigmentaria
Restauración Neurológica
Vitiligo, Psoriasis, Alopecia
Cirugía Estética
Oncología
Ortopedia
Cirugía Cardiovascular
Transplantología
Pediatría
Clínico Quirúrgicos

Programas de Calidad de Vida
Centros de Calidad de Vida
Servicios de Estética y Belleza
Regulación del Peso Corporal
Regulación del Estrés
Programa Antienvejecimiento

Clínicas Internacionales en Centros Turísticos

Red de Opticas MIRAMAR
Armaduras Oftálmicas
Lentes Blancos y Transitions
Gafas de Sol con
Lentes Polarizados

Red de Farmacias Internacionales

Eventos y Cursos Internacionales

cubanacan
TURISMO Y SALUD
Con la Savia de la Vida
Calle 43 #1418 esq. a calle 18, Miramar, Playa, Ciudad de La Habana, Cuba.
Telfs: (537) 24 4811 al 13. Fax: (537) 24 1630. e-mail: medicos@sermed.cha.cyt.cu. http://www.cubanacan.cu/turismo/salud.html

FIGURE 31. Cuban medicine: Experience, know-how, and techniques for healing. Source: *Avances Médicos de Cuba* 6(20) (1999), back cover.

provision of credit.[15] The economic benefits for Cuba were great. Earnings from medical services reportedly equaled 28 percent of the total export receipts and net capital payments in 2006. This amounted to 212 million U.S. dollars, generating more money than both nickel and cobalt exports and tourism.[16]

Cuba's medical missions also greatly benefitted from the country's inclusion in strategic partnership agreements such as the Alternativa Bolivariana para los Pueblos de Nuestra América (ALBA) (Bolivarian alternative for the Americas). Originally conceived as a means of forging a unified front against the United States by Cuba and Venezuela, ALBA now includes Nicaragua, Honduras, the Dominican Republic, and Bolivia. ALBA was grounded on the fundamental belief that true international exchange must be directed through states and public action rather than through individuals and private markets. With the financial backing of ALBA, driven by the petroleum capital of Venezuela, Cuba has been able to expand the scope of its medical cooperation programs, exemplified by the launching of Operation Miracle. Given this massive scaling up, what are some of the domestic ramifications of Cuba's recent export of health personnel, or human capital, to foreign locales?

CONSULTORIO LOS MOLINOS

In 2004 Consultorio Los Molinos was vacant. Louis Pérez had been selected to join the MBA in Venezuela but after a year there he returned to Cuba for what became a short-lived stay. Within several weeks of his return he was once again dispatched with a medical brigade team, this time to Pakistan after the earthquake in October 2005. In his absence, the conditions of the neighborhood he serviced in Los Molinos deteriorated significantly. Many of the patients who had regarded Pérez as their first line of defense for many of their medical emergencies had taken to self-medicating and to making ad hoc diagnoses spread by word of mouth.

Bení Ortiz, with whom Pérez was personally working to address his alcoholism, was consumed by the illness when I visited in 2005. Since the consultorio was closed, Mariella Ortiz was forced to visit the municipal *policlínico* to see if she could get her husband into some kind of treatment program. The inconvenience of getting there, compounded by the lack of personal care by the attending physicians, quickly led Mariella to abandon the prospect of returning to the policlínico. Tired of the drama, as she called it, she tried to make her problems more bearable by indulging in a steady diet of coffee and sleeping pills. Had all of Pérez's work been in vain?, she asked.

In a reversal of roles, Mariella's concerns echoed those of people in countries that had been the recipients of provisional humanitarian medical aid: what happens when the doctors leave?[17] In an ironic twist, Pérez's departure

We Have to Think Like Capitalists

to engage in humanitarian work in other parts of the globe left his own patients without the personalized care that had been the very benchmark of the MEF program.[18] Because most of the patients in his *ficha familiar* were categorized, classified, and tabulated for individualized health care programs under the *dispensarización* program, Pérez's departure left a void. The overworked staff at the local policlínico had neither the time nor the mandate to circulate in the communities they served. As Mariella complained, the health workers were, in effect, strangers: they quickly reviewed your file, wrote prescriptions, and ushered you out the door. They couldn't comment on or assess your living conditions, whether you had enough to eat, or even if you had a roof over your head. This signaled the return to an impersonal, disembodied style of health care delivery. Many of the residents in Pérez's *área de salud* nostalgically recalled the days when having a doctor on the block or *en el terreno* making house calls was a luxury. In effect, they had lost their personalized "first line of defense."

Shortly after he returned to Cuba in 2006 I interviewed Pérez. He was preparing to depart for Venezuela on another mission. The formerly tall, lanky physician was now considerably heavier. "Viste! Estoy gordo!" (Look, I am fat!), he proudly exclaimed when we met at my apartment. Riffling through the pictures he had taken in Pakistan and Venezuela, Pérez excitedly described the travails of his life as an internacionalista. While the hardships of life in Venezuela were trying, he enjoyed his work. His new patients, he said, were extremely appreciative and warm. He described also the extreme pride he felt in finally being more financially secure and able to realize many of his dreams of traveling and having certain material luxuries. During his absence the state continued to deposit his monthly peso salary (about 20 U.S. dollars) into a bank account in Cuba as well as a monthly stimulus of 50 *pesos convertibles* (52 U.S. dollars). The stimulus funds could be accessed only upon his return to the island. These payments, he added, were in addition to the stipend of approximately 180 U.S. dollars per month he received in Venezuela. Financially, he was in a privileged position now.

Pérez had arrived on the island with several cargo boxes of luxury goods, including a television set, a DVD player, and a stereo, brand-name clothes, and some small furniture. Several of his patients were vocal in their complaints about the physician's newly acquired wealth. Another family doctor in a nearby community who was required to take on Pérez's caseload of infant and maternal health cases, in addition to her already busy caseload, was boiling when I interviewed her: "Nobody pays me a higher wage for doing twice the amount of work I used to. We all have to make sacrifices for this profession, so it really annoys me to see these internacionalistas talking about *humanidad* [humanity]. It is also a shopping expedition. You have to be chosen to be an internacionalista. Trust me, it is like finding a pot of gold to be able to go, especially in the crisis we are experiencing now."

Aware of what he termed "an epidemic of *envidia* [envy]," Pérez had made a concerted effort to bring *regalitos* for many of his patients and colleagues to defuse the issues of his long absence and the symbols of his new jet-setter lifestyle. This was all the more jarring given that many of the people in his community did not even have a passport, much less ever boarded a plane in their lives. An elderly woman I interviewed in Pérez's área de salud, commenting outspokenly on the Venezuelan oil-for-aid deal, remarked bitterly, "My doctor is helping to keep the lights on" (prior to Chávez's agreement, *apagones* [blackouts] were a regular occurrence throughout Havana). Her sentiments were reflected in other interviews I conducted, in which citizens increasingly vocalized their anger and resentment at the loss of medical personnel as a result of what several individuals referred to as "their sale" to Venezuela. Peoples' conversations suddenly took on a more critical tone. During my visit to the island in 2005 the sudden appearance at the local *bodega* and dollar stores of sundry items marked "Products of the Bolivarian Revolution, Venezuela," were met with great fanfare and excitement. The canned sardines, packages of chocolate drink mix, and tinned meats at reasonable prices were welcome additions to the limited fare traditionally available. When I returned in 2007, these very same items were met with derision and disappointment. Several people asked, "What exactly were the benefits of the agreement with Venezuela for the average citizen?"

SURPLUS AND DEFICITS IN A
SHIFTING MORAL ECONOMY

The concerns raised by citizens were, in many ways, prompted by the confession of several physicians that they were eager to be selected as internacionalistas. For a profession that is typically remunerated very little in comparison to people engaged in private businesses or tourism, many physicians highlighted their view that material rewards were not insignificant. "I can't live off of feeling good," one physician joked when I prodded him that he was, theoretically, participating in these missions to do good. His response revealed that the humanitarian ethic was merged with a personal desire not only to travel, but also to acquire material goods.

When I interviewed Alberto Navarro in 2007, he had just returned from Caracas, where he was working as a consultant with the Venezuelan Ministry of Public Health. He was unhappy about his temporary return to Havana. "The city looks so dark," he complained. The main thoroughfares in Havana were dimly lit. The streetlights either had blown out and not been replaced or were broken. He had returned to Cuba only to visit his family and purchase a house in Cienfuegos, an incentive the government provided for some of the returning internacionalistas.[19] However, this had created some tensions in his previous área de salud.

While his old consultorio stood vacant, Navarro was now in the process of setting up house a couple of blocks away, complete with the material luxuries he had acquired abroad. To make matters worse, he announced that he would be extending his contract for an additional two years in Venezuela. Planning to leave his house with family members, he intended to "make the best" of his time in Venezuela. He was well aware that several of the residents in his área de salud had responded to this announcement by calling him a medical *jinetero*, hustling medicine for money. He had, in their eyes, reduced himself to a commodity. While hurt by these comments, he said that while these trips made good financial sense, Caracas was not an easy place to live. The constant fear of crime and the resentment of various sectors of Venezuelan society, including the middle class and the elite, about the growing presence of Cubans in their country made life there tense. As he concluded, ultimately, he had to live in a foreign country without seeing his family for long stretches of time. This was a sacrifice he was willing to undertake to be able to save enough money to return to Cuba and live well. This was not, he added, an unworthy or unjust pursuit.

While Cuba boasts of one of the highest physician-per-inhabitant ratios in the world, the massive deployment of doctors on foreign missions has left noticeable absences in the country's domestic primary health care programs. In his address to the nation on 26 July 2007, then–acting president Raúl Castro called on Cubans to hold meetings to discuss the country's most pressing problems. In the public community meetings that ensued, citizens became increasingly vocal about the daily constraints they encountered in trying to solve their immediate health problems. In March 2008 Raúl Castro announced that the MEF program would be reorganized to address some of the structural and staffing problems that were created as a result of the increasing foreign demands for the country's primary health care physicians. Rather than emphasize consultorios, the capstone of Cuba's primary health sector, polyclinics were to take on a considerably more important role. The aim of these changes, health officials noted, was to strengthen their roles in the communities they serviced and to add a host of specialty services previously available only in hospitals, including X-rays, ultrasounds, psychiatry, and cardiology, among other services.

Most individuals were content with the added services. However, many were equally saddened by the slow disappearance of the family physicians stationed in their respective communities. The traditional physician en el terreno, making house calls and visiting patients with chronic health problems, was increasingly becoming the exception rather than the rule. As many citizens point out, the Cuban model of primary health care being exported is, in many ways, not the one being practiced at home. While individual complaints have not translated into poor health outcomes (for example, Cubans are not dying for lack of a physician), and the country's health profile remains stable amidst massive socioeconomic changes, the popular support for medical internationalism such as MBA has decreased among certain sectors of the population. For example, one individual commented, "Sometimes I wonder if we weren't better off with the lights off. At least we weren't forced to see what we were lacking."

A conference I presented in May 2009 focused on assessing the Cuban revolution on its fiftieth anniversary. The conference featured a special panel devoted to Cuba's medical internationalism. After the various presentations, audience members asked about complaints made by Cubans living in Cuba that, because of MBA and other medical missions, their medical needs were no longer being met. Various panelists quickly dismissed such complaints. As one panelist stated, such complaints needed to be put in the context of "an overmedicalized population, who have been spoiled by too many years of having a doctor on every block." The conclusion to be drawn here: Cuba does not need so many physicians. While there may be much truth to this conclusion, it does not take away from the lived experience of Cubans who, for more than fifty years, have been trained by the state not only to accept, seek out, and desire medical intervention—from the most basic first-aid problem to the most severe medical matter—but equally to feel entitled to and expect those very services. The Cuban revolution built its legitimacy, in part, on the provision of a universal, accessible health care system as a basic human right.

As Cuban health officials increasingly assert, it is the very success of the primary health programs of the past, such as the MEF, that make it possible for Cuba to begin the process of restructuring health care to meet the populations' new health needs. Yet another narrative emerges from the perspective of the average citizen. That is, the moral economy of the gift is increasingly being called into question. While daily shortages during Cuba's socialist and economic crisis have become embodied in people's everyday lived experiences, the sudden deficit of physicians is created by an entirely different market rationality. Physicians, traditionally understood to possess no economic value, but who impart their knowledge and expertise through a moral imperative of socialism, are now entangled in an economy of exchange. The surplus of Cuban-trained physicians who were supposed to cure the social ills of society and work to foster socialist morals and values are now luxury commodities, like those advertised in the campaigns for Turismo y Salud S.A., bartered and contracted out to foreign destinations to serve as accessible, affordable medical labor.

BODIES ENTANGLED IN HISTORY

To make a topic of the body is to study cultural, natural, and historical variation in whole worlds. **Judith Farquhar and Margaret Lock,** *Beyond the Body Proper*

Writing against the grain of many scholarly and popular analyses of Cuba's health sector, I have explored here how bodily health and physical well-being, in a context of economic insecurity, are interpreted through ethical and moral valences that embody the past and reflect new reconfigurations of power and statecraft. I have employed a genealogical method of individual bodily practices to unravel, separate, and analyze the multiple threads that make up the fabric of the country's primary health care system. One should be hesitant, I argue, to subscribe too readily to neatly bounded discursive oppositions such as static understandings of socialism vis-à-vis capitalism or the demarcation and bracketing of the crisis in a before-and-after chronology. This elides nuanced understandings of the implicit complexities involved in these relations, reducing the plural, multifaceted, and multivocal aspects of the situation to a unidirectional movement, expressed as a linear view of history, and, ultimately, to singularity. This book, by contrast, has opened a new field of inquiry that addresses the coproduction and coexistence of different forms of capital, whether centralized or dispersed, and explores the emergence of new subjectivities in the island's changing social and political landscape as well as the reemergence of older ones. The themes highlighted here contribute to ongoing debates and larger dialogues that touch upon several important ethnographic and theoretical concerns that warrant further investigation.[1]

SOCIALIST GOVERNMENTALITY

The emergence of socialism in the eighteenth century as a political philosophy in European intellectual and worker movements centered on the belief that mass industrialization and the exploitative characteristics of the so-called capitalist crisis were unsustainable. Seeking to harness socialism as a form of liberation, the redefining of state–society relations was to bring about radical changes to the operation of state power, thereby freeing individuals from the vise of class stratification. While grounded in a redemptive worldview, national socialism—from the former USSR to Cuba, China, and several African countries—quickly fell prey to the mounting criticism in the international arena and among dissident groups that, in practice, it operated as a technology of discipline. The state, rather than withering away, was said to have become an all-too-powerful machine of domination and oppression, squelching individual freedom by an overwrought, centralized bureaucracy. Socialism, from this perspective, rendered citizens objects of state rule rather than subjects capable of speaking about any notion of a self. Socialist governance in its many variants quickly became the textbook case for examining the disciplinary thesis. This thesis predominated as the privileged analytical lens through which to project the vision of a strong sovereign state presiding over docile bodies. The rationale driving this approach was that "socialism itself does not possess and has never possessed its own distinctive art of governing."[2]

Central to these interpretations was the conceptual distinction of what constitutes a liberal subject. The rise of the liberal subject is linked to "the radical change in Western thought towards the end of the eighteenth century, whereby each individual was no longer considered an object on which repressive state power could be 'unleashed' . . . [but] the individual [could] be considered a subject, capable of speaking about its own identity, self-image, [and] emotional states."[3] Highlighting the coercive and noncoercive strategies that the state and other institutions urge upon subjects, seemingly for their own benefit, various studies have mapped the inextricable relationship between subject formation, bodies, and differing modalities of regulation, containment, governance, incitement, and resistance.[4] These relationships, however, are embedded in an epistemological and ontological understanding of the rise of the liberal (and decidedly capitalist) state.

Rather than take the universality of the modern liberal, autonomous subject as formulaic, this book argues that such a subject should be the starting point of the discussion or seen as an exception.[5] Finite analyses of the lived experiences of socialism reveal how, historically, socialism as a political practice was invested in reforming the mind, body, and soul through state-sponsored programs of economic restructuring and the "étatization" of everyday life.[6] While generated through a different sociohistoric and political process, the "arts of governing" in socialist societies such as Cuba's engendered, cultivated, and constructed a unique form of biopolitical self-governance. This process was not entirely unrelated or incomparable to construction of the Western autonomous subject.[7] One should recognize that "the exercise of government in all modern states entails the articulation of a form of pastoral power with one of sovereign power."[8] As I argued in chapter 5, the link between power and subject formation profoundly shapes an understanding of power as constituting a diverse set of apparatuses that operate along a continuum. On one side, power can be oppressive, constraining individual agency. On the other, power has the potential to construct "an all-pervasive, normative and positive presence, internalized by, and thus creating, the subject."[9] Power, in this context, is both constructive and oppressive. Cuba's primary health sector provides an exceptional case study in which to examine the paradoxical nature of the operation of state power.

SOCIALIST AND POSTSOCIALIST EPISTEMOLOGIES

Cuba's biopolitical project has done an extraordinary job of creating medicalized subjectivities by reworking state power through, among other venues, an exhaustive program of biomedical intervention, health education, and disease prevention campaigns. Through the universal provision of health and social welfare since 1959 this project has inscribed individuals' social and physical environment, shaping definitions of the body, personhood, productivity, space, and time.[10] This fostered expectations of what the state was morally responsible to provide. In effect, it encouraged feelings of entitlement, grounded in a discourse of "access to health care is a basic human right."

Since the fall of the Soviet bloc, the state has increasingly found it hard to maintain this cradle-to-grave welfare apparatus while remaining a small developing nation with, at least, in theory, a socialist-based economy, rare in today's age of global capitalism. The collapse of this worldview produced a number of crises, for both individual citizens and the state. In the twenty-first century Cuba has come to represent what I call the pragmatic state. I purposely chose this turn of phrase because the term *state* is polysemic, and its two definitions warrant closer examination. The first denotes the condition that somebody or something is in at a particular moment in time. Capitalizing it as the State often differentiates the other meaning, commonly used to define a sovereign independent government. I have employed both meanings in this book. The pragmatic state can be read in two ways, one inseparable from the other.

The *período especial* magnified the importance of *lo informal*, as individual citizens responded to the *lucha* (struggle) of everyday life with a renewed pragmatism, trying to negotiate the tenuous, sometimes ill-defined withdrawal of the state in the political economy of heath care. Interestingly, individual citizens creatively inverted the metaphor of la lucha to describe their actions in a way that parallels the historical use by *la Revolución* of the Cuban independence fighter José Martí's notion of lucha and *sacrificio*. This metaphor was pivotal in Cuba's struggles in the nineteenth century to gain independence from Spain. Present-day understandings of la lucha are transformed and embodied through a politics of entitlement, for example, access to health services is a right, serving as a central symbol to describe individual citizens' forging of social relationships based on material and spiritual interests. Current iterations of la lucha reformulate some of the informal ideals and values of the prerevolutionary past and combine them with a pragmatic twist to confront the new challenges of everyday life.

On the other hand, in recent years, responding to the challenges of selective forms of neoliberal governance evident in everyday practices, the institutions of the State have increasingly modified their policies, objectives, and age-old ideological positions, thus exemplifying the pragmatic State. I have argued that rather than imagine the State as a tangible, monolithic entity, one must see it as being disaggregated in multiple forms, dynamic and responsive, to global and external pressures. Such multiplicity has influenced how medicine is practiced, experienced, and imagined in the post-Soviet era. In the process, Cuban socialism is itself being redefined and transformed. Such transformations in Cuba cannot be unhinged from the great social, political, and economic upheaval that followed the collapse of European socialism and heralded a rupture in socialist imaginings of the past, present, and future.

For scholars working on contemporary Cuba and international political observers alike, including the vociferous community of Cubans living abroad, one of the foremost questions concerns whether the socialist state is in transition. The emergence of postsocialist studies in universities in North America and Europe has contributed to comparative studies of societies emerging from the embrace of socialism. They often track the penetration of capital into noncapitalist modes of production, which leads to the supposed transition of formerly socialist countries into liberal market economies.[11] With the abundance of terms such as "late socialist"[12] and "socialism under siege," there has long been the anticipation that recent changes to Cuba's socialist project are harbingers of its imminent collapse. In a similar vein, Cuba's flexible ideological posturing in the global arena, from the expansion of private enterprise to the increasing commodification of health and medical services, among other notable changes in diverse sectors of the economy, has led to the conclusion that the island is replicating the policies of China or Vietnam in reforming its political philosophy to be a form of market socialism, more flexible, open, and responsive to neoliberal reforms.

In addressing the question of transition in socialist and postsocialist studies, one should heed the warning of Karl Polanyi, who expounded on the importance of cultural approaches to economics and the way economies are embedded in society and culture.[13] Increasingly, the teleological assumptions of analytical concepts such as the market or market-based reforms are being challenged. The recurring trope of a freely roaming market is no longer a given in most critical social science writing. Rather, these concepts are slowly being detached from the evolutionary framework by which so many analysts have often triumphantly declared the inevitability of market-based reform in postsocialist countries on the path to capitalist modes of production. My intention in this book is not to enter the fray of predictive forecasting. As more than fifty years of Cuban socialism have demonstrated, collapse, like transition, is not always obvious, or even expected.

This book has focused more broadly on the sociocultural dimensions of Cuba's primary health sector as a departure point to discuss how crisis narratives of bodily health are metonyms of larger political processes. The Cuban State and, by association, Cuban socialism are in flux. This observation, however, should not direct attention away from the historically significant accomplishments of the socialist State in health and social welfare. Almost half of the globe's human population lacks basic health care, and there is a growing economic gap between the North and the South. It is therefore necessary to conduct research into how cultural, political, and economic differences affect illness experiences and health outcomes in specific contexts. Similarly, it is necessary to question some of the entrenched practices and ideas in the arena of policy formation in connection with health and development. In spite of this, I am not promoting the exportation of the Cuban model for health reform elsewhere. The conditions of la Revolución are materially, culturally, and historically situated and, as I have argued, have produced particular kinds of subjects who embody these conditions. Combined, these conditions were influential not only in transforming the body politic but also in crafting the individual and social body through the socialist *doxa* that was to emerge. One should be cautious, then, of engaging in the project that Che Guevara once termed "exporting revolution."

LIVED EXPERIENCE OF BODIES

Since the Cuban revolution of 1959, history, as something that is both made and reinvented, has once again greatly influenced what it means to be Cuban. Cubans, whether in Cuba, in exile (*exilio*), or, the newest category to emerge, living abroad (*residentes permanentes en el exterior*)—as opposed to being in a self-declared state of exile—all construct narratives of the Cuban experience in a variety of ways; some are patriotic, some are bitter, some angry, while others are embellished, confused, betrayed, or content, and so on. Through an examination of such narratives of health and the body, this book has traced the shifting terrain in which many Cubans on the island define themselves in opposition to or in legion with (or both) events, people, and politics on (*en Cuba*) and off (*en el exterior*) the island. These narratives express ranges of experiences that are sometimes contradictory. For example, a self-declared revolutionary or *fidelista* (supporter of Fidel Castro) may also be a self-professed anticommunist; others, adamantly anti-Castro, may lament the crumbling of Cuba's socialist policies and the complicit role of U.S. foreign policy in this process. Equally, another history would emerge if this research had included the Cuban diaspora in Miami or Cubans in other parts of the United States, Canada, or Europe. They, too, participate in constructing narratives that shape history and bodies in Cuba's post-Soviet era.

For example, Ana Menéndez's novel *In Cuba I Was a German Shepherd*, masterfully weaves together several short stories of Miami's exile community to interrogate how longing, memory, nostalgia, and the past are all complicit in the political project of writing or rewriting history. The provocative title of the novel derives from the story of a dog, Juanito, "just off the boat from

Cuba."[14] The story of Juanito, recounted among a group of elderly Cuban men playing dominoes, addresses the leitmotif of loss and the recuperative, therapeutic quality of memory.

Juanito, making his way down Brickwell Avenue in downtown Miami, crosses the path of an elegant white poodle. A provocateur of sorts, Juanito blurts out, "Si cocinas como caminas . . . [If you cook like you walk . . .]," but the white poodle abruptly interrupts, "I beg your pardon. This is America—kindly speak English." So Juanito pauses for a moment to consider and in his broken English spurts out, "Mamita, you are one hot doggie, yes? I would like to take you to the movies and fancy dinners. I would like to marry you, my love, and have gorgeous puppies with you and live in a castle." The white poodle, snout in the air, looks at Juanito and says, "Do you have any idea who you're talking to? I am a refined breed of considerable class and you are nothing but a short, insignificant mutt." Juanito is stunned for a moment, but he gets in the final shot: "Pardon me, your highness. Here in America, I may be a short, insignificant mutt, but in Cuba I was a German shepherd."

The elderly man narrating the plight of Juanito in Menéndez's novel ends his story, tellingly, with tears in his eyes. Juanito, the mangy dog, is emblematic of much more. He is the reimagination of Cuba's past, the painful reality of the present, and the constant reminder of the identity, rooted in temporal and physical space, that gets left behind, *en la isla* (on the island).

But what of the Cubans who have remained en la isla? Rather than rush to postulate, classify, code, and identify different ideological positions on either side of the Straits of Florida, I argue that one also needs to pause and critically reflect on the everyday lived experience of socialism that has shaped and influenced subject formation in Cuba. A genealogy of individual bodily practices opens a domain through which to examine how different sociopolitical fields create and transform political subjectivities. It forces scholars to delve into the nebulous field of embodiment, asking pointed questions about how subjects respond, enact, and rearticulate ideological assumptions in their everyday practices. It is important to probe Cubans on the island to determine how their experience of state-sponsored programs of holistic health care not only has shaped their definitions of individual bodily health, but also has surpassed biological understandings of the body and become entangled in a mesh of rights, entitlements, and expectations that are products of the island's revolutionary history.

The Cuban State, in the face of multiple machinations, now must reorient the country's political project to stay afloat as a marginalized member of the global arena. However, it has another, equally daunting task. That State must now seriously contend with the very bodies, souls, and minds of the populace it historically shaped and influenced through rhetoric, deeds, and actions to believe la Revolución was even possible.

I do not feel deceived by the state because Fidel warned the population ahead of time that this period would be a difficult time for us and that many changes would occur. I can never say that I have lost all of my optimism. I have total confidence in *la Revolución*. The current *período especial* has existed for some ten years now, and I don't like it but we have to make sacrifices for our goals. We still have many problems, but the problems we have are not the product of one year. These are problems that have accumulated over many years, because la Revolución has had to face many difficult situations. The revolutionary government has never been given any breaks. La Revolución has had to be like a tree: you plant it and you wait to harvest the fruits. It may turn out that not all the fruits turn out good or do not turn out the way you wanted them to, but you have to start over again, and plant another tree and wait. It is like this.

Olga Dilme, university professor and local CDR
president, born in Pinar del Río in 1947

I can remember when we were in primary school. We used to have to recite, "¿Pioneros por el Comunismo? ¡Seremos Como El Che!" [Pioneers for Communism? We will be like Che!]. In those days we were supposed to be dedicated to communism and follow the example of Che Guevara. For example, the teacher would ask, "What kind of person was Che?" We would always respond, "Brave, honest, and determined." Similarly, the teachers would ask, "What was it like before the revolution?" We would respond, "Misery, hunger, and exploitation." In secondary school we had classes in the Russian language and courses in Marxism and Leninism. Now, this has all changed. The Youth Pioneers recite, "¡Somos felices aquí!" [We are happy here]. Students learn basic human values and political orientation or something. What happened to communism? It was the utopia that Fidel knew could never be accomplished and that is why he abandoned it.

Dimitri Martínez, state newspaper
editor, born in Havana in 1974

Communism is a beautiful idea, but in practice it cannot work, especially not in the tropics. In Cuba we are supposed to be a socialist country. But really, I don't know what we are.

María Luisa Rodríguez, accounting
assistant, born in Havana in 1953

PREFACE

1. In November 2004 Cuba's dual economy became further mired in controversy when Cuban authorities eliminated the circulation of U.S. dollars throughout the country. The Cuban Central Bank (BCC) issued a new currency, the Cuban *peso convertible*, popularly referred to as the *chavito*. This new currency is necessary, Castro argued in a speech in October 2004, because the United States has discouraged banks from sending U.S. cash to Cuba. Although those in possession of U.S. dollars are not penalized, only pesos convertibles are currently accepted in all establishments that formerly used the U.S. dollar. In an attempt to discourage use of dollars, which had been in free circulation for nearly ten years, the BCC issued resolution 80/2004, which established that from 8 November 2004 on the exchange of U.S. dollars for pesos convertibles would bear a 10 percent tax. In April 2005 the BCC further revalued the peso convertible by 8 percent in relation to the U.S. dollar, thereby levying a whopping 18 percent exchange rate (10 percent penalty plus 8 percent revaluation) on U.S. dollars. All other foreign currencies are exchanged according to the international currency market, taking into consideration the 8 percent revaluation of the peso convertible.

2. The plight of Oscar Lewis, the late American anthropologist, is one of the most noteworthy cases. The studies of Lewis, Lewis, and Rigdon (1977a, 1977b, 1978) were carried out in 1969–70. They were controversial and were terminated by the Cuban government in 1970. Raúl Castro, then minister of the Revolutionary Army, declared that the study "departed from the [agreed-upon research] proposals" and carried out counterrevolutionary activities with the aim of conducting "political, economic, social, cultural, and military espionage, making use of their progressivist facade" (cited in Lewis 1977a: xxii). Lewis and his research team denied these allegations. The full details of the events can be found in the foreword of volume 1 of their two-part anthology (1977a).

3. See Fernández (2000a) for a detailed description of this term.

4. Rationing of food began in March 1962. In principle, the system ensures equality of food consumption among the population since every Cuban is, in theory, legally permitted to buy the same amount of basic food products at the same prices. Ration cards (*libretas*) set limits on the quantities that one person can purchase at

subsidized prices, although rationing does not guarantee that those products will be available for purchase every month (Benjamin, Collins, and Scott, 1984). See, for example, Premat (1998) and Garth (1988) for an ethnographic account of the ways in which Cubans negotiated food shortages and rationing during the *período especial.*

INTRODUCTION

1. From 1991 to 1993 an epidemic of optic and peripheral neuropathy—commonly associated with a painful inflammation of nerves—affected more than fifty thousand people in Cuba. The number of new cases decreased after vitamin supplements were distributed through family doctors to every citizen.

2. In Cuban Spanish, all references to the Cuban revolution of 1959 are capitalized. The term conveys how individuals express feelings and ideas about *la Revolución* as an agent capable of acting on an individual.

3. In times of crisis, Agamben (2005, 5) asserts, the "state of exception" refers to the expansion of the powers of government to issue decrees that have the force of law. As the government engages in the process of claiming this power, questions of sovereignty, citizenship, and individual rights can be diminished, superseded, and rejected.

4. For instance, the government introduced reforms that sought to restore import capacity and stimulate domestic supply; increase the economy's responsiveness to the world market; search for foreign capital and technology; allow free-market sales of surplus produce, handcrafts, and some manufactured goods; increase the categories of self-employment allowed by the state to cover an additional one hundred freelance occupations; and permit the registration and taxation of private rental activity (Economist Intelligence Unit 1999).

5. Cited in Eckstein 1994, 103.

6. Crisis, as an isolated event or discursive category of a prolonged period of unrest, is hardly new in Cuba's revolutionary vernacular and arguably could be extended back to the country's formation as a republic in 1902. Since 1959 the island has experienced multiple crises: the Bay of Pigs invasion (1961), the Cuban Missile Crisis (1962), the era of *perestroika* and *glasnost* (mid-1980s), and the ongoing U.S. embargo (1962–present), among other notable events in the island's historical trajectory.

7. While I have traveled extensively throughout Cuba in the past decade, and much of the analysis I present in this book resonates with my experiences in other regions of the country, I am both cognizant of and careful about misrepresenting the experience of *habaneros* (residents of the city of Havana) as the general experience of all Cubans. "Working in Havana and talking about Cuba is paramount to working in Manhattan and generalizing about the United States," an independent scholar who worked in Santiago de Cuba in the eastern region of the island complained at a conference at which I presented a paper in 2007. The scholar was uncomfortable with the privileging of Havana as the benchmark of most of the research carried out on the island. Recognizing this regionalist divide and the scholarly bias in the pursuit of knowledge production, I argue that Havana, despite revolutionary efforts to change this fact, is still home to Cuba's prized hospitals, burgeoning research and

biotechnology institutions, and a plethora of health tourist clinics and pharmacies. The capital city is a significant draw for Cubans from other provinces seeking out medical treatment and specialized medical services, both formally and informally. For the questions being explored in this book, the city of Havana is an ideal site for addressing changes to the country's health care system.

8. The bulk of my field research was carried out with residents within a regional division of the MEF program, which I will describe in detail in chapter 4.

9. To elicit a wide cross section of opinions and experiences of the health care sector every effort was made in this research to interview people who cut across the lines of professional status, class, gender, local categories of race, and sexuality. For example: informants ranged from twenty-one to seventy-five years of age; 65 percent of those interviewed were women; monthly official state salaries, for those who were employed, ranged from the equivalent of 7.50 to 30 U.S. dollars, with no access to other income; other individuals supplemented their state income or relied solely upon income generated from trading on the black market, renting rooms to tourists and Cubans, both legally and illegally, and receiving remittances from abroad (these individuals made between 20 to 400 U.S. dollars per month); educational levels ranged from university graduates to people with no formal education. All the names of the people and places—for example, the *consultorios* and the specific subdivision in which they are located—used in the book are pseudonyms to protect the identity of those who participated in the research. Moreover, published English translations of original Spanish texts have been used whenever available. Unless otherwise noted, the author translated all published texts and quotations from interviews.

10. Bourdieu's (1977, 1990) "theory of practice" is pivotal to this discussion, particularly the idea of practice as part of his broader argument on the relationship between belief and what he calls *habitus*, which he defines in terms of structures, or "systems of durable, transportable dispositions, structured structures" (1990, 53) that are internalized by the subject and that come to generate and organize social practices and representations. The habitus, then, is constituted through the past experiences, both individual and collective, of subjects within the world. Bourdieu argues that the habitus "is always oriented towards practical functions," since it regulates human practices and behavior (1990, 52). Individual bodily practices also build on earlier works on bodily techniques and *hexis* (Mauss 2006 [1934]); and the civilizing process (Elias 2000).

11. See Foucault 1991, 83.

12. This builds on Lacombe's (1996, 348) definition of the genealogical method.

13. See Abu-Lughod 1990.

14. As Farquhar (2002, 9) notes, Bourdieu's concept of habitus has been criticized as ahistorical and deterministic: "To be useful to social anthropology at all, it must be seen as open to history and many unexpected variations." Other scholars have examined this variation; see, for example, Lock and Kaufert 1998; Lock 1993b; Lock and Farquhar 2007; Boddy 1989; Comaroff 1985; Fassin 2007; Scott 1990; Lock and Schepher-Hughes 1987; and de Certeau 1988.

15. This book also contributes to recent literature on governmentality and subjec-

tivity in socialist and postsocialist contexts (see, for example, Palmié 2004; Philips 2005; Rigi 2005; and Yurchak 2005) as well as to studies that focus on science and medicine (see Petryna 2002; Farquhar 2002; Greenhalgh and Winckler 2005; Rivkin-Fish 2005; Hyde 2007; Ninetto 2005; and Reid-Henry 2003, 2007). It also contributes to emerging ethnographies of capital (see, for example, Elyachar 2005; Fisher and Downey 2006; Ong 2006; Roitman 2004a, 2004b; and Sunder Rajan 2006).

16. See Butler's (1997, 2) important discussion on the paradoxical nature of state power.

17. See Hardt and Negri 2000, 23.

18. Foucault 1983, 208. Also see Verdery's (1996) application of *étatization* to examine the regulation of time in European socialism. Similarly, Farquhar's discussion of how the Maoist past is embodied in the political and historical character of pleasure in modern-day China also speaks to variants of the genealogical method.

19. See José Quiroga (2005), *Cuban Palimpsests*.

20. Fernández (2000a), for example, identifies three major cultural paradigms that can be identified in Cuba's history: the liberal, the corporatist, and the informal (*lo informal*). Central to the liberalist project were the ideas that individual rationality and self-interest were to be wedded with the autonomy of social organization in a free market economy. Corporatism, Fernández argues, "endorsed the notion of law, order, stability, and elite leadership through a centralized bureaucratic authority— the state—that would rule over, and function in coordination with, sectoral groups hierarchically and organically integrated" (2000a, 27). Lo informal, on the other hand, subverted the institutions and regulation of daily life in order to satisfy the material and nonmaterial needs of the self, the family, and the community.

21. This book privileges the analysis of the way in which the creation and transformation of medicalized subjectivities are part and parcel of a broader matrix of socioeconomic and political changes. This is not to suggest that other factors, such as gender and local categories of racial classification, among others, are not equally important factors. Yet this form of finite analysis should be elaborated on in separate scholarly works: for example, gendering *la lucha* or discussions of race and the dual economy. I only briefly touch upon these latter themes in chapter 1.

22. See Hardt and Negri 2000, 23.

23. There are several notions of citizenship in relation to biomedicine and medical practice with which this work is in dialogue. See, for example, biological citizenship (Petryna 2002; Rose 2006; Rose and Novas 2004); and therapeutic citizenship (Nguyen 2010).

24. See DelVecchio Good's (2007) work on the "political economy of hope" and the "biotechnical embrace." This work demonstrates how biomedical intervention, in fields such as oncology, increasingly take on affective and imaginative dimensions, enveloping physicians, patients, and the public. She argues that analyzing the "multiple regimes of truth" circulating in high-technology medicine serves as a nexus for examining the subjective experiences of patients, clinical scientists, and the political economy of biomedicine.

25. This is not to suggest that the informal economy is a new phenomenon in Cuba. As many Cubans pointed out during interviews, a black and gray market had existed since the mid-1960s, before the advent of the período especial. However, as several informants also pointed out, the private informal economy tended to be in nonessential items (e.g., blue jeans and electronic equipment), not in basic medical provisions (e.g., medicine, medical supplies, and access to medical services). I highlight the qualitative differences in the informal economy from before and after 1989 in chapters 1 and 2.

26. See the work of Alena Ledeneva (1998).

27. One of the greatest sources of U.S. dollars before the law changed allowing Cubans to legally hold them was through remittance payments from Cubans abroad. The government had an official procedure by which the state would exchange these dollars at a one-to-one exchange for Cuban pesos.

28. I borrow the term from Augé and Herzlich 1983.

29. These speculations were made more complex when, in February 2008, Fidel Castro retired. Raúl Castro, Fidel's younger brother (younger by only a few years), was shortly thereafter officially recognized as the president of the Cuban Council of State. As recently as August 2010 Fidel's reappearance to give speeches, grant media interviews, and pose for public photos has only thickened the plot on the various speculations of the associations between his bodily health and the socialist state. This has led to a resurgence of questions about the longevity of both.

30. These categories not only take the meanings of terms such as *weak* and *strong* or *authoritarian* and *democratic* to be self-evident, but also are premised on a certain set of assumptions about the nature and function of states. In the end, scholars fall prey to a Eurocentric logic and take for granted that the so-called fully developed or ideal states are Western liberal democratic ones and that they are the norm by which other states are judged (see the work of Sharma and Gupta 2006).

31. For example, the state carries out periodic crackdowns on black market ringleaders (*macetas*, literally "flowerpots"), illegal renters, and *jineteros*, among others, who are publicly arrested and denounced for their activities. While these selective displays of sovereign state power are relatively ineffectual in curtailing the widespread existence of informal activities, they serve to keep them in check. In April 2003, for instance, the socialist government infiltrated several dissident movements operating in Cuba, which state security agents suggested were sponsored and funded by the U.S. government. All of the dissidents were sentenced to long jail terms, mostly ranging from fourteen to twenty-eight years. Shortly after this incident, three men who hijacked a passenger ferry and attempted to steer it to Florida before running out of fuel were sentenced with "very grave acts of terrorism" and were executed by firing squad. While there are clear differences between political repression and the control of the private informal economy in Cuba, several of my interlocutors in Cuba commented that the state's severe, brutal response to the dissidents and hijackers had temporarily resulted in a noticeable decrease in certain sectors of the private informal economy (namely, the black market trade in food items, electronics, and construction materials). As one Cuban I interviewed shortly after the

crackdown noted, the government's response was harkening back to the old days and the state's hard-line approach to illegal practices.

32. The gradual dismantling of prevailing forms of the state's social and political control has led to what some scholars argue is the gradual emergence of civil society (see Dilla 1999; Eckstein 1994; Fernández 1998; and León 1997). "Civil society," argues the Cuban sociologist Haroldo Dilla, provides "independent spaces for activities and debate" and "must be seen as the interaction—in words or deeds—among groups that form new power relations or affect existing ones, either by consolidating or chipping away at them" (1999, 32).

33. I take this lead from Roitman's (2004a; 2004b) work.

34. Roitman 2004b, 194.

35. See Aretxaga 2003; Bendix, Ollman, Sparrow, and Mitchell 1992; Coronil 1997; Das and Poole 2004; Gupta 1995; Masquelier 2001; Mitchell 1991a, 1991b; Montoya 2007; Sunder Rajan 2006; and Trouillot 2001.

36. See de Certeau 1988; Hacking 1986; and Pels 1997.

37. Elyachar 2005, 67. Much has been written (critically) about informal economies and shadow economies, and this scholarship informs my analysis (see Burawoy and Verdery 1999; Ferguson 2006; Ledeneva 1998, 2006; Nordstrom 2004; Roitman 1990, 2004b; Verdery 1996; Yang 1994; and Yurchak 1997, 2002, 2005).

38. See Harvey 2003.

39. See Roitman 2004b.

40. Ibid., 192.

41. This linear metanarrative that posits a progression for socialism to capitalism has been classified as a form of "transitology," and highlighted by several scholars who work in postsocialist studies (see, for example, Burawoy and Verdery 1999; Humphrey 2002; Humphrey and Mandel 2002; Verdery 1996, 2002; Yang 1994; Yurchak 1997, 2002; and Zhang 2001).

42. Lo informal in Cuba's health sector is in contrast to former Soviet bloc countries in which informal networks known as *blat* networks undermined the state (see, for example, Field 1995; Ledeneva 1998; Rivkin-Fish 2000, 2005; and Salmi 2003).

43. Garcia 1992, 215.

44. Cited in Constantín 1981, 1.

45. See, for example, Barberia and Castro 2003; Danielson 1979, 1981; Díaz-Briquets 1983; Feinsilver 1993; Farmer and Castro 2004; Huish 2008; Kath 2010; Perez 2008; Santana 1987, 1990; Whiteford and Branch 2008; and Ubell 1989.

46. For the purposes of this discussion, the best way to define *fetishism*, following the anthropologist Michael Taussig, is a state in which "definite social relationships are reduced to the magical matrix of things" (2002, 479). Taussig is building on Marx's discussion of the relationship between capital, workers, and social relations in capitalist nations.

47. Geertz's (1973) paradigm was primarily concerned with how religious symbols provide a representation of the way things are (the "model of") as well as guides and programs directing human activity (the "model for").

48. Scheper-Hughes 1994, 997.

49. See Dalton 1993; Werner 1983; and Hirschfeld 2008.

50. Ernesto "Che" Guevara was a strong proponent of "exporting revolution" to other Latin American countries. See Fidel Castro's speech of 4 February 1962 entitled "The Duty of a Revolutionary Is to Make Revolution: The Second Declaration of Havana," in which he stated, "The duty of every revolutionary is to make the revolution. It is known that the revolution will triumph in America and throughout the world, but it is not for revolutionaries to sit in the doorways of their houses waiting for the corpse of imperialism to pass by. The role of Job doesn't suit a revolutionary" (Castro Ruz 1969a, 104). Che was killed in 1967 while attempting to aid rebel fighters in "making revolution" in Bolivia.

51. Escobar 1995, 213.

52. This echoes Appadurai's (1988) discussion of the complex mechanisms that imbue meaning and value to things.

53. See the work of Hacking (1982) on the rise of statistics in governing society.

1. THE BIOPOLITICS OF HEALTH

1. See Brotherton 2008; Doyon and Brotherton 2008; and Spiegel and Yassi 2004.

2. The Council for Mutual Economic Assistance, 1949–91, was an organization composed of the countries of the Eastern bloc and a select number of socialist countries elsewhere in the world.

3. See Pastor and Zimbalist 1995, 8.

4. See Pan American Health Organization (PAHO) 2001.

5. The Torricelli Act forbids foreign subsidiaries of U.S. companies from trading with Cuba and places a six-month U.S. port ban on ships that have called at Cuban ports.

6. The Helms-Burton bill temporarily halted all direct flights and remittances to Cuba and allowed U.S. investors to take legal action in American courts against foreign companies that were utilizing their confiscated property in Cuba.

7. Brenner and Kornbluh 1995, 39

8. A number of other causal factors are responsible for the current crisis. These include what the policy analysts Ritter and Kirk (1995, 3) argue was the dysfunctional economic architecture, which was inadequate in dealing with a set of three interlinked crises as a result of the cessation of foreign exchange earnings. First, an energy crisis emerged with the reduction of petroleum. Second, an agricultural food-nutrition crisis resulted from reduced agricultural production, including the sugar harvest. Third, a general macroeconomic crisis was reflected in open unemployment, hidden "unemployment-on-the-job" (people being paid but not producing anything), high absenteeism, and a shift to legal or illegal economic activities.

9. See the work of the noted Cuban public health historian Delgado-García 1996c.

10. See PAHO 2001; see also A. Chomsky 2000.

11. See, for example, American Association for World Health (AAWH) 1997; Kirkpatrick 1996, 1997.

12. AAWH 1997, 2.

13. See, for example, Burns's statement of 1997 from the U.S. Department of State.

14. See Nayeri 1995, 326.

15. See also Kirkpatrick 1996, 1997; American Association for World Health 1997, for similar arguments.

16. See McKeown 1976a, 1976b; see also Navarro 2000.

17. It is important to distinguish between clinical medicine and public health. Clinical medicine (or intervention), such as pharmaceutical prophylaxis, may be effective in treating the prevalence of a condition (that is, the number of people who currently have the condition) but is relatively ineffective statistically at the population level. Whereas public health, composed of a spectrum of interventions aimed at the environment, human behavior and lifestyle, and medical care, is more effective at targeting the incidence of a particular condition (that is, the occurrence of new cases). Statistically speaking, public health efforts have been effective at controlling and preventing infectious diseases at the local and population levels, but there is still considerable debate over their impact on treating and preventing chronic illnesses (see Crabb 2001 for review of this debate, particularly in the context of Cuba).

18. In 1993 the government opened a series of Cadecas (that is, Casa de Cambio, S.A.), an operation designed specifically for currency exchange, where Cubans could legally exchange U.S. dollars into *moneda nacional*, or Cuban pesos (or vice versa), at a rate higher than that on the black market. Cuba thus entered into a state-approved dual economy.

19. This term is used in Cuba to refer to anyone who does not support the Cuban revolution. Often used in reference to Cubans who live in exile in Miami, it is also known as the Mafia of Miami.

20. Mutual benefit societies, known as *mutualistas*, consisted of medical insurance collectives; the members paid monthly dues (see chapter 3).

21. My research suggests that individuals tend to prefer products, including drugs, produced and manufactured abroad because they believe the quality of Cuban-made products is poor. While individuals discuss with admiration Cuba's scientific research community (*el pueblo científico*) (see chapter 6), they attribute the poor quality of drugs manufactured in Cuba to the widespread theft in state-run industries, which results in employees cutting corners to steal the basic ingredients to sell on the black market.

22. See Eckstein (2009, 190) for a detailed discussion of this subject.

23. See Dilla 2001.

24. This figure is reflective of the formal routes of sending money to Cuba, that is, the large and small money agencies that are dedicated to remittances to the island. Manuel Orozco (2002) notes that informal sources (for example, sending money via Canada, money provided to individuals by tourism, and money sent through friends and family members) may push this figure above one billion dollars. In 2002 over 90 percent of the reported remittances sent to Cuba originated from Cubans living in the United States. There is a growing body of literature that addresses the critical role of remittances in both the formal and informal economy in Cuba (see, for example,

Díaz-Briquets and Pérez López 1997; Eckstein 2009; Kildergaard and Orro Fernández 2000).

25. Some scholars estimate that the proportion of the population that has access to dollars through various channels reached 62 percent in 1999 (Ritter and Rowe 2000, 11–12). This number is difficult to estimate, but I suspect the figure is much higher, especially given that in addition to remittances, many individuals are involved in *trabajo por cuenta propia*, or self-employment for private profit (see Henken 2008).

26. There is an ongoing debate over the use of the terms *Afro-Cuban* and *black* (see, for example, Pérez Sarduy and Stubbs 2000). Arguably, all Cubans are Afro-Cuban if one considers their shared African cultural heritage. On the other hand, the term *black* is contentious because it fails to address the mixed racial heritage of many Cubans with darker skin tones. Acknowledging the wider debate surrounding these terms, all references in this book to Cubans of color, or *Cubanos de color*, indicate blacks and people of mixed racial heritage (*mulattos*). The problem of race is complex in Cuba's postrevolutionary environment, which in official state discourse is extolled as a harmonious racial mosaic. Historically, the revolutionary government, informed by Marxist teachings, had emphasized issues of class over race in overcoming Cuba's highly stratified society. The state had hoped that once class-based inequalities were overcome, other forms of discrimination would be overcome as well. However, the concept of race must be situated in reference to the prerevolutionary past, in which a discriminatory social order shaped the lives and experiences of people of color in Cuba. Many Cubans of color have long been considered by many as the main beneficiaries of the postrevolutionary social order and therefore have been deemed a group from which the current government draws unconditional political support. No longer relegated to the discussion of Cuba's postrevolutionary racial harmony, issues of race, racism, and discrimination are now being considered seriously as topics of popular debate (see, for example, Castillo Bueno 2000; de La Fuente and Glasco 1997, 53; de la Fuente 2001; N. Fernández 2010; Pérez Sarduy and Stubbs 2000).

27. See the discussion of campaigns in chapter 3.

28. See, for example, Andaya 2007; Smith and Padula 1996.

29. See León's 1997 work on the rise of *sociolismo*.

2. EXPANDING THERAPEUTIC ITINERARIES

1. The case study of this section examines Santería because of the clear links that are drawn between the spiritual and material, particularly by those interviewed about their physical health and well-being. An examination of individuals returning to Evangelical churches, Catholicism, and other religious traditions is also relevant (cf. Hearn's 2008 discussion of the increasing role of religion in Havana's urban renewal projects). However, Santería was by far the most commonly followed religious tradition among those formally interviewed for this research.

2. See Lewis, Lewis, and Rigdon, *Living the Revolution* (1977a, 1977b): *Four Men* (vol. 1), and *Four Women* (vol. 2).

3. Cf. Barnet 1997.

4. Arnold 1988, 1992; Comaroff 1993; Gilman 1985.

5. Until a new law took effect on 10 November 2011, property sales were not permitted in Cuba, but Cubans can exchange apartments; for example, someone can trade a two-bedroom apartment for two separate one-bedroom apartments (and vice versa), in the case of divorce, family expansion, or to live in a better area or apartment. While simplistic, at least in theory, the practice of housing exchange, popularly known as *permuta*, is rife with illegality involving cash interactions above and beyond the trades. A growing number of informal real estate agents have emerged to facilitate these illegal acts, which people effectively use for profit by manipulating the laws regulating the terms and conditions of housing exchange. See Lewis, Lewis, and Rigdon's ethnography *Neighbors* (1978) for an examination of the politics of housing exchange in Cuba in the 1960s and 1970s.

6. Katherine Hagedorn notes, "The potential to negotiate with, and *resolver* [to solve one's problems] through the *orichas* is inherent in the philosophy of Santería. All of the *orichas* can be favorably influenced by offerings of water, flowers, candles, fruit, honey, candy, liquor, money, fish, birds, or, in serious situations, four-legged animals. . . . Santeria is not only a polytheistic religion with many *orichas*, but each *oricha* also has at least several (and sometimes several hundred) *caminos* [paths or roads to follow]. Each *oricha* is generally associated with certain colors, foods, natural phenomena, and sacred attributes, and these associations and preferences become more specific with each *camino* or avatar of the particular *oricha*" (2001, 213).

7. Castro enjoyed the popular support of *santeros*, practitioners of Santería. Known as *El Caballo* (the horse) in these circles, Castro was assumed to have mysterious qualities similar to those of santeros, who are also known as the horses for the saints. Moreover, the colors of the flag of the Movement of July 26th rebel army, which are red and black, symbolize the colors of Changó, the warrior god in Santería.

8. The work of the anthropologist Roger Lancaster (1988), who examined the rise of liberation theology (the fusion of folk Catholicism and Marxism) in Nicaragua in the early 1980s, is an exceptional example of the way in which religious beliefs can be framed and reinterpreted within the context of solving the material problems of daily life. Moreover, as the Cuban American anthropologist Mercedes Sandoval, who carried out research on the role of Santería as a mental health care system among Cuban refugees in Dade County, Florida, in the 1970s noted, "In an amoral, materialistic, present-oriented society, gods which are conceptualized in pragmatic terms are seen as more real and efficient than sublime deities. The reasoning appears to be that the supernatural powers must be as amoral and manipulative as society today is perceived to be. Consequently, there need be little concern about moral behavior, which is to be rewarded in the afterlife" (Sandoval 1979, 144).

9. Cf. Cabrera 1999.

10. Marx 1977, 64.

11. Neophytes in Santería often stand out because they are required to wear white clothes and coverings from head to toe during the first year as santeros. In downtown Havana countless individuals are dressed in this fashion. As my informant Angela Ulloa pointed out, this was not the case before the *período especial*.

12. Wedel (2003) focuses on the aesthetics of healing in Santería. The author does not examine the theme of medical pluralism in contemporary Cuba.

13. Nichter and Lock 2002, 3.

14. In this context, the word *war* does not necessarily correspond to any war in particular. Rather, in the mid-1980s, the FAR, under the banner "La Guerra de Todo El Pueblo" (The war of all the people), began investigating a number of alternative strategies for ensuring the survival of Cuban socialism in the event it was ever threatened. This included training the militia and individual citizens for combat, building underground tunnels and safe havens, and investigating MTN and methods for water and food conservation.

15. Ministerio de Salud Pública (MINSAP) 1996, 25.

16. MINSAP 1999, 7.

17. Ibid., 9.

18. See MINSAP 2001, 31.

19. Ferzacca 2002, 50.

20. See Castro Ruz 2002, 2.

3. MEDICALIZED SUBJECTIVITIES

1. Danielson 1979, 2.

2. Cf. Burchell, Gordon, and Miller 1991; Foucault 1991.

3. See Quiroga 2005, 22.

4. See Whitney 2001, 121.

5. See, for example, Ortiz 1995; Barnet 1980; McGillivray 2009; and Mintz 1985 for a historical discussion of the sugar industry.

6. Cited in Lockwood 1967, 104.

7. Gilpin 1989; Gilpin and Rodriguez-Trias 1978, 4; Nelson 1950.

8. See Danielson 1979, 127–63; Gilpin 1989; Díaz Novas and Fernández Sacasas 1989.

9. As several scholars have noted, those left without formalized health care in prerevolutionary Cuba were mostly drawn from the black and colored population (Danielson 1979). The racial and demographic composition of Cuba's social stratification during the *período republicano burgués* was parallel to the color and class hierarchy of the colonial period. Furthermore, as Danielson notes, blacks were excluded from many of the prepaid medical plans (mutualistas) during the prerevolutionary period (1979, 6).

10. Modest estimates at the time placed the infant mortality rate at sixty per one thousand live births and life expectancy at approximately sixty-one years (Díaz Novas and Fernández Sacasas 1989). In addition, in the 1940s Cuba had the highest ratio of hospital beds to population in the Caribbean, of which 80 percent were in the city of Havana (Benjamin, Collins, and Scott 1984).

11. Hirschfeld 2008, 212.

12. See A. Chomsky 2000, 332.

13. Many individuals also used the services of traditional healers (*curanderos*) or healers who were practitioners of Santería (*santería espiritualistas*). Traditional and religious healing services played an active role in the lives of poor rural and urban

Cubans in the prerevolutionary context (see, for example, Lewis, Lewis, and Rigdon 1977a, 1977b, 1978).

14. See also Gilpin 1989.

15. See Gilpin and Rodriguez-Trias 1978, 4.

16. On 26 July 1943 more than one hundred revolutionaries led by Fidel Castro attacked Batista's troops in the Moncada Barracks (Santiago de Cuba), the second most important garrison in Cuba. They were captured and imprisoned before being exiled. This speech formed part of his legal defense. The date, the 26th of July, became the defining symbol of Castro's revolutionary rebel army, which later became known as the 26th of July Movement.

17. Castro Ruz 1983, 72–73.

18. One of the first formalized processes of nationalization was the Agrarian Reform Law, adopted on 17 May 1959. This law prohibited private farms larger than four hundred hectares. The expropriated lands were to be distributed among former tenant farmers and sharecroppers, but during 1961 and 1962 most of the land was turned into state farms. In addition, in March 1968 approximately forty-four thousand small businesses, largely family owned and operated, were closed down by the government as part of a new so-called revolutionary offensive to avoid private ownership. These were small steps in the revolutionary government's greater plan to return the means of production to state ownership. The underlying logic of these reform policies, through the interpretive lens of a Marxist–Leninist framework espoused by the state, would reduce class stratification in Cuban society.

19. Fidel Castro declared the year 1961 the Year of Education, dedicated to eradicating illiteracy in Cuba. Schools were closed and one hundred thousand students from junior high to college level were mobilized as *brigadistas* (brigades), trained, and sent into rural and poor urban areas to teach reading and writing. The program was reported to be successful in reducing the illiteracy rate from 23 percent to approximately 3 percent (Lockwood 1967, 126). Other programs included the campaign to eliminate prostitution, which began in 1961 and lasted five or six years. In addition, the state ran a number of reeducation training programs, such as the Educación Obrera-Campesina (Worker peasant programs), offered to unskilled laborers to provide high school equivalency education in order to be eligible for university preparation programs.

20. There have been no formal diplomatic relations between the United States and Cuba since 1961, although both governments maintain Interest Sections in other embassies in each other's capitals.

21. The PCC is the only legal political party in Cuba, and it exercises de facto control over government policies.

22. Eckstein 1994, 33; Castro Ruz 1969a.

23. Castro Ruz 1969b, 199.

24. Eckstein 1994, 34.

25. The Comités de Defensa de la Revolución (CDRs) were founded in 1960. Organized as *frentes*, or fronts, CDRs are active in a broad range of programs, including recruiting volunteers to participate in public health campaigns, providing education, promoting urban reform, carrying out local administration as well as actively

pursuing surveillance work against counterrevolutionary activities. CDR members are known as *cederistas*.

26. The Federación de Mujeres Cubanas (FMC) was founded primarily as a women's movement and played a major role in mobilizing women to pursue postsecondary education, join the labor force, and participate in community defense and surveillance.

27. The Central de Trabajadores de Cuba (CTC) brought together members of sixteen industry-based unions. This organization serves as a channel through which government directives affecting constituencies are disseminated to bolster support and participation (Eckstein 1994). In effect, the CTC is like a labor union organizing all employees at a workplace.

28. Given the selective nature of membership in the PCC, mass organizations often serve as a primary source for recruiting *militantes* (members of the PCC, also known as cadres).

29. See Dilla 1999.

30. Ibid., 32.

31. In addition to the religious and symbolic affiliation of Castro as a messiah (see Fernández 2000a for a more elaborate discussion), Castro enjoyed the popular support of santeros, practitioners of Santería, as I mentioned in the previous chapter.

32. Fernández 2000a, 64.

33. Cited in Lewis, Lewis, and Rigdon, 1977a, 218.

34. The early revolutionary years were not without casualties. While mass organizations grouped ordinary citizens into miniature polities, they also served as a prime means of surveillance and control of daily life. Under siege by both direct and indirect counterrevolutionary activities being carried out by the U.S. government and communities of Cuban Americans in exile, mass organizations responded by becoming active participants in weeding out certain ideas, values, and individuals who were believed to be opposed to the collective vision of a communist Cuba. In 1964, for example, a special program (now defunct), the notorious Military Units to Assist Production (UMAP), was created to reform, through hard labor, people deemed to be socially dangerous, antisocial, or antithetical to revolutionary principles. Interns in the UMAP included, among others, militant Catholics, artists, academics, and homosexuals, self-identified or not. All interns were subject to reform under Castro's vaguely worded pronouncement of the early 1960s: "Inside the Revolution, everything; against the Revolution, nothing." As a result of these repressive practices, the revolutionary government quickly earned an international reputation as a violator of human rights. Domestically, there was a conspicuous absence of dissenting voices, especially those who openly criticized government practices or polices. As Fernández notes, "The many benefits provided (education, health care, guaranteed employment, among others) came with a price attached: conformity to official dogma, and a dosage of control (closely resembling corporatism)" (2000b, 84).

35. Eckstein 1994, 128.

36. Fidel Castro identified health welfare as a basic human right. It was codified as such in the Cuban Constitution of 1976.

37. For example, China and the former USSR.

38. The state's narrowly defined vision of science and development in the health sector meant a disavowal of alternative perspectives and approaches to health care. For example, the role of midwives, curanderos (traditional healers), Santería, and herbal medicine, among other alternatives to biomedicine, were actively marginalized and effectively criminalized as occult sciences in the postrevolutionary environment. This situation changed in the período especial, as I noted in chapter 2.

39. Guevara 1968b, 114.

40. Ibid. This phrase is reflective of the overall philosophy of the revolutionary government, which emphasizes a materialist approach to health, viewing the individual as a social being (worker) in harmony with the physical environment.

41. Guevara 1968a, 119.

42. Eckstein 1994, 130.

43. Gilpin and Rodriguez-Trias 1978, 4.

44. Admissions to medical school were open to everybody in the country, and campaigns were organized to recruit medical students. This differed from the prerevolutionary context, in which the medical school tended to cater to students who could afford to attend. Under the revolutionary administration, free tuition and residential scholarships changed the socioeconomic makeup of the student body. The selection of medical students is based not only on good examination results from grade twelve, but also on the reference from the applicant's CDR. Macdonald, a health care specialist who has carried out extensive research on Cuba's education system, writes, "The CDR record of a person will show, for instance, to what extent a candidate's hobbies throughout his/her school life have been socially oriented" (1999, 94–96). Moreover, as Dalton (1993) has noted, the selection process seeks to promote those students who have most actively participated in la Revolución and are more likely to espouse the values of the dominant state ideology.

45. The training of auxiliary medical personnel also increased during the early years of the revolution. By 1968 there were 17,084 graduates of basic training in nursing and the paramedical professions, and 1,470 of these had completed specialty training after two years of practice (Danielson 1979, 184).

46. Werner 1983, 24.

47. For example, in 1960 the revolutionary government introduced Law Number 723, El Servicio Médico Social Rural. The law required doctors to spend a set amount of time in rural areas, thereby guaranteeing medical and social services to the most marginalized areas of the country. See Gilpin and Rodriguez-Trias 1978; Danielson 1979.

48. See Danielson 1979.

49. MINSAP was created in 1949. It existed as various governing bodies before the revolution. For example, public health was under the direction of the Secretary of Sanitation in 1909, the Ministry of Health and Social Assistance in 1940, and the Ministry of Health and Hospital Assistance in the early months of 1949 (cf. ACIMED 1998).

50. Danielson 1979, 143–44.

51. Dalton 1993; Delgado García 1996a, 1996c; Eckstein 1994.

52. See Gilpin and Rodriguez-Trias 1978, 4; Danielson 1979, 168.

53. Gilpin and Rodriguez-Trias 1978, 4–6.

54. See Feinsilver 1993; Díaz Novas and Fernández Sacasas 1989, 446–64.

55. See Gilpin and Rodriguez-Trias 1978, 7–8.

56. See Díaz Novas and Fernández Sacasas 1989.

57. Ordóñez Carceller 1976, 12.

58. Feinsilver 1993, 37.

59. See Werner 1983.

60. See MINSAP, *Programas básicos* 1977, 79–84; Eckstein 1994, 136–37; Feinsilver 1989, 17.

61. See Eckstein 1994, 136–37; Feinsilver 1989: 17; Andaya 2007.

62. Delgado García 1996b: 11. Feinsilver (1993) has argued that Cuba's impressive health statistics have been the basis for the island's "global empowerment" and a significant source of Cuban nationalism (see also Eckstein 1994, 128, for a similar argument).

63. Díaz-Briquets 1983, 118–19; Santana 1987, 117.

64. See, for example, Cardelle 1994 for a detailed description of curriculum reform; see also *Granma Weekly Review* 1986, 4; Dalton 1993, 123.

65. Fernández Sacasas and López Benítez 1976, 1.

66. Cited in *Granma Weekly Review* 1986, 4.

4. CURING THE SOCIAL ILLS OF SOCIETY

1. MINSAP 2001, 10.

2. Ibid., 11.

3. According to the MINSAP, over 50 percent of Cuban physicians remain family practitioners.

4. In 2009 approximately 70 percent of Cuba's total health sector staff was made up of women; women also comprised about 50 percent of the island's family doctors. These figures are indicative of the feminization of medical labor and care giving on the island (MINSAP 2009).

5. My ethnographic field research suggests that, owing to a severe housing shortage in Havana, a significant number of physicians and nurses do not live in the communities they serve. Rather, the health teams commute daily to the *consultorios* in their respective neighborhoods. Only two physicians in the more than fifteen consultorios I researched extensively lived in the same complex, and all the nurses lived elsewhere.

6. Cited in Gilpin 1989, 470.

7. Central to the Alma Ata Declaration (1978) is a definition of health. The declaration asserts that "a state of complete physical, mental and social wellbeing, and not merely the absence of disease or infirmity, is a fundamental human right and . . . the attainment of the highest possible level of health is a most important world-wide social goal whose realization requires the action of many other social and economic sectors in addition to the health sector" (WHO 1978, 1).

8. See, for example, Rodríguez and Zayas 1997.

9. Historically the increasing participation of the citizenry in state health reforms

through mass organizations effectively led to the extension of the state surveillance apparatus into everyday local practices under the umbrella of collective health and well-being (for example, the CDR's campaign for weeding out allegedly antisocial individuals in the 1960s and 1970s).

10. The Hermanos Ameijeiras Hospital "stands as a striking symbol of Cuba's zeal for high-technology medicine" (Ubell 1989, 439). It is the first major hospital to be built in Havana since the revolution. The twenty-four-story tower was under construction for ten years. "The $45-million center, designed for postgraduate work, offers 36 specialties, primarily in six areas: advanced heart, brain, and reconstructive surgery, gastroenterology, psychiatry, and nuclear medicine. Five of the center's 25 operating rooms are used for microsurgery. . . . The hospital is well-equipped with high-powered diagnostic tools from all over the world; the latest and most sophisticated equipment is mostly from Japan" (Ubell 1989, 440).

11. Páez and Rodríguez 1997, 2. In chapter 6 I expand on the theme of high-technology medicine in Cuba and, in particular, on the politics associated with the MINSAP's significant financial investment in biotechnology and medical specialist clinics for foreigners, especially given the overall financial contraction occurring in other areas of the primary health care sector.

12. All health services in Cuba, regardless of level of specialization, are provided free of charge. The only out-of-pocket expenditures for individuals include drugs prescribed for outpatient treatment, hearing aids, dental and orthopedic apparatuses, and so on. The prices for all these items are low and are subsidized by the state.

13. Lock and Scheper-Hughes 1987, 10.

14. C. Gordon 1991, 2.

15. Fieldwork suggests, for instance, that some municipalities are stigmatized for being resettlement communities, that is, they contain former shantytown dwellers who have moved to new state-built apartment complexes or individuals who were provided with the apartments, located in formerly middle-class suburbs of Cuba, who fled the country after the revolution. For example, the municipality of Central Havana and certain areas of El Cerro, which has a high population of Afro-Cubans, are often associated with crime, danger, and filth. This contrasts with municipalities like Miramar and certain parts of Plaza of the Revolution, previously wealthy suburbs that are perceived by many citizens to have preserved many of their former characteristics, among them, a high percentage of professionals and diplomats.

16. I distinguish these communities socio-demographically on the basis of extensive participant observation and interviews with citizens who live in these municipalities. I was unable to get specific information from the MINSAP on the consultorios under study owing to the multiple levels of bureaucracy I encountered. Formal written requests, which the MINSAP requires, would have compromised the anonymity of the participating physicians and individuals in their health areas. Only in September 2002, after a twenty-one-year hiatus of demographic data collection, did Cuba initiate a census of population and housing. The census took three years to process, becoming available in 2005. I take these numbers from that report.

17. According to PAHO, in 2001, 75.5 percent of the population in Cuba was urban and 24.5 percent was rural.

18. For family physicians fortunate enough to be granted housing in the communities in which they work, generally speaking, they do not have to pay rent or utilities. However, in the general population, the many Cubans who have legal title to their property usually do not pay rent either, unless the property was inherited. If they do, the figure is usually a nominal sum of ten to fifteen Cuban pesos a month, and all utilities are subsidized: for example, one peso per person per month for water, and so on.

19. Campbell 2001.

20. Several longitudinal studies implemented before and after the incorporation of the MEF program also argue that the MEF program has, statistically speaking, greatly affected the level of health awareness of the general population in the City of Havana Province (see the studies by Vera Castillo, Iglesias Díaz, Milían Montesino, Torres Ruiz, and Diaz Narváez 1989; Jova and Padrón 1989; Pérez Peña 1989).

21. See Cortiñas 1993 and Werner 1983, who draw on Ivan Illich's *Medical Nemesis* (1975).

5. PREVENTIVE STRATEGIES

1. The president of the FMC, Vilma Espín, later changed this term to the "new human being."

2. Dalton 1993, 126.

3. Most studies of biomedicine and power have presumed a liberal democratic and capitalist context (see, for example, Comaroff 1982; Foucault 1991; Gordon 1998; Lupton 1995; Miller and Rose 2008; Navarro 1977; Petersen and Lupton 1996; Rabinow and Rose 2006; Rose 2006; Rose and Novas 2004; Taussig 1992; Young 1978). The relationship between medicine and politics is demonstrated in Vincanne Adams's (1998) *Doctors for Democracy*, which ethnographically examines the paradoxical connections between science and politics in the rhetoric and activities of medicine and development in Nepal's revolutionary changes in the 1990s.

4. I am indebted to Stacey Leigh Pigg for pushing me to develop this argument.

5. Evans 1993, 1.

6. Butler 1997; Lock 1993b; Foucault 2008; and Rabinow and Dreyfus 1982.

7. This builds on the theoretical work of Lacombe 1996, 334 and Foucault 1990a, 1991.

8. MINSAP 2009.

9. MINSAP 1996, 4.

10. See DiGiacomo 1999, 440.

11. See Aronowitz 1998, 144.

12. Cf. PAHO 2001, 2–3.

13. The two remaining programs for individuals include integral care of children (under fifteen) and dental care.

14. See Batista, Salabarría, and Díaz González 1996; Waitskin, Wald, Kee, Danielson, and Robinson 1997, 1–2; Reed 2001.

15. *Granma Weekly Review* 1986, 4.

16. Fidel Castro [1984] in MINSAP 2001, 4.

17. As was evident in interviews, many Cubans informally refer to various sedatives such as diazepam as *la pastilla de la felicidad*, or the happiness pill, a way to temporarily forget the struggles and anxieties of everyday life. A study of the relationship between medicalized understandings of the body and formal and informal consumption of prescription drugs in Cuba would contribute to a fascinating body of literature on the anthropology of pharmaceuticals (see, for example, Geest, Whyte, and Hardon 1996 and Petryna, Kleinman, and Lakoff 2006).

18. While this book does not discuss the problem of mental illness, such as depression, anxiety disorder, and so on, in contemporary Cuba, it would be interesting to explore the relationship between the recent economic crisis and suicide or, more generally, the diagnoses of psychological health-related problems. For example, according to Pérez (2006) since the nineteenth century and throughout the twentieth, the per capita rate of suicide in Cuba was the highest in Latin America and among the highest in the world. He argues that this formed part of the Cubans' unique form of social protest. Official numbers on mental illness and suicide in contemporary Cuba are scarce or, some argue, underreported, but several journalistic accounts claim that both are quite high (cf. Navarro 2009). Given the high rates of self-diagnoses and self-medication (particularly the abuse of sedatives) and the widespread informal networks that trade in prescription drugs, a separate study is required.

19. See Rodríguez and Zayas 1997.

20. Gifford 1986, 215.

21. Gifford (1986) illustrates her argument by focusing on the relationship between risk factors for breast cancer and the complexities of accurately defining epidemiological risk. She argues that because of the uncertainty that a woman with a benign condition will develop breast cancer, "the condition comes to take on the double meaning of being both normal and pre-malignant at the same time" (225). As a result, the women whom epidemiological risk discourses have classified as having high risk factors are predisposed to a higher degree of clinical medical surveillance and must live with the belief that a benign lump can become, cause, or mask breast cancer.

22. Scholars are starting to examine how genetic risk complicates the surveillance of women's bodies, for example, in screening for genetic disorders such as sickle cell anemia or physical disabilities on expectant mothers' fetuses (see Andaya 2007 on genetic counseling and abortion). Other work examines the screening and targeting of genes that are linked to breast cancer (see Gibbon 2009).

23. In Castilian Spanish the use of *tú* (you) denotes familiarity and is often used informally. The use of *usted* (you) is for formal contexts, such as speaking to strangers. Forty years of Cuban socialism and the rhetoric of egalitarianism have drastically affected the way in which Cubans oscillate between formal and informal Spanish. The use of informal language among the population reflects an idiom of camaraderie; for instance, the terms *compañero* and *colega* both denote colleague, friend, and compatriot. These terms are used in tandem with the tú form. According to several of my informants, the formal use of usted became more frequent only with

the influx of tourists. Tourists and foreigners generally are almost without exception addressed by usted.

24. Dengue is a viral disease characterized by "high fever, rash, severe headaches, and pain behind the eyes, but the disease can also present with very mild symptom or no symptoms at all. It is rarely fatal, but epidemics can cause considerable disruption, especially in countries dependent on tourism. A severe and relatively new variant known as dengue hemorrhagic fever or DHF makes dengue particularly dangerous" (Kendall, Hudelson, Leonstini, Winch, Lloyd, and Cruz 1991, 259).

25. Water is provided intermittently in different areas of Havana owing to frequent overall water shortages. For example, in the building I lived in from 2000 until 2003 most apartments had installed internal storage tanks for water. When the main water supply serving the building was shut off, which was the case except for three hours in the evening, people switched to internal tanks.

26. Feinsilver 1993, 82.

27. There are four known strains, labeled dengue-1 through dengue-4.

28. A. Chomsky 2000, 338.

29. At the time, Castro argued that the strain of dengue affecting Cuba was not found anywhere else in the world. Castro's suspicions were compounded by the admission of several counterrevolutionary groups that they had exposed the Cuban population to a form of germ warfare (see Feinsilver 1993 for discussion of these events).

30. Cited ibid., 89.

31. All university graduates must complete two years of social service to the government. The exception is men, who, at the age of sixteen, must complete two years of mandatory military service; military service is optional for women. In theory, this means that the majority of individuals completing the social service program are women, but increasingly men are avoiding military service for a variety of reasons, such as openly declaring their homosexuality (whether genuine or not) or by obtaining medical certificates for specific ailments, certificates which, in recent years, could be purchased illegally from state officials.

32. This can be seen as a parallel to city-dwelling high school students being required to complete a number of months of agricultural labor each year, popularly known as Escuela al Campo (country school).

33. Castro, cited in *Granma Internacional Digital*, 21 October 2002, 16.

34. See Feinsilver 1989, 1993.

35. The physician often expressed his discontent with certain aspects of la Revolución, such as the lack of material resources at his disposal, by setting up mock scenarios and then turning to me and asking, "Now, do you think I can do my job with what I have?" Inevitably, the answer, from my limited perspective, was no. (For example, a physician whose only stethoscope is broken is unable to take people's blood pressure, for a primary health care physician an essential operation.)

36. Hirschfeld (2008) discusses the controversy between the rumored and the official dengue epidemic in the spring of 1997 in Santiago de Cuba. She contends the Cuban authorities made concerted efforts to cover up the epidemic. During my stay

in Havana during the dengue campaigns in the early 2000s, public health authorities were transparent about the possible risks and the need to be vigilant. While the term *epidemic* was not used frequently, the term *risk* and the factors that put one at risk were made very clear by the daily visits of sanitation inspectors.

37. These forms of collectives can be traced back to the early 1960s. The socialist government has formed everything from literacy brigades to construction brigades, youth brigades, and public health brigades, all based on the philosophy of popular participation in the development of social transformation. Using the rhetoric of the state, these activities promote social cohesion and the importance of putting the collective well-being before individual wants and desires.

38. Fagen 1969, 7.

39. Spiegel, Bonet, Ibarra, Pagliccia, Ouellette, and Yassi (2007) note in their study of the social and environmental determinants of *Aedes aegypti* infestations in central Havana that Cuban health authorities may need to pay closer attention to the religious observances of santeros. In Santería it is common to regularly provide "spiritual vases" of water as part of a ritualized practice. As the authors of this study note, in other countries with similar religions offerings of water, there were statistically significant increases of *A. aegypti* breeding grounds. In short, the practice of Santería is effectively linked to risky practices, opening up the distinct possibility of further scrutiny and regulation (see chapter 2 for a more detailed discussion of this theme).

40. See Treichler 1987.

41. Programa Nacional ITS/VIH/SIDA. Dirección de Epidemiología. La Habana (Cuba): Ministerio de Salud Pública; June 2008.

42. Opponents of Cuba's socialist government have argued that Cuba's HIV/AIDS statistics do not reflect the actual numbers (cf. Chesnut 1991; Pérez-Stable 1991). However, as Lumsden notes, "Critics have not been able to demonstrate why Cuba's AIDS statistics would not have the same integrity as its other highly reliable epidemiological statistics" (1996, 102).

43. The mandatory testing of Cuban soldiers returning from Africa in the mid-1980s, several of whom were found to be seropositive, was the underlying reason the AIDS sanitarium was initially under the authority of the MINFAR (see Scheper-Hughes 1994).

44. See Lumsden's (1996) use of this term.

45. See Chestnut's (1991) use of this phrase.

46. See Leiner 1994, 133–35. He argues that popular stereotypes such as "men naturally cheat" or "men will be men" posit male sexuality as somewhat inherent and assume that men are biologically programmed to be sexually promiscuous. He notes that literature on Latin American *machismo* and male sexuality, rather than diminish these popular stereotypes, has reinforced them.

47. Castro cited in Lockwood 1967, 107.

48. For example, see the *Diagnostic and Statistical Manual of Mental Disorders* (*DSM-I*) (1952), which categorized homosexuality as "sexual deviation" under the general psychiatric category of "socio-pathic personality disturbance," or in the *DSM-II* (1968) that classified homosexuality as a "personality disorder."

49. See Young 1981.

50. See Lumsden (1996) for a discussion of this.

51. Systematic oppression of homosexuals was common practice during the period of the UMAP programs in the 1960s (as I discussed briefly in chapter 3). The internationally acclaimed film *Fresa y chocolate* (Strawberry and chocolate), made in 1993, deals with the theme of homosexual oppression in contemporary Cuba. In a considerably more polemic vein, the movie, based on the autobiography of the late exiled Cuban writer Reynaldo Arenas, *Antes que anochezca* (Before night falls), also deals with the theme of homosexual repression in Cuba. An article in the Cuban magazine *Alma Mater* suggests that in recent years the Cuban population has become more relaxed about homosexuality, though, as the article further contends, this does not necessarily suggest that the population is more tolerant (see Jiménez 2003).

52. See, for example, the criticism voiced by Feinsilver 1993 and Lumsden 1994.

53. Nancy Scheper-Hughes's (1994) article "AIDS and the Social Body" provides a very cursory, yet supportive examination of the HIV/AIDS prevention program in Cuba; see also A. Chomsky 2000; Santana 1990; Pérez-Stable 1991. Of the other limited studies available, which are characterized by the conflicting claims of ethnographic accounts, for example, "AIDS in Cuba: Patients Speak Out" (Ross 1991), most commentators are firmly planted in a tug-of-war of ideological posturing, doing little to sway ardent critics or supporters.

54. Feinsilver 1993, 83–84.

55. Cuba's domestic pharmaceutical industry, in opposition to the international patenting laws, produces its own HIV/AIDS medications (cf. Pérez Avila, Peña Torres, Joanes Fiol, Lantero Abreu, and Arazoza Rodriguez 1996). For instance, after 1996 Cuba produced generic equivalents of the antiretroviral (ARV) drugs, including Zidovudine (AZT), Didanosine (DDI), Lamivudine (3TC), Stavudine (4T), Zalcitabine (DDC), Nevirapine (NVP), Indinavir (IDV) (*Pautas cubanas para el tratamiento y manejo de los pacientes VIH/SIDA sometidos a Terapéutica Antiretroviral. Instituto de Medicina Tropical Pedro Kourí 2003*). Following the Cuban guidelines, the treatment for HIV-positive patients begins after the development of an opportunistic infection or a CD4 less than 200. After 2001 all HIV patients were receiving therapy. Cuba also receives internationally donated HIV medication and currently has 120 individuals on triple therapy (the combination of various HIV medications, argued to be more effective in combating the virus). According to an article in *Granma* from 2003, Cuba also sold over one million U.S. dollars worth of antiretroviral drugs to other developing countries (cf. Riera 2003).

56. See Allen 2007; Cabezas 1998, 2004, 2009; Fusco 1998.

57. See Lugones Botell, Yamilé, and Riverón 1995, 114.

58. "Adolescence" in this study is defined as the following: early adolescence (ten to fifteen years of age) and middle to late adolescence (fifteen to nineteen years of age).

59. Other forms of contraception, for example, birth control pills and intrauterine devices, are widely available in Cuba at very low cost. The rate of induced abortion, which was legalized in Cuba in 1969, decreased from 70.0 per 100 deliveries in 1992

to 59.4 in 1996 (PAHO 2001). Cuban health officials have noted that the latter number is still relatively high (cf. Peláez Mendoza, Rodríguez Izquierdo, Lammers, and Blum 1999). Currently, there are health promotion campaigns to reduce the number of induced abortions.

60. See Cortés Alfaro, Garcia Roche, Gutiérrez, Fuentes Abreu, and Pérez Sosa 2000, 253–60.

61. See, for example, Fernández 2000 and M. Pérez-Stable 1998.

62. The problem of *la doble moral* is best summarized in comments made in 1993 by Raúl Castro, then-minister of the FAR: "We all know we don't say anything in meetings, but we talk a lot in the hallways," in reference to the duplicity prevalent in PCC meetings (cited in M. Pérez-Stable 1998, 28).

63. On 10 October 1961 the Castro government formed the CDRs as community-based surveillance units to work "side by side with the army, the militia, and the police" to carry out "denunciations, arrests, and imprisonment" of so-called counterrevolutionaries (Colomer 2000, 122). In the 1960s and 1970s the CDRs, which were quickly labeled models of social control by outside observers, lived up to their reputation by carrying out twenty-four-hour community patrols, holding neighborhood courts headed by elected community members to denounce people, and monitoring in detail the comings and goings of vehicles, people, and packages within their defined territories.

64. This is not to suggest, however, that *jineterismo* is widely acceptable in the general population. Rather, many individuals who date foreigners (one or several) discuss these relationships in terms of love in order to avoid the stigma of calling them clients. Passing by any of the foreign embassies in Havana during business hours, one sees a long lineup of foreigners paired with their Cuban sweethearts. I stress that jineterismo is much more complex than a simple exchange of sex for money (see, for example, Brennan's 2004 work on transnational desire, agency, and commercial sex work in the Dominican Republic). Many of these men and women end up marrying the foreigners they date—the ultimate goal—and are able to travel freely in and out of the country, unlike the rest of the population. According to D. Fernández, jineterismo, in its most inclusive sense, refers to "any activity outside of one's salaried employment that generates hard currency or the possibility of foreign travel" (2000a, 85). Soon, however, sexual relationships between tourists and Cuban men and women came to be seen as a predominant form of jineterismo.

65. Lupton 1997, 102.

66. I make this statement on the basis of my experiences in the several communities in which I lived and worked beginning in 1997. My opinion is supported by the work of Colomer (2000), who notes that empirical evidence shows decreasing levels of CDR membership, mobilization, and effectiveness. As various informants argued, in rural communities and several cities in other provinces revolutionary fervor is still high and, by extension, the role of the CDR retains much of its original force. See, for example, Rosendahl's (1997) ethnography of a small municipality in Santiago de Cuba.

6. TURISMO Y SALUD, S.A.

1. See Centeno and Font 1997; Eckstein 1994; Pérez-López 1994.

2. See Sullivan 2002.

3. Turismo y Salud was originally launched in the Soviet era but expanded rapidly in the mid-1990s with changes to the foreign investment laws.

4. An advertisement by the state-run travel agency Cubanacán in *Avances Médicos de Cuba* 2000 (VI), 20.

5. In 1995 the total value of Cuban biotechnology and pharmaceutical exports was two hundred million U.S. dollars (Pastor and Zimbalist 1995, 8). One of Cuba's prized discoveries, the meningitis-B vaccine, developed through genetic engineering and patented, has been exported to Brazil and Argentina. The vaccine has also been licensed to GlaxoSmithKline, which now markets it in Europe. A detailing of Cuba's budding biotechnology industry can be found in Feinsilver 1989, 1992, 1993, 1994; Quezada 2006; Reid-Henry 2003, 2010; and Cuba's biotechnology magazine, *Avances Médicos de Cuba*.

6. Act 77 reformulated earlier legislation on foreign investment, Decree-Law 50 of 15 February 1982 (Law 50). This original law authorized the formation of economic associations between foreign investors and state-owned enterprises. Despite the formalization of this law, there were a number of restrictions on investment (e.g., the inability for foreign investors to own property) that resulted in very few foreign investors in the country.

7. Alarcón de Quesada 1995, 1.

8. Ibid.

9. Ibid., 2.

10. Ibid.

11. See Díaz-Briquets and Pérez-López 2006, 147–56.

12. Pastor and Zimbalist 1995, 233. Interestingly, Act No. 77 reverses a hallmark of the revolution, the transformation of the Cuban economy from one of entrepreneurial capitalism to a centrally planned system. This transformation included land reforms, under the Agrarian Reform Law adopted on 17 May 1959 and the nationalization and socialization of private property. See note 18 of chapter 3 for more detailed description of these reforms.

13. Tourism constituted revenues close to 1.9 billion U.S. dollars in 1999, and by 2008 had an estimated value of 2.7 billion U.S. dollars (MINTUR 2008).

14. See Rojas Ochoa and López Pardo 1996.

15. See http://www.aduana.co.cu/, accessed on 25 October 2010.

16. See, for example, CIMTI Financial Services Ltd.; "Medicines to Cuba," http://www.medicines2cuba.com, accessed on 1 March 2003.

17. MINSAP 1996.

18. For individual Cubans who leave the country for official purposes, for example, as physicians, professors, athletes, students, and so forth, the failure to return after the completion of that trip is seen by the government as a form of betrayal. Normally, severe sanctions are imposed against such individuals, such as denying

reentry to the country for a set period of time or denying family members still in Cuba exit permits to visit their families abroad.

19. Sharma and Gupta 2006.

20. See, for example, Gordy's (2006) examination of the rise of consumer capitalism in Cuba's dollar economy.

21. See Hernández-Reguant's (2000) article "Socialism with Commercials: Consuming Advertising in Today's Cuba."

22. Sunder Rajan 2006, 80.

23. Ong 2006, 19.

24. Yurchak 2002.

7. MY DOCTOR KEEPS THE LIGHTS ON

1. See the works of Huish and Kirk 2007; Kirk and Erisman 2009.

2. The embassy regularly features the empirical results of such efforts; for example, from the inception of the medical internationalism program, medical attention has been provided to more than 4,666,913 persons, including more than 42,611 surgical operations. They have also assisted at 22,655 births and provided vaccinations to 142,975 people, against 10 kinds of illness. See http://embacu.cubaminrex.cu, accessed October 2010.

3. Feinsilver 2008.

4. See Mauss's (1990) anthropological discussion of the role of the gift in establishing reciprocal exchanges; see also Andaya 2009 on the "gift of health" in Cuba's post-Soviet medical sector.

5. See Huish 2008, 553.

6. Ibid.

7. Http://www.saludthefilm.net/ns/synopsis.html, accessed 1 June 2009.

8. According to Huish (2008, 553), "as of February 2008, a total of 9,264 students from 24 countries were studying at ELAM. . . . In addition, students from as many as 29 countries have come to ELAM." By 2007 ELAM had produced over four thousand graduates (Huish 2009). More recently, scholarships have been extended to include minorities from the United States, whom the Cuban government contends are victims of systematic discrimination.

9. See, for example, Gordon 2001; Huish and Kirk 2007; Huish 2008, 2009.

10. See, for example, Fox 1995; Nguyen 2009, 2010; Pandolfi 2003, 2007; Peterson 2012; Redfield 2005, 2006.

11. See the works of Eckstein 1994; Feinsilver 1993.

12. See Feinsilver's (2008) argument on this.

13. The first agreement, known as the "Convenio Integral de Cooperación entre la República de Cuba y la República Bolivariana de Venezuela" (Integral cooperation accord), was signed on 30 October 2000. In April 2005 Castro and Chávez signed the Regional Integration Project to expand, build, and collaborate on various joint projects, including the MBA program.

14. According to statistics cited by Briggs and Mantini-Briggs 2009, 550.

15. Feinsilver 2008, 73.

16. Ibid., 85.

17. See Redfield's work on Médecins Sans Frontières (2005, 2006).

18. Data collected from Cuba's Office of National Statistics has reported a 22 percent increase in the number of emergency visits to *policlínicos* between 2004 and 2006. An analysis of these figures can be found in Pérez and Haddad (2008).

19. In August 2007 U.S. officials announced the Cuban Medical Professional Parole program that allows Cuban medical personnel, identified by the Department of Homeland Security as doctors, physical therapists, laboratory technicians, nurses, sports trainers, and others, to apply for entry to the United States at U.S. embassies in the countries where they serve. In essence, they were opening the door for Cuban personnel on missions to defect to the United States. Cuba's generous incentives to return to the island could be a response to this policy.

CONCLUSION

1. This work contributes to a burgeoning field of research on health, the body, and the changing practice of science and medicine in socialist and postsocialist contexts; among others, several notable studies are Andaya 2009; Chen 2003; Farquhar 1994, 2002; Gibbon 2009; Greenhalgh 2008; Greenhalgh and Winkler 2005; Hyde 2007; Kohrman 2005; Ninetto 2005; Petryna 2002; Raikhel 2010; Rivkin-Fish 2005; and Song 2010.

2. Gordon 1991, 6.

3. Van-Dijk 1994, 431.

4. For several examples, see Burchell, Gordon, and Miller 1991; Faubion 2001; Lock and Kaufert 1998.

5. Foucault's lack of attentiveness, or short-sightedness, in identifying the important relationship between metropolis and colonies or different regimes of governance begs the question of whether a Foucauldian framework is at all applicable or even relevant to the study of resistance, authority relations, and power outside the modern state in Europe or in colonial and postcolonial contexts. See, for example, the works Anderson 2006a; Clarke 2009; Gupta 1999; Mitchell 1991b; Mudimbe 1988; Spivak 1985; Stoler 1995; Thomas 1995; and Vaughan 1994. These scholars call for the refining of the Foucauldian framework in diverse sociopolitical fields.

6. Foucault (1991) refers to the "étatization of society" as the process through which the state slowly encroaches into more and more areas of everyday life. This is evident from Katherine Verdery's application of "étatization" as the regulation and control of time in European socialism.

7. I thank Amy Ninetto for pushing me to stress this comparison.

8. Dean 2001, 53.

9. Evans 1993, 1; for a critical discussion on subject formation, see also the works of Butler 1997; Foucault 2008; and Rabinow and Dreyfus 1982.

10. Comaroff's (1985) analysis of colonialism and consciousness, especially with reference to the powerful ways in which the material and symbolic are incorporated

into practice, is insightful for examining how ideology becomes inscribed in people's taken-for-granted assumptions of the world.

11. Among others, see the following work in postsocialist studies: Verdery 1991, 1996; Hann, Humphrey, and Verdery 2001; Hann 2002; Burawoy and Verdery 1999; Davydova and Franks 2006; Humphrey and Mandel 2002; Rogers 2006; Stan 2005.

12. The term is used by Yurchak 1997 and Zhang 2001.

13. See Polayni's (1944) theory of substantivism.

14. I have paraphrased the story, only integrating a small number of direct quotes, to provide a more detailed context for this discussion. See Menéndez for the complete version (2001, 27–28).

Abu-Lughod, Lila. 1990. "The Romance of Resistance: Tracing Transformations of Power through Bedouin Women." *American Ethnologist* 17: 41–55.

ACIMED. 1998. "Los Ministros de salud pública." *Revista Cubana de Información en Ciencias de la Salud* 6: 206–20.

Ackerknecht Erwin H. 1953. *Rudolf Virchow: Doctor, Statesman, Anthropologist.* Madison: University of Wisconsin Press.

Adams, Vincanne. 1998. *Doctors for Democracy: Health Professionals in the Nepal Revolution.* Cambridge: Cambridge University Press.

Agamben, Giorgio. 2005. *State of Exception.* Chicago: University of Chicago Press.

Alarcón de Quesada, Ricardo. 1995. "Cuba: Law Number (77) Foreign Investment Act." *Official Gazette*, Special Issue 3. Havana.

Allen, Jafari. 2007. "Means of Desire's Production: Male Sex Labor in Cuba." *Identities: Global Studies in Culture and Power* 14(1): 183–202.

Álvarez, Alvin. 2001. "La doble moneda." *Tribuna de La Habana*, March 20: 3.

American Association for World Health (AAWH). 1997. *Denial of Food and Medicine: The Impact of the U.S. Embargo on the Health and Nutrition in Cuba—An Executive Summary.* Washington.

Anagnost, Ann. 1995. "A Surfeit of Bodies: Population and the Rationality of the State in Post-Mao China." *Conceiving the New World Order: The Global Politics of Reproduction*, ed. Faye D. Ginsburg and Rayna Rapp, 22–41. Berkeley: University of California Press.

Andaya, Elise. 2007. "Reproducing the Revolution: Gender, Kinship, and the State in Contemporary Cuba." Ph.D. diss., New York University.

——. 2009. "The Gift of Health: Socialist Medical Practice and Shifting Material and Moral Economies in Post-Soviet Cuba." *Medical Anthropology Quarterly* 23(4): 375–74.

Anderson, Jon Lee. 1997. *Che Guevara: A Revolutionary Life.* New York: Grove Press.

Anderson, Warwick. 2006a. *The Cultivation of Whiteness: Science, Health, and Racial Destiny in Australia.* Durham: Duke University Press.

——. 2006b. *Colonial Pathologies: American Tropical Medicine, Race, and Hygiene in the Philippines.* Durham: Duke University Press.

Appadurai, Arjun. 1991. "Global Ethnoscapes: Notes and Queries for a Transnational Anthropology." *Recapturing Anthropology: Working in the Present,* ed. Richard Fox, 191–210. Santa Fe: School of American Research Press.

——. 1997. *Modernity at Large: Cultural Dimensions of Globalization.* Minneapolis: University of Minnesota Press.

——. 1988. *The Social Life of Things: Commodities in Cultural Perspective.* Cambridge: Cambridge University Press.

Appiah, Kwame A. 1996. "Is the Post in Postmodernism the Same as Post in Postcolonialism?" *Contemporary Postcolonial Theory: A Reader,* ed. Padmini Mongia, 55–71. New York: Arnold.

Armstrong, David. 1983. *Political Anatomy of the Body: Medical Knowledge in Britain in the Twentieth Century.* Cambridge: Cambridge University Press.

Arnold, David. 1988. *Imperial Medicine and Indigenous Societies.* Manchester: Manchester University Press.

——. 1992. *Colonizing the Body: State Medicine and Epidemic Disease in Nineteenth Century India.* Berkeley: University of California Press.

Aronowitz, Robert A. 1998. *Making Sense of Illness: Science, Society and Disease.* Cambridge: Cambridge University Press.

Aretxaga, Begoña. 2003. "Maddening States." *Annual Review of Anthropology* 32: 393–410.

Ashcroft, Bill, Gareth Griffiths, and Helen Tiffin. 1989. *The Empire Writes Back: Theory and Practice in Post-Colonial Literature.* London: Routledge.

——. 1995. *The Post-Colonial Studies Reader.* London: Routledge.

——. 1998. *Key Concepts in Post-Colonial Studies.* London: Routledge.

Augé, Marc, and Claudine Herzlich. 1983. *Le sens du mal: Anthropologie, histoire, sociologie de la maladie.* Paris: Editions des archives contemporaines.

Avances Médicos de Cuba. 1999. 6(20).

——. 2000. 7(23).

——. 2001. 7(26).

Barberia, Lorena, and Arachu Castro, eds. 2003. "Seminar on the Cuban Health System: Its Evolution, Accomplishments and Challenges." Working Papers on Latin America, 02/03–4. Cambridge: David Rockefeller Center for Latin American Studies at Harvard University.

Barnet, Miguel. 1980. "The Culture that Sugar Created." *Latin American Literary Review* 8: 38–46.

——. 1995. "Rethinking the Revolution: Nine Testimonies from Cuba." NACLA *Report on the Americas—Cuba, Adapting to a Post-Soviet World* 29: 30.

——. 1997. "La Regla de Ocha: The Religious System of Santería." *Sacred Possessions: Vodou, Santería, Obeah, and the Caribbean,* ed. Margarite Fernández Olmos and Lizabeth Paravisini-Gebert, 70–100. New Brunswick: Rutgers University Press.

Batista Moliner, Ricardo, Luis Salabarría, and Lázara Díaz González. 1998. "Sistema de vigilancia de salud a nivel de la atención primaria." *Revista Cubana de Medicina General Integral* 12: 1–11.

Behar, Ruth, ed. 1995. *Puentes a Cuba/Bridges to Cuba: Cuban and Cuban American Artists, Writers and Scholars Explore Identity, Nationality and Homeland.* Ann Arbor: University of Michigan Press.

Beinfield, Harriet. 2001. "Dreaming with Two Feet on the Ground: Acupuncture in Cuba." *Clinical Acupuncture and Oriental Medicine* 2: 66–69.

Bendix, John, Bertell Ollman, Bartholomew H. Sparrow, and Timothy P. Mitchell. 1992. "Going Beyond the State?" *American Political Science Review* 86: 1007–21.

Bengelsdorf, Carollee. 1994. *The Problem of Democracy in Cuba: Between Vision and Reality.* Oxford: Oxford University Press.

Benjamin, Medea, Joseph Collins, and Michael Scott. 1984. *No Free Lunch: Food and Revolution in Cuba Today.* San Francisco: Institute for Food and Development Policy.

Bhabha, Homi. 1984. "Of Mimicry and Man: The Ambivalence of Colonial Discourse." *October* 28 (Spring): 125–33.

——, ed. 1994. *Nation and Narration.* London: Routledge.

Biehl, João, Byron Good, and Arthur Kleinman, eds. 2007. *Subjectivity: Ethnographic Investigations.* Berkeley: University of California Press.

Blackburn, Robin. 1963. "Prologue to the Cuban Revolution." *New Left Review* 21(October): 59–60.

Boddy, Janice. 1989. *Wombs and Alien Spirits: Women, Men, and the Zar Cult in Northern Sudan.* Madison: University of Wisconsin Press.

Bourdieu, Pierre. 1977. *Outline of a Theory of Practice.* Cambridge: Cambridge University Press.

——. 1990. *The Logic of Practice.* Cambridge: Polity Press.

Brandon, George. 1993. *Santería from Africa to the New World.* Bloomington: Indiana University Press.

Bravo, Ernesto Mario. 1998. *Development within Underdevelopment? New Trends in Cuban Medicine.* Havana: Editorial José Martí.

Brennan, Denise. 2004. *What's Love Got to Do With It? Transnational Desires and Sex Tourism in the Dominican Republic.* Durham: Duke University Press.

Brenner, Philip, and Peter Kornbluh. 1995. "Clinton's Cuba Calculus." NACLA *Report on the Americas—Cuba, Adapting to a Post-Soviet World* 29: 33–39.

Briggs, Charles, and Clara Mantini-Briggs. 2009. "Confronting Health Disparities: Latin American Social Medicine in Venezuela." *American Journal of Public Health* 99(3): 549–55.

Brotherton, P. Sean. 2008. "We have to think like capitalists but continue being socialists": Medicalized Subjectivities, Emergent Capital, and Socialist Entrepreneurs in Post-Soviet Cuba. *American Ethnologist* 35(2): 259–74.

Buckley Green, Linda. 1989. "Consensus and Coercion: Primary Health Care and the Guatemalan State." *Medical Anthropology Quarterly* 3: 246–57.

Burawoy, Michael, and Katherine Verdery, eds. 1999. *Uncertain Transition: Eth-*

nographies of Change in the Postsocialist World. Lanham, Md.: Rowman and Littlefield.

Burchell, Graham, Colin Gordon, and Peter Miller, eds. 1991. *The Foucault Effect: Studies in Governmentality.* Chicago: University of Chicago Press.

Burns, Nicholas. 1997. *The U.S. Embargo and Health Care in Cuba: Myth Versus Reality.* U.S. Department of State.

Butler, Judith. 1997. *The Psychic Life of Power: Theories in Subjection.* Stanford: Stanford University Press.

Cabezas, Amalia L. 1998. "Discourses of Prostitution: The Case of Cuba." *Global Sex Workers: Rights, Resistance, and Redefinition,* ed. Kamala Kempadoo and Jo Doezema, 79–86. New York: Routledge.

———. 2004. "Between Love and Money: Sex, Tourism, and Citizenship in Cuba and the Dominican Republic." *Journal of Women in Culture and Society* 29(4): 247–74.

———. 2009. *Economies of Desire: Sex and Tourism in Cuba and the Dominican Republic.* Philadelphia: Temple University Press.

Cabrera, Eddie. 1999. *At the Crossroads: Faith in Cuba* (documentary film). Edited by Anton Wagner. New York: Filmmakers Library.

Calderón Rodríguez, Mirta. 1995. "Life in the Special Period." *NACLA Report on the Americas—Cuba, Adapting to a Post-Soviet World* 29: 18–19.

Campbell, Colin. 2001. "The Changing Face of Inner-City Havana." *IDRC Reports: News from the Developing World.* Ottawa: International Development Research Centre (IDRC).

Campo, José, Antonio López Espinosa, and Soledad Díaz del Campo. 1995. "Los médicos de la familia y los recursos informativos." *Revista Cubana de Medicina General Integral* 11: 134–38.

Canedy, Dana. 2003. "Cuban Exiles Finding Spirit of Reconciliation." *New York Times,* March 23, A20. New York.

Canizares, Raul. 1992. *Walking with the Night: The Afro-Cuban World of Santería.* Rochester: Destiny Books.

Cardelle, Alberto J. F. 1994. "The Preeminence of Primary Care within Cuban Predoctoral Medical Education." *International Journal of Health Services: Planning, Administration, Evaluation* 24(3): 421–29.

Castel, Robert. 1991. "From Dangerousness to Risk." *The Foucault Effect: Studies in Governmentality,* ed. Graham Burchell and Colin Gordon, Peter Miller, 281–98. Chicago: University of Chicago Press.

Castillo Bueno, María de los Reyes. 2000. *Reyita: The Life of a Black Cuban Woman in the Twentieth Century.* Durham: Duke University Press.

Castro Ruz, Fidel. 1969a. "The Duty of a Revolutionary Is to Make Revolution: The Second Declaration of Havana." *Fidel Castro Speaks,* ed. Martin Kenner and James Petras, 85–106. New York: Grove Press.

———. 1969b. "We Will Never Build a Communist Conscience with a Dollar Sign in the Minds and Hearts of Men." *Fidel Castro Speaks,* ed. Martin Kenner and James Petras, 199–213. New York: Grove Press.

——. 1983. *La Historia Me Absolverá*. Havana: Editorial de Ciencias Sociales, Ediciones Políticas.

——. 1998. *Fidel: My Early Years*. New York: Ocean Press.

——. 2002. "The Effort to Achieve Excellence in Our Health. Speech commemorating the 40th anniversary of the Victoria de Girón Institute of Basic Medical Sciences, on October 17, 2002." *Granma Internacional Digital*, 1–16.

Centeno, Miguel Angel, and Mauricio Font, eds. 1997. *Toward a New Cuba? Legacies of a Revolution*. Boulder: Lynn Rienner.

Chalgub Moreno, Ana María, Oria Susana Acosta Cabrera, Enrique A. Abraham Marcel, and Luisa Paz Sendin. 1999. "Municipios por la salud: Proyecto provincial de la Ciudad de la Habana." *Revista Cubana de Medicina General Integral* 15: 334–41.

Chambers, Lain, and Lidia Curti. 1996. *The Post-Colonial Question: Common Skies, Divided Horizons*. New York: Routledge.

Chen, Nancy. 2003. *Breathing Spaces: Qigong, Psychiatry, and Healing in China*. New York: Columbia University Press.

Chestnut, Mark. 1991. "Cuban AIDS Centres Prompt Accusations." *The Advocate* (September 10): 8.

Chomsky, Aviva. 2000. " 'The Threat of a Good Example': Health and Revolution in Cuba." *Dying for Growth: Global Inequality and the Health of the Poor*, ed. Jim Yong Kim, Joyce V. Millen, Alec Irwin, and John Gershman, 331–57. Monroe, Me.: Common Courage Press.

Chomsky, Noam. 2000. "Cuba and the U.S. Government: David vs. Goliath." *Rogue States: The Rule of Force in World Affairs*, 82–92. Cambridge, Mass.: South End Press.

Clarke, Kamari. 2009. *Fictions of Justice: The International Criminal Court and the Challenge of Legal Pluralism in Sub-Saharan Africa*. Cambridge: Cambridge University Press.

Cockerham, William C. 1999. *Health and Social Change in Russia and Eastern Europe*. New York: Routledge.

Cohn, Bernard S. 1998. *Colonialism and Its Forms of Knowledge: The British in India*. Princeton: Princeton University Press.

Colomer, Josep M. 2000. "Watching Neighbours: The Cuban Model of Social Control." *Cuban Studies* 31: 118–38.

Comaroff, Jean. 1982. "Medicine: Symbol and Ideology." *The Problem of Medical Knowledge*, ed. Peter Wright and Andrew Treacher, 49–68. Edinburgh: Edinburgh University Press.

——. 1985. *Body of Power, Spirit of Resistance: The Culture and History of a South African People*. Chicago: University of Chicago Press.

——. 1993. "The Diseased Heart of Africa: Medicine, Colonialism, and the Body." *Knowledge, Power, and Practice: The Anthropology of Medicine in Everyday Life*, ed. Shirely Lindenbaum and Margaret Lock, 305–29. Berkeley: University of California Press.

Comaroff, Jean, and John Comaroff. 1991. *Of Revelation and Revolution: Chris-*

tianity, Colonialism, and Consciousness in South Africa. Chicago: University of Chicago Press.

———. 1992. *Ethnography and the Historical Imagination.* Boulder: Westview.

———. 2001. "Millennial Capitalism: First Thoughts on a Second Coming." *Millennial Capitalism and the Culture of Neoliberalism,* ed. Jean Comaroff and John Comaroff, 1–55. Chicago: University of Chicago Press.

Constantín, Elio E. 1981. *Granma Weekly Review.* August 9: 1.

Cooper, Frederick, and Ann Laura Stoler. 1997. *Tensions of Empire: Colonial Cultures in a Bourgeois World.* Berkeley: University of California Press.

Coronil, Fernando. 1995. "Introduction." *Cuban Counterpoint: Tobacco and Sugar.* Durham: Duke University Press.

———. 1997. *The Magical State: Nature, Money, and Modernity in Venezuela.* Chicago: University of Chicago Press.

Cortés Alfaro, Alba, René García Roche, Pedro Monterrey Gutiérrez, Jorge Fuentes Abreu, and Dania Pérez Sosa. 2000. "SIDA, adolescencia y riesgos." *Revista Cubana de Medicina General Integral* 16: 253–60.

Cortiñas, Jorge. 1993. "Laws that Say So: A Dialogue with Residents of Cuba's AIDS Sanitorium." *Socialist Review* 23(1): 107–34.

Crabb, Mary Katherine. 2001. "Socialism, Health and Medicine in Cuba: A Critical Re-appraisal." Ph.D. diss., Emory University.

Cuba Review. 1978. "A Promise Kept, Health Care in Cuba." 3(1).

Dalton, Thomas C. 1993. *Everything within the Revolution.* Boulder: Westview.

Danielson, Roswell S. 1979. *Cuban Medicine.* New Brunswick, N.J.: Transaction.

———. 1981. "Medicine in the Community: The Ideology and Substance of Community Medicine in Socialist Cuba." *Social Science and Medicine* 15C: 239–47.

Das, Veena, and Deborah Poole, eds. 2004. *Anthropology in the Margins of the State.* Santa Fe: School of American Research Press.

Davydova Irina, and J. R. Franks. 2006. "Responses to Agrarian Reforms in Russia: Evidence from Novosibirsk Oblast." *Journal of Rural Studies* 22: 39–54.

Dean, Mitchell. 1997. "Sociology after Society." *Sociology after Postmodernism,* ed. David Owen. London: Sage.

———. 1999. "Risk, Calculable and Incalculable." *Risk and Sociocultural Theory: New Directions and Perspective,* ed. Deborah Lupton, 131–59. Cambridge: Cambridge University Press.

———. 2001. " 'Demonic Societies': Liberalism, Biopolitics, and Sovereignty." *States of Imagination: Ethnographic Explorations of the Postcolonial State, Politics, History, and Culture,* ed. Thomas Blom Hansen and Finn Stepputat, 41–64. Durham: Duke University Press.

de Certeau, Michel. 1988. *The Practice of Everyday Life.* Berkeley: University of California Press.

de La Fuente, Alejandro. 2001. *A Nation for All: Race, Inequality, and Politics in Twentieth-Century Cuba.* Chapel Hill: University of North Carolina Press.

de La Fuente, Alejandro, and Laurence Glasco. 1997. "Are Blacks 'Getting Out of

Control?' " Racial Attitudes, Revolution and Political Transition in Cuba." *Toward a New Cuba? Legacies of a Revolution*, ed. Miguel Angel Centeno and Mauricio Font, 53–71. Boulder: Lynne Rienner.

Delgado García, Gregorio. 1996a. "Etapas del desarollo de la salud pública revolucionaria cubana." *Revista Cubana de Salud Pública* 22 (1). http://bvs.sld.cu/re vistas/spu/ (accessed 5 July 2011).

——. 1996b. "La salud pública en Cuba en el período de la república burguesa." *Cuaderno de Historia* 81. http://bvs.sld.cu/revistas/his/ (accessed 5 July 2011).

——. 1996c. "La salud pública en Cuba en el período revolucionario socialista." *Cuaderno de Historia* 82. http://bvs.sld.cu/revistas/his/ (accessed 5 July 2011).

DelVecchio Good, Mary-Jo. 2007. "The Medical Imaginary and the Biotechnical Embrace." *Subjectivity*, ed. Joäl Biehl and Arthur Kleinman, 362–80. Berkeley: University of California Press.

Departamento de Estadístico, República de Cuba. 2001. *El Anuario Estadístico de Cuba.*

——. 2007. *El Anuario Estadístico de Cuba.*

Díaz-Briquets, Sergio. 1983. *The Health Revolution in Cuba.* Austin: University of Texas Press.

Díaz-Briquets, Sergio, and Jorge Pérez-López. 1997. "Refugee Remittances: Conceptual Issues from the Cuban and Nicaraguan Experiences." *International Migration Review* 31: 411–37.

——. 2006. *Corruption in Cuba: Castro and Beyond.* Austin: University of Texas Press.

Díaz Cerveto, Ana Margarita, Ofelia Pérez Cruz, and Minerva Rodriguez Delgado. 1994. "Religious Beliefs in Today's Cuban Society: Basic Characteristics According to the Level of Elaboration of the Concept of the Supernatural." *Social Compass* 41: 225–40.

Díaz Novas, José. 1989. "La familia como unidad de atención." *Revista Cubana de Medicina General Integral* 5: 231–34.

Díaz Novas, José, and José A. Fernández Sacasas. 1989. "Del policlínico integral al Médico de la Familia." *Revista Cubana de Medicina General Integral* 5: 556–64.

DiGiacomo, Susan M. 1999. "Can There Be a 'Cultural Epidemiology?' " *Medical Anthropology Quarterly* 13: 436–57.

Dilla, Haroldo. 1999. "The Virtues and Misfortunes of Civil Society." NACLA *Report on the Americas—Inside Cuba* 32: 30–36.

——. 2001. "Local Government and Economic and Social Change in Cuba." FOCAL: *Canadian Foundation for the Americas* (May): 1–7.

Dirks, Nicholas B. 1991. *Colonialism and Culture.* Michigan: University of Michigan Press.

Dirlik, Arif. 1994. "The Postcolonial Aura: Third World Criticism in the Age of Global Capitalism." *Critical Inquiry* 20: 356–82.

Doyon, Sabrina and Pierre Sean Brotherton, eds. 2008. "Mondes socialistes et (post)socialistes." Special issue of *Anthropologie et sociétés*, 32 (2–1).

Dreyfus, Hubert, and Paul Rabinow. 1982. *Michel Foucault: Beyond Structuralism and Hermeneutics.* Chicago: University of Chicago Press.

Duany, Jorge. 2000. "Reconstructing Cubanness: Changing Discourses of National Identity on the Island and in the Diaspora during the Twentieth Century." *Cuba, the Elusive Nation: Interpretations of National Identity,* ed. Damian J. Fernández and Madeline Cámara Betancourt. Gainesville: University Press of Florida.

Dunning, Thad. 2001. "Structural Reform and Medical Commerce: The Political Economy of Cuban Health Care in the Special Period." Paper presented at the Latin American Studies Association Conference, Washington.

Eckstein, Susan Eva. 1994. *Back from the Future: Cuba under Castro.* Princeton: Princeton University Press.

———. 1997. "Limits of Socialism in a Capitalist World Economy: Cuba since the Collapse of the Soviet Bloc." *Toward a New Cuba? Legacies of a Revolution,* ed. M. Angel Cenento and Mauricio Font. Boulder: Lynne Rienner.

———. 2009. *The Immigrant Divide: How Cuban Americans Changed the U.S. and Their Homeland.* New York: Routledge.

Economist Intelligence Unit (E.I.U.). 1999. *Cuba: A Country Profile.*

Eisen, George. 1996. "La atención primaria en Cuba: El equipo del médico de la familia y el policlínico." *Revista Cubana de Salud Pública* 2: 345–50.

Elias, Norbert. 2000. *The Civilizing Process: Sociogenetic and Psychogenetic Investigations.* Malden, Mass.: Blackwell Publishing.

Elyachar, Julia. 2005. *Markets of Dispossession: NGOs, Economic Development, and the State in Cairo.* Durham: Duke University Press.

Escobar, Arturo. 1995. *Encountering Development: The Making and Unmaking of the Third World.* Princeton: Princeton University Press.

Estrada, Isidro. 1999. "¿De qué color es el cubano?" *prismA* 29: 19–24.

Evans, David T. 1993. *Sexual Citizenship: The Material Construction of Sexualities.* London: Routledge.

Ewald, Francois. 1991. "Insurance and Risk." *The Foucault Effect: Studies in Governmentality,* ed. Graham Burchell, Colin Gordon, and Peter Miller, 197–10. Chicago: University of Chicago Press.

Fabian, Johannes. 1983. *Times and the Other: How Anthropology Makes Its Object.* New York: Columbia University Press.

Fagen, Richard. 1969. *The Transformation of Political Culture in Cuba.* Stanford: Stanford University Press.

Fanon, Franz. 1959. *The Wretched of the Earth.* New York: Grove Press.

Farmer, Paul, and Arachu Castro. 2004. "Pearls of the Antilles? Public Health in Haiti and Cuba." *Unhealthy Health Policy: A Critical Anthropological Examination,* ed. Arachu Castro and Merrill Singer, 3–28. Walnut Creek, Calif.: Altamira Press.

Farquhar, Judith. 1994. *Knowing Practice: Clinical Encounter of Chinese Medicine.* Boulder: Westview.

———. 2002. *Appetites: Food and Sex in Post-Socialist China.* Durham: Duke University Press.

Farquhar, Judith, and Margaret Lock. 2007. "Introduction." *Beyond the Body Proper: Reading the Anthropology of Material Life,* ed. Judith Farquhar and Margaret Lock, 1–16. Durham: Duke University Press.

Fassin, Didier. 2007. *When Bodies Remember: Experiences and Politics of AIDS in South Africa.* Berkeley: University of California Press.

Faubion, James, ed. 2001. *Power: Essential Works of Foucault, 1954–1984.* Volume 3. New York: New Press.

Feinsilver, Julie M. 1989. "Cuba as a 'World Medical Power:' The Politics of Symbolism." *Latin American Research Review* 24: 1–34.

———. 1992. "Will Cuba's Wonder Drugs Lead to Political and Economic Wonder? Capitalizing on Biotechnology and Medical Exports." *Cuban Studies* 22: 79–111.

———. 1993. *Healing the Masses: Cuban Health Politics at Home and Abroad.* Berkeley: University of California Press.

———. 1994. "Cuban Biotechnology: A First World Approach to Development." *Cuba at a Crossroads,* ed. Jorge F. Pérez-López, 167–89. Florida: University Press of Florida.

———. 2008. "Oil for Doctors: Cuban Medical Diplomacy Gets a Little Help from a Venezuelan Friend." *Nueva Sociedad* 216 (July–August). http://www.nuso.org (accessed 12 July 2011).

Ferguson, James. 2006. *Global Shadows: Africa in the Neoliberal World Order.* Durham: Duke University Press.

Fernández, Damián J. 1998. "(Desperately) Seeking Civil Society in Cuba." *Cuba Today: The Events Taking Place in Cuba and the Ensuing Issues for Canadian Policy (FOCAL),* 30–32. Ottawa, Canada.

———. 2000a. *Cuba and the Politics of Passion.* Austin: University of Texas Press.

———. 2000b. "Cuba and *lo Cubano,* or the Story of Desire and Disenchantment." *Cuba, the Elusive Nation: Interpretations of National Identity,* ed. Damián J. Fernández and Madeline Cámara Betancourt, 79–99. Gainesville: University Press of Florida.

Fernández, Damián J., and Madeline Cámara Betancourt, eds. 2000. *Cuba, the Elusive Nation: Interpretations of National Identity.* Gainesville: University Press of Florida.

Fernández, Nadine. 2001. "The Changing Discourse of Race in Contemporary Cuba." *Qualitative Studies in Education* 14: 117–32.

———. 2010. *Revolutionizing Romance: Interracial Couples in Contemporary Cuba.* New Brunswick: Rutgers University Press.

Fernández Sacasas, José, and Julio López Benítez. 1976. "El profesor en la comunidad." *Revista Cubana de Administración de Salud* 2(1).

Ferzacca, Steve. 2002. "Governing Bodies in New Order Indonesia." *New Horizons in Medical Anthropology: Essays in Honour of Charles Leslie,* ed. Mark Nichter and Margaret Lock, 35–57. New York: Routledge.

Field, Mark G. 1995. "The Health Crisis in the Former Soviet Union: A Report from the 'Post-war' Zone." *Social Science and Medicine* 41(11): 1469–78.

Field, Mark G., David M. Kotz, and Genee Bukhman. 2001. "Neoliberal Economic Policy, 'State Desertion,' and the Russian Health Crisis." *Dying for Growth: Global Inequality and the Health of the Poor*, ed. Jim Yong Kim, Joyce V. Millen, Alec Irwin, and John Gershman, 155–73. Monroe, Maine: Common Courage Press.

Fisher, Melissa, and Greg Downey, eds. 2006. *Frontiers of Capital: Ethnographic Reflections on the New Economy*. Durham: Duke University Press.

Fisher, William F. 1997. "Doing Good? The Politics and Antipolitics of NGO Practices." *Annual Review of Anthropology* 26: 439–64.

Foucault, Michel. 1980. "The Politics of Health in the Eighteenth Century." *Power/ Knowledge: Selected Interviews and Other Writings*, ed. Colin Gordon, 166–82. Brighton: Harvester Press.

——. 1983. "The Subject and Power." *Michel Foucault: Beyond Structuralism and Hermeneutics*, ed. Hubert L. Dreyfus and Paul Rabinow, 208–28. Chicago: University of Chicago Press.

——. 1988. *The Care of the Self: The History of Sexuality*. Volume 3. New York: Vintage Books.

——. 1990a. *The History of Sexuality: An Introduction*. Volume 1. New York: Vintage Books.

——. 1990b. *The Use of Pleasure: The History of Sexuality*. Volume 2. New York: Vintage Books.

——. 1991. "Governmentality." *The Governmentality Effect: Studies in Governmentality*, ed. Graham Burchell, Colin Gordon, and Peter Miller, 87–104. Chicago: University of Chicago Press.

——. 1994. *The Birth of the Clinic: An Archaeology of Medical Perception*. New York: Vintage Books.

——. 1995. *Discipline and Punish: The Birth of the Prison*. New York: Vintage Books.

——. 2008. *The Birth of Biopolitics: Lectures at the Collège de France, 1978–1979*. New York: Palgrave Macmillan.

Fox, Renée. 1995. "Medical Humanitarianism and Human Rights: Reflections on Doctors without Borders and Doctors of the World." *Social Science Medicine* 41(12): 1607–16

Friedman, Sara L. 2005. "The Intimacy of State Power: Marriage, Liberation, and Socialist Subjects in Southeastern China." *American Ethnologist* 32(2): 312–27.

Fusco, Coco. 1998. "Hustling for Dollars: *Jineterismo* in Cuba." *Global Sex Workers: Rights, Resistance, and Redefinition*, ed. Kamala Kempadoo and Jo Doezema, 151–60. New York: Routledge.

Gal, Susan, and Gail Kligman. 2000a. *The Politics of Gender after Socialism*. Princeton: Princeton University Press.

——. 2000b. *Reproducing Gender: Politics, Publics, and Everyday Life after Socialism*. Princeton: Princeton University Press.

García, Cristina. 1992. *Dreaming in Cuban*. New York: Columbia Press.

Garfield, R., F. Kirkpatrick, and R. M. Philen. 1995. "Epidemic Optic Neuropathy in Cuba—Clinical Characterization and Risk Factors." *New England Journal of Medicine* 333: 1176–82.

Garfield, Richard, and Sarah Santana. 1997. "The Impact of the Economic Crisis and the U.S. Embargo on Health in Cuba." *American Journal of Public Health* 87: 15–20.

Garth, Hannah. 1988. "Things Became Scarce: Food Availability and Accessibility in Santiago de Cuba Then and Now." NAPA *Bulletin* 32: 178–92.

Geertz, Clifford. 1973 [1966]. *The Interpretation of Cultures.* New York: Basic Books.

Geest, Sjaak van der, Susan R. Whyte, and Anita Hardon. 1996. "The Anthropology of Pharmaceuticals: A Biographical Approach." *Annual Review of Anthropology* 25: 153–78.

Gerassi, John, ed. 1968. *Venceremos: The Speeches and Writings of Che Guevara.* New York: Macmillan.

Gestaldo, Denise. 1997. "Is Health Education Good for You? Re-thinking Health Education Through the Concept of Bio-power." *Foucault, Health, and Medicine,* ed. Alan Peterson and Robin Bunton, 113–34. London: Routledge.

Gibbon, Sahra. 2009. "Genomics as Public Health? Community Genetics and the Challenge of Personalised Medicine in Cuba." *Anthropology and Medicine* 16(2): 131–46.

Gifford, Sandra M. 1986. "The Meaning of Lumps: A Case Study of the Ambiguities of Risk." *Anthropology and Epidemiology: Interdisciplinary Approaches to the Study of Health and Disease,* ed. Craig Janes, Ron Stall, and Sandra Gifford. Dordrecht: D. Reidel.

Gigerenzer, Gerd, and David J. Murray. 1987. "Introduction: Two Revolutions— Cognitive and Probabilistic." *Cognition as Intuitive Statistics,* ed. Gerd Gigerenzer and David J. Murray, 162–74. Hillsdale, N.J.: Lawrence Erlbaum.

Gilman, Sander. 1985. *Difference and Pathology: Stereotypes of Sexuality, Race, and Madness.* Ithaca: Cornell University Press.

Gilpin, Margaret. 1989. "Cuba on the Road to a Family Medicine Nation." *Family Medicine* 21: 405–71.

Gilpin, Margaret, and Helen Rodriguez-Trias. 1978. "Looking at Health in a Healthy Way." *Cuba Review* 7: 3–15.

Gilroy, Paul. 1993. *The Black Atlantic: Modernity and Double Consciousness.* New York: Verso Books.

Golden, Tim. 1995. "Health Care in Cuba." *Cuban Communism 1959–1995.* 8th ed. Ed. Irving Horowitz, 483–88. New Brunswick: Transaction.

González-Wippler, Migene. 1999. *Santería: Mis Experiencias en la Religión.* St. Paul, Minn.: Llewellyn Español.

Gordon, Antonio. 2001. "Cuba's Free Medical Education for U.S. Students." *The Lancet* 357: 1884–85

Gordon, Colin. 1991. "Governmental Rationality: An Introduction." *The Foucault Effect: Studies in Governmentality,* ed. Graham Burchell, Colin Gordon, and Peter Miller, 1–52. Chicago: University of Chicago Press.

Gordon, Deborah. 1998. "Tenacious assumptions in western biomedicine." *Biomedicine Reexamined,* ed. Margaret Lock and Deborah Gordon, 19–56. New York: Kluwer.

Gordon, Joy. 1997. "Cuba's Entrepreneurial Socialism." *Atlantic Monthly* 279(1): 18.

Gordy, Katherine. 2006. "Sales + Economy + Efficiency = Revolution? Dollarization, Consumer Capitalism, and Popular Responses in Special Period Cuba." *Public Culture* 18(2): 383–412.

Granma Weekly Review. 1985. "Supplement," 3. Havana.

———. 1986. "Fidel Speaks on the Family Doctor Program," 4. Havana.

———. 1991. "Foreign Investment in Cuba," 15. Havana.

Greenhalgh, Susan. 2005. "Globalization and Population Governance in China." *Global Assemblages: Technology, Politics, and Ethics as Anthropological Problems,* ed. Aihwa Ong and Stephen Collier, 354–72. Malden, Mass.: Blackwell Publishing.

———. 2008. *Just One Child: Science and Policy in Deng's China.* Berkeley: University of California Press.

Greenhalgh, Susan, and Edwin A. Winckler. 2005. *Governing China's Population: From Leninist to Neoliberal Biopolitics.* Stanford: Stanford University Press.

Guevara, Ernesto. 1967 [1965]. *Man and Socialism.* Havana: Guairas Book Institute.

———. 1968a. "On Revolutionary Medicine." *Venceremos: The Speeches and Writings of Che Guevara,* ed. John Gerassi. New York: Macmillan.

———. 1968b. "On Creating a New Attitude." *Venceremos: The Speeches and Writings of Che Guevara,* ed. John Gerassi. New York: Macmillan.

———. 1987. *Che Guevara and the Cuban Revolution: Writings and Speeches of Ernesto Che Guevara,* ed. David Deutschmann. Sydney: Pathfinder.

Guillermoprieto, Alma. 1994. *The Heart that Bleeds: Latin America Now.* New York: Vintage Books.

Gupta, Akhil. 1995. "Blurred Boundaries: The Discourse of Corruption, the Culture of Politics, and the Imagined State." *American Ethnologist* 22(2): 375–402.

———. 1999. *Postcolonial Developments: Agriculture in the Making of Modern India.* Durham: Duke University Press.

Hacking, Ian. 1982. "Biopower and the Avalanche of Printer Numbers." *Humanities in Society* 5: 275–95.

———. 1985. "Styles of Reasoning." *Postanalytic Philosophy,* ed. John Rajchman and Cornel West, 145–64. New York: Columbia University Press.

———. 1986. "Making Up People." *Reconstructing Individualism: Autonomy, Individuality, and the Self in Western Thought,* ed. Thomas C. Heller, Morton Sosna, and David E. Wilibery, 222–36. Stanford: Stanford University Press.

———. 1990. *The Taming Chance.* Cambridge: University of Cambridge Press.

———. 1991. "How Should We Do the History of Statistics?" *The Foucault Effect: Studies in Governmentality,* ed. Graham Burchell, Colin Gordon, and Peter Miller, 181–96. Chicago: University of Chicago Press.

Hagedorn, Katherine J. 2001. *Divine Utterances: The Performance of Afro-Cuban Santería.* Washington: Smithsonian Institution Press.

Halebsky, Sandor, and Richard L. Harris, ed. 1995. *Capital, Power, and Inequality in Latin America.* Boulder: Westview.

Hammond, Jack. 1999. "The High Price of Dollars." NACLA *Report on the Americas— Inside Cuba* 32: 24.

Hann C. M., ed. 2002. *Postsocialism: Ideals, Ideologies and Practices in Eurasia*. London: Routledge.

Hann Chris, Caroline Humphrey, and Katherine Verdery. 2001. "Introduction: Postsocialism as a Topic of Anthropological Investigation." *Postsocialism: Ideals, Ideologies and Practices in Eurasia*, ed. C. M. Hann, 1–28. London: Routledge.

Hardt, Michael, and Antonio Negri. 2000. *Empire*. Cambridge: Harvard University Press.

Hartsock, Nancy. 1990. "Foucault on Power: A Theory for Women." *Feminism/Postmodernism*, ed. Linda J. Nicholson, 157–75. London: Routledge.

Harvey, David. 2003. *The New Imperialism*. Oxford: Oxford University Press.

Hearn, Adrian. 2008. *Cuba: Religion, Social Capital, and Development*. Durham: Duke University Press.

Henken, Ted. 2008. "*Vale Todo* in Cuba's *Paladares*, Everything is Prohibited but Anything Goes." *A Contemporary Cuba Reader: Reinventing the Revolution*, ed. P. Brenner, J. Kirk, W. LeoGrande, M. Jiménez, 166–176. Lanham, Md.: Rowman and Littlefield.

Hernández Cisneros, Freddie, José A. Calvo Rodriguez, Marlene Sifontes Ballagas, Gladys Díaz Garcia, Bárbara Pino García, and Livia Quiles Viamontes. 1989. "Riesgo materno perinatal: Comportamiento en 4 consultorios del Médico de la Familia." *Revista Cubana de Medicina General Integral* 5: 174–77.

Hernández-Reguant, Ariana. 2008. "Writing the Special Period." *Cuba in the Special Period: Culture and Ideology in the 1990s*, ed. Ariana Hernández-Reguant, 1–19. New York: Palgrave Macmillan.

———. 2004. "Copyrighting Che: Art and Authorship under Cuban Late Socialism." *Public Culture* 16(1): 1–29.

———. 2000. "Socialism with Commercials: Consuming Advertising." drclas *News* (Winter).

Hindess, Barry. 1993. "Liberalism, Socialism and Democracy: Variations on a Governmental Theme." *Economy and Society* 22: 300–313.

Hirschfeld, Katherine. 2008. *Health, Politics, and Revolution in Cuba since 1898*. New Brunswick: Transaction.

Horowitz, Irving. 1995. "Preface." *Cuban Communism 1959–1995*. New Brunswick: Transaction.

Huish, Robert. 2008. "Going Where No Doctor Has Gone Before: The Role of Cuba's Latin American School of Medicine in Meeting the Needs of Some of the World's Most Vulnerable Populations." *Public Health* 122: 552–57.

———. 2009. "How Cuba's Latin American School of Medicine Challenges the Ethics of Physician Migration." *Social Science and Medicine* 69(3): 301–4.

Huish, Robert, and John M. Kirk. 2007. "Cuban Medical Internationalism and the Development of the Latin American School of Medicine." *Latin American Perspectives* 34(6): 77–92.

Huish, Robert, and Jerry Spiegel. 2008. "Integrating Health and Human Security into Foreign Policy: Cuba's Surprising Success." *International Journal of Cuban Studies* 1(1): 1–13.

Humphrey, Caroline. 2002. *The Unmaking of Soviet Life: Everyday Economies after Socialism.* Ithaca: Cornell University Press.

Humphrey, Caroline, and Ruth Mandel, eds. 2002. *Markets and Moralities: Ethnographies of Postsocialism.* Oxford: Berg.

Hyde, Sandra T. 2007. *Eating Spring Rice: The Cultural Politics of AIDS in Southwest China.* Berkeley: University of California Press.

Illich, Ivan. 1975. *Medical Nemesis: The Expropriation of Health.* London: Calder and Boyars.

Inhorn, Marcia C. 1995. "Medical Anthropology and Epidemiology: Divergences and Convergences." *Social Science and Medicine* 40: 285–90.

JanMohammed, Abdul R. 1985. "The Economy of Manichean Allegory: The Function of Racial Difference in Colonial Literature." *Critical Inquiry* 12: 18–23.

Janzen, John M. 1978. *The Quest for Therapy in Lower Zaire.* Berkeley: University of California Press.

Jardines Méndez, José B. 1995. "Cuba: El reto de la atención primaria y la eficiencia en salud." *Revista Cubana de Educación Médica Superior* 9(1–2). http://bvs.sld .cu/re vistas/ems (accessed 5 July 2011).

Jiménez Garcia, Eduardo. 2003. "La sociedad Cubana ante la homosexualidad: Más relajados, no más tolerantes." *Alma Mater.* May 23. http://www.almamater.cu (accessed 6 July 2011).

Jova Casañas, Rodolfo, and René Padrón Martínez. 1989. "El Médico de la Familia: Estudio preliminar en ciudad de Havana." *Revista Cubana de Salud Publica* 13: 128–37.

Kath, Elizabeth. 2010. *Social Relations and the Cuban Health Miracle.* New Brunswick: Transaction.

Kendall, Carl, Patricia Hudelson, Elli Leonstini, Peter Winch, Linda Lloyd, and Fernando Cruz. 1991. "Urbanization, Dengue, and the Health Transition: Anthropological Contributions to International Health." *Medical Anthropology Quarterly* 5: 257–68.

Kildergaard, Anne C., and Roberto Orro Fernández. 2000. "Dollarization in Cuba and Implications for the Future Transition." Papers and Proceedings of the 9th Annual Meeting of the Association for the Study of the Cuban Economy (ASCE). *Cuba in Transition.* Volume 9: 25–35. Miami: Florida International University.

Kim, Jim Yong, Joyce V. Millen, Alec Irwin, and John Gershman. 2000. *Dying for Growth: Global Inequality and the Health of the Poor.* Monroe, Maine: Common Courage Press.

Kirk, John. 2009. "Cuba's Medical Internationalism: Development and Rationale." *Bulletin of Latin American Research* 28(4): 497–511.

Kirk, John, and Michael Erisman. 2009. *Cuban Medical Internationalism: Origins, Evolution, and Goals.* New York: Palgrave Macmillan.

Kirkpatrick, Anthony F. 1996. "Role of the USA in Shortage of Food and Medicine in Cuba." *Lancet* 348: 1489–91.

——. 1997. "The U.S. Attack on Cuba's Health." *Canadian Medical Association Journal* 157: 281–84.

Kohrman, Matthew. 2005. *Bodies of Difference: Experiences of Disability and Institutional Advocacy in the Making of Modern China*. Berkeley: University of California Press.

Kunitz, Stephen. 1987. "Explanations and Ideologies in Mortality Patterns." *Population and Development Review* 13: 379–408.

Lacombe, Danny. 1996. "Reforming Foucault: A Critique of the Social Control Thesis." *British Journal of Sociology* 47: 332–52.

Lakoff, Andrew. 1995. *Pharmaceutical Reason: Knowledge and Value in Global Psychiatry*. Cambridge: Cambridge University Press.

Lancaster, Roger N. 1988. *Thanks to God and the Revolution: Popular Religion and Class Consciousness in the New Nicaragua*. Berkeley: University of California Press.

Ledeneva, Alena. 1998. *Russia's Economy of Favors: Blat, Networking and Informal Exchange*. Cambridge: Cambridge University Press.

——. 2006. *How Russia Really Works: The Informal Practices that Shaped Post-Soviet Politics and Business*. Ithaca: Cornell University Press.

Leiner, Marvin. 1994. *Sexual Politics in Cuba—Machismo, Homosexuality and* AIDS. Boulder: Westview.

Lemke, Thomas. 2001. " 'The Birth of Bio-Politics': Michel Foucault's Lecture at the Collège de France on Neo-Liberal Governmentality." *Economy and Society* 30(2): 190–207.

León, Francisco. 1997. "*Socialism* and *Sociolism*: Social Actors and Economic Change in 1990s Cuba." *Toward a New Cuba? Legacies of a Revolution*, ed. Angel Centeno and Mauricio Font, 39–52. Boulder: Lynne Rienner.

Lewis, Oscar. 1959. *Five Families: Mexican Case Studies in the Culture of Poverty*. New York: Basic Books.

Lewis, Oscar, Ruth M. Lewis, and Susan M. Rigdon. 1977a. *Four Men: Living the Revolution—An Oral History of Contemporary Cuba*. Urbana: University of Illinois Press.

——. 1977b. *Four Women: Living the Revolution—An Oral History of Contemporary Cuba*. Urbana: University of Illinois Press.

——. 1978. *Neighbors: Living the Revolution—An Oral History of Contemporary Cuba*. Urbana: University of Illinois Press.

Lilienfeld, Abraham M. 1976. *Foundations of Epidemiology*. New York: Oxford University Press.

Lindenbaum, Shirley, and Margaret Lock. 1993. *Knowledge, Power, and Practice: The Anthropology of Medicine in Everyday Life*. Berkeley: University of California Press.

Liu, Xin. 2000. *In One's Own Shadow*. Berkeley: University of California Press.

Lock, Margaret. 1993a. *Encounters with Aging: Mythologies of Menopause in Japan and North America*. Berkeley: University of California Press.

——. 1993b. "Cultivating the Body: Anthropology and Epistemologies of Bodily Practice and Knowledge." *Annual Review of Anthropology* 22: 133–55.

——. 1997. "Decentering the Natural Body: Making Difference Matter." *Configurations* 5: 267–92.

Lock, Margaret, and Judith Farquhar, eds. 2007. *Beyond the Body Proper: Reading the Anthropology of Material Life*. Durham: Duke University Press.

Lock, Margaret, and Deborah R. Gordon, eds. 1987. *Biomedicine Examined.* Dordrecht: Kluwer Academic.

Lock, Margaret, and Patricia Kaufert, eds. 1998. *Pragmatic Women and Body Politics.* Cambridge: Cambridge University Press.

Lock, Margaret, and Nancy Scheper-Hughes. 1987. "The Mindful Body: A Prolegomenon to Future Work in Medical Anthropology." *Medical Anthropology Quarterly* 1: 6–41.

Lockwood, Lee. 1967. *Castro's Cuba, Cuba's Fidel.* Boulder: Westview.

Loomba, Anita. 1998. *Colonialism/Postcolonialism.* New York: Routledge.

Lugones Botell, Miguel, Tania Yamilé, and Quintana Riverón. 1995. "Análisis del riesgo preconcepcional en un grupo básico de trabajo." *Revista Cubana de Medicina General Integral* 11:12–116.

Lumsden, Ian. 1996. *Machos, Maricones, and Gays: Cuba and Homosexuality.* Philadelphia: Temple University Press.

Lupton, Deborah. 1995. *The Imperative of Health: Public Health and the Regulated Body.* London: Sage.

———. 1997. "Foucault and the Medicalisation Critique." *Foucault, Health, and Medicine,* ed. Alan Peterson and Robin Bunton, 94–110. London: Routledge.

———. 1999. *Risk.* London: Routledge.

Macdonald, Theodore. 1999. *A Developmental Analysis of Cuba's Health Care System Since 1959.* Lewiston, N.Y.: Edwin Millen Press.

Martí, José. 1959. *La cuestión racial.* Havana: Editorial Lex.

Martinez-Alier, Verena. 1974. *Marriage, Class and Colour in Nineteenth-Century Cuba.* Cambridge: Cambridge University Press.

Marx, Karl. 1977. "Towards a Critique of Hegel's Philosophy of Right: Introduction." *Karl Marx: Selected Writings,* ed. David McLellan, 150–70. Oxford: Oxford University Press.

Masquelier, Adeline. 2001. "Behind the Dispensary's Prosperous Facade: Imagining the State in Rural Niger." *Public Culture* 13(2): 267–91.

Mauss, Marcel. 2006 (1934). "Techniques of the Body." *Beyond the Body Proper: Reading the Anthropology of Material Life,* ed. Judith Farquhar and Margaret Lock, 50–68. Durham: Duke University Press.

———. 1990 (1922). *The Gift: Forms and Functions of Exchange in Archaic Societies.* London: Routledge.

McClintock, Anne. 1995. *Imperial Leather: Race, Gender, and Sexuality in the Colonial Contest.* London: Routledge.

McFayden, Deirdre. 1995. "The Social Repercussions of the Crisis." NACLA *Report on the Americas—Cuba, Adapting to a Post-Soviet World* 29: 20–23.

McGillivray, Gillian. 2009. *Blazing Cane: Sugar Communities, Class, and State Formation in Cuba, 1868–1959.* Durham: Duke University Press.

McKeown, Thomas. 1976a. *The Modern Rise of Population.* London: Edward Arnold.

———. 1976b. *The Role of Medicine.* London: Nuffield Provincial Hospital Trust.

Medina Lorente, Gertrudis M., Juan M. Vargas Torres, Rolando Romero Villar, Elvira M. Crespo Bello, and Juan J. Lemes Báez. 1998. "Satisfacción de la población con el Médico de la Familia." *Revista Cubana de Medicina General Integral* 14: 571–80.

Menéndez, Ana. 2001. *In Cuba I Was a German Shepherd.* New York: Grove Press.

Mesa-Lago, Carmelo. 2000. "The Resurrection of Cuban Statistics." *Cuban Studies* 31: 139–50.

Mesa-Lago, Carmelo, Alberto Arenas de Mesa, Ivan Brenes, Verónica Montecinos, and Mark Samara, eds. 2000. *Market, Socialist, and Mixed Economies: Comparative Policy and Performance; Chile, Cuba, and Costa Rica.* Baltimore: Johns Hopkins University Press.

Millen, Joyce V., Alec Irwin, and Kim Yong. 2000. "Introduction: What Is Growing? Who Is Dying?" *Dying for Growth: Global Inequality and the Health of the Poor*, ed. Jim Yong Kim, Joyce V. Millen, Alec Irwin, and John Gershman, 3–10. Monroe, Maine: Common Courage Press.

Miller, Peter, and Rose, Nikolas. 2008. *Governing the Present: Administering Economic, Social and Personal Life.* Cambridge: Polity Press.

Ministerio de Salud Pública (MINSAP), República de Cuba. 1976. *Programas básicos.* Havana.

——. 1977. *Fundamentación para un nuevo enfoque de la medicina en la comunidad.* Havana.

——. 1983. *Salud para todos: 25 años de experiencia cubana.* Havana.

——. 1988. *Médico de la Familia: Información estadística.* Havana.

——. 1991. *Evaluación de estrategias de salud todo en el año 2000: Informe de Cuba 1990.* Havana.

——. 1996. *Análisis del sector salud en Cuba—Resumen ejecutivo.* Havana.

——. 1997. *Programa Nacional de Medicina Tradicional y Natural (MTN).* Havana.

——. 2001. *Carpeta Metodológica de Atención Primaria de Salud y Medicina Familiar, VII Reunión Metodológica del MINSAP.* Havana.

——. 2009. *Sistema de información estadística de salud.* Havana.

Ministerio de Turismo (MINTUR), República de Cuba. 2008. http://www.cubagob.cu (accessed on 1 June 2009).

Mintz, Sidney. 1985. *Sweetness and Power: The Place of Sugar in Modern History.* Chicago: University of Chicago Press.

Mitchell, Timothy. 1991a. "The Limits of the State: Beyond Statist Approaches and Their Critics." *American Political Science Review* 85: 77–96.

——. 1991b. *Colonizing Egypt.* Berkeley: University of California Press.

Mol, Annemarie. 1998. "Lived Reality and the Multiplicity of Norms: A Critical Tribute to George Canguilhem." *Economy and Society* 7: 274–84.

Molina-Esquivel, E., G. Pita-Rodríguez, P. A. Monterrey Gutiérrez, and A. M. Clúa-Calderín. 1998. "Factores de riesgo en la neuropatía epidémica cubana." *Revista Investigación Clínica* 50: 105–11.

Monreal, Pedro. 1999. "Sea Changes: The New Cuban Economy." *NACLA Report on the Americas—Inside Cuba* 32: 21–29.

Montoya, Rosario. 2007. "Socialist Scenarios, Power, and State Formation in Sandinista Nicaragua." *American Ethnologist* 34(1): 71–90.

Morgan, Lynn M. 1989. "'Political Will' and Community Participation in Costa Rican Primary Health Care." *Medical Anthropology Quarterly* 3: 232–45.

———. 1993. *Community Participation in Health: The Politics of Primary Care in Costa Rica.* Cambridge: Cambridge University Press.

Mudimbe, Valentin Y. 1988. *The Invention of Africa: Gnosis, Philosophy and the Order of Knowledge.* Bloomington: Indiana University Press.

Navarro, Lydia. 2009. "Tropical Depression." *Virginia Quarterly Review* (Winter): 26–47. http://www.vqronline.org (accessed 2 June 2009).

Navarro, Mireya. 1999. "Cuba Draws the Curious, Despite the Law." *New York Times*, 31 January, 8–9.

Navarro, Vincente. 1972. "Health, Health Services, and Health Planning in Cuba." *International Journal of Health Services* 2: 397–432.

———. 1977. *Medicine under Capitalism.* New York: Prodist.

———. 1984. "A Critique of the Ideological and Political Positions of the Willy Brandt Report and the WHO Alma Ata Declaration." *Social Science and Medicine* 18: 467–74.

———. 2000. "Assessment of the World Health Report 2000." *The Lancet* 356: 1598–1601.

Nayeri, Kamran. 1995. "The Cuban Health Care System and Factors Currently Undermining It." *Journal of Community Health* 20: 321–35.

Nelson, Lowry. 1950. *Rural Cuba.* Minneapolis: University of Minnesota Press.

———. 1971. *Cuba: The Measure of a Revolution.* Minneapolis: University of Minnesota Press.

Nettleford, Rex. 1993. *Inward Stretch, Outward Reach: A Voice from the Caribbean.* London: Macmillan.

Nguyen, Vinh-Kim. 2009. "Government-by-Exception: Enrolment and Experimentality in Mass HIV Treatment Programmes in Africa." *Social Theory and Health* 7: 196–217.

———. 2010. *The Republic of Therapy: Triage and Sovereignty in West Africa's Time of AIDS.* Durham: Duke University Press.

Nichter, Mark, and Margaret Lock. 2002. "Introduction: From Documenting Medical Pluralism to Critical Interpretations of Globalized Health Knowledge, Policies, and Practices." *New Horizons in Medical Anthropology: Essays in Honour of Charles Leslie*, ed. Margaret Lock and Mark Nichter, 1–34. London: Routledge.

Ninetto, Amy. 2005. "An Island of Socialism in a Capitalist Country." *Postsocialist Russian Science and the Culture of the State Ethnos* 70(4): 443–64.

Nordstrom, Carolyn. 2004. *Shadows of War: Violence, Power, and International Profiteering in the 21st Century.* Berkeley: University of California Press.

Ong, Aihwa. 2006. *Neoliberalism as Exception: Mutations in Citizenship and Sovereignty.* Durham: Duke University Press.

———. 1995. "Making the Biopolitical Subject: Cambodian Immigrants, Refugee

Medicine and Cultural Citizenship in California." *Social Science and Medicine* 40: 1243–57.

Ordóñez Carceller, Cosme. 1976. *La medicina en la comunidad.* Havana: MINSAP.

Orozco, Manuel. 2002. *Challenges and Opportunities of Marketing Remittances to Cuba.* Washington: Inter-American Dialogue.

Orozco Muñoz, Calixto. 1996. "Reflexión acerca de la labor del Médico de la Familia." *Revista Cubana de Medicina General Integral* 12: 34–78.

Ortiz, Fernando. 1995. *Cuban Counterpoint: Tobacco and Sugar.* Durham: Duke University Press.

Oxhorn, Philip. 1995. "From Controlled Inclusion to Coerced Marginalization: The Struggle for Civil Society in Latin America." *Civil Society: Theory, History, Comparison,* ed. John Hall, 250–77. Cambridge, UK: Polity Press.

Páez Prats, Isidoro, and José Rodríguez Abrines. 1997. "Intregrated Work Between Hospitals and Community-Level Primary Care Facilities: A Practical Approach." *Revista Cubana de Medicina General Integral* 13: 1–4.

Palmié, Stephan. 2004. "Fascinans or Tremendum? Permutations of the State, the Body, and the Divine in Late-Twentieth Century Havana." *New West Indian Guide* 78(3–4): 229–68.

Pan American Health Organization (PAHO). 2001. *Country Health Profile: Cuba.*

Pandolfi, Mariella. 2003. "Contract of Mutual (In)Difference: Governance and Humanitarian Apparatus in Albania and Kosovo." *Indiana Journal of Global Legal Studies* 10(1): 369–81.

——. 2007. "Laboratory of Intervention: The Humanitarian Governance of the Post-Communist Balkan Territories." *Postcolonial Disorders,* ed. Sandra T. Hyde, Byron Good, and Sarah Pinto, 157–86. Berkeley: University of California Press.

Parker, Dick. 1999. "The Cuban Revolution: Resilience and Uncertainty." NACLA *Report on the Americas—Inside Cuba* 32: 17–20.

Partido Comunista de Cuba (PCC). 1975. *Primer Congreso del Partido Comunista de Cuba: Informe Central.* Departamento de Orientación Revolucionaria del Comité Central del Partido Comunista de Cuba.

——. 1980. *Estatutos del Partido Comunista de Cuba: Aprobados por el I Congreso, con las modificaciones acordadas por el II Congreso.* Havana: Editora Política.

Pastor, Manuel, Jr., and Andrew Zimbalist. 1995. "Cuba's Economic Conundrum." NACLA *Report on the Americas—Cuba, Adapting to a Post-Soviet World* 29: 7–12.

Patico, Jennifer. 2005. "To Be Happy in a Mercedes: Tropes of Value and Ambivalent Visions of Marketing." *American Ethnologist* 32(3): 479–96.

Patico, Jennifer, and Melissa L. Caldwell. 2002. "Consumers Exiting Socialism: Ethnographic Perspective on Daily Life in Post-Communist Europe." *Ethnos* 67(3): 285–94.

Patton, Cindy. 1990. *Inventing AIDS.* New York: Routledge.

——. 1996. *Fatal Advice: How Safe-Sex Education Went Wrong.* Durham: Duke University Press.

Peláez Mendoza, Jorge, Aldo Rodríguez Izquierdo, Cristina Lammers, and Robert

William Blum. 1999. "Abortion among Adolescents in Cuba." *Journal of Adolescent Health* 24: 59–62.

Pels, Peter. 1997. "The Anthropology of Colonialism: Culture, History, and the Emergence of Western Governmentality." *Annual Review of Anthropology* 26: 163–83.

Perez, Cristina. 2008. *Caring for Them from Birth to Death: The Practice of Community-Based Cuban Medicine*. Lanham, Md.: Lexington Books.

Pérez, Louis A., Jr. 1995. *Cuba: Between Reform and Revolution*. New York: Oxford University Press.

———. 1999. *On Becoming Cuban: Identity, Nationality, and Culture*. Chapel Hill: University of North Carolina Press.

———. 2006. *To Die in Suicide: Suicide and Society*. Chapel Hill: University of North Carolina Press.

Pérez, Orlando, and Angela T. Haddad. 2008. "Cuba's New Export Commodity: A Framework." *Changing Cuba/Changing World*, ed. Mauricio Font, 327–44. New York: Bildner Center for Western Hemisphere Studies, CUNY.

Pérez Avila, J., R. Peña Torres, J. Joanes Fiol, M. Lantero Abreu, and H. Arazoza Rodriguez. 1996. "HIV Control in Cuba." *Biomedicine and Pharmacotherapy* 50: 216–19.

Pérez Peña, Julian. 1989. "Impacto del Médico de la Familia en el funcionamiento de los servicios de medicina interna." *Revista Cubana de Salud Pública* 15: 309–15.

Pérez Sarduy, Pedro, and Jean Stubbs, eds. 2000. *Afro-Cuban Voices: On Race and Identity in Contemporary Cuba*. Gainesville: University Press of Florida.

Pérez-López, Jorge F., ed. 1994. *Cuba at a Crossroads: Politics and Economics after the Fourth Party Congress*. Florida: University Press of Florida.

Pérez-Stable, Eliseo J. 1991. "Cuba's Response to the HIV Epidemic." *American Journal of Public Health* 81(5): 563–67.

Pérez-Stable, Marifeli. 1998. *The Cuban Revolution: Origins, Course, and Legacy*. New York and Oxford: Oxford University Press.

Petersen, Allan, and Deborah Lupton, eds. 1996. *The New Public Health: Health and Self in the Age of Risk*. Sydney: Allen and Unwyn.

Peterson, Kristin. 2012. "AIDS Policies for Markets and Warriors: Dispossession, Capital, and Pharmaceuticals in Nigeria." *Lively Capital: Biotechnologies, Ethics, and Governance in Global Markets*, ed. Kaushik Sunder Rajan. Durham: Duke University Press.

Petras, Martin, and James Kenner, eds. 1969. *Fidel Castro Speaks*. New York: Grove Press.

Petryna, Adriana. 2002. *Life Exposed: Biological Citizens after Chernobyl*. Princeton: Princeton University Press.

Petryna, Adriana, and Arthur Kleinman. 2006. "The Pharmaceutical Nexus." *Global Pharmaceuticals: Ethics, Markets, and Practices*, ed. Adriana Petryna, Arthur Kleinman, and Andrew Lakoff, 1–32. Durham: Duke University Press.

Philips, Sarah D. 2005. "Postsocialism, Governmentality, and Subjectivity: An Introduction." *Ethnos* 70(4): 437–42.

Polanyi, Karl. 2001 [1944]. *The Great Transformation: The Political and Economic Origins of Our Time.* Boston: Beacon Press.

Porter, Theodore. 1986. *The Rise of Statistical Thinking, 1820–1900.* Princeton: Princeton University Press.

Potts, Ricardo. 1999. "Revolución verde." *Avances Médicos de Cuba* 20: 44–46.

Poupeye, Veerle. 1998. *Caribbean Art.* London: Thames and Hudson.

Premat, Adriana. 1998. "Feeding the Self and Cultivating Identities in Havana, Cuba." M.A. thesis, York University.

Quezada, Fernando. 2006. "Commercial Biotechnology in Latin America: Current Opportunities and Challenges." *Journal of Commercial Biotechnology* 12(3): 192–99.

Quiroga, José. 2005. *Cuban Palimpsests.* Minneapolis: University of Minnesota Press.

Rabinow, Paul, ed. 1984. *The Foucault Reader.* New York: Pantheon.

Rabinow, Paul, and Hubert L. Dreyfus, eds. 1982. *Michel Foucault—Beyond Structuralism and Hermeneutics.* Chicago: University of Chicago Press.

Rabinow, Paul, and Nikolas Rose. 2006. "Biopower Today." *BioSocieties* 1(2): 195–217.

Rabkin, Rhoda P. 1992. "Cuban Socialism: Ideological Responses to the Era of Socialist Crisis." *Cuban Studies* 22: 27–50.

Raikhel, Eugene. 2010. "Post-Soviet Placebos: Epistemology and Authority in Russian Treatments for Alcoholism." *Culture, Medicine and Psychiatry* 34(1): 132–68.

Read, Jason. 2009. "A Genealogy of Homo-Economicus: Neoliberalism and the Production of Subjectivity." *Foucault Studies* 6: 25–36.

Redfield, Peter. 2005. "Doctors, Borders and Life in Crisis." *Cultural Anthropology* 20(3): 328–61.

——. 2006. "A Less Modest Witness: Collective Advocacy and Motivated Truth in a Medical Humanitarian Movement." *American Ethnologist* 33(1): 3–26.

Reed, Gail. 2001. "Health News from Cuba." MEDICC *Review* 2: 1–2.

Reid-Henry, Simon. 2003. "Under the Microscope: Fieldwork Practice and Cuba's Biotechnology Industry, A Reflexive Affair?" *Singapore Journal of Tropical Geography* 24(2): 184–97.

——. 2007. "The Contested Spaces of Cuban Development: Postsocialism, Postcolonialism and Development." *Geoforum* 38(3): 445–55.

——. 2010. *The Cuban Cure: Reason and Resistance in Global Science.* Chicago: University of Chicago Press.

Reinoso, Ana T. Fariñas, and Héctor Gómez de Haz. 1998. "Evaluación de la vigilancia de la sífilis congénita en ciudad de Havana." 1996. *Revista Cubana de Salud Pública* 24: 73–77.

República de Cuba. 1976. *Constitución.* Departamento de Orientación Revolucionaria de Comité del Partido Comunista de Cuba.

Riera, Lilliam. 2003. "Cuba Produces Anti-Retroviral Medicine for AIDS Patients." *Granma International Digital* 16 May. http://www.granma.cu/ingles/mayo03/vier16/20sida.html (accessed 6 July 2011).

Rigi, Jakob. 2005. "State and Big Capital in Russia." *Social Analysis* 49(1): 198–205.

Ritter, Archibald R. M., and John M. Kirk, eds. 1995. *Cuba in the International System: Normalization and Integration.* New York: St. Martin's Press.

Ritter, Archibald R. M., and Nicholas Rowe. 2000. *Cuba: From "Dollarization" to "Euro-ization" or "Peso Re-Consolidation?"* Carleton University, Department of Economics CEP 00–13.

Rivera, Juan Carlos. 1995a. "A Pueblo Chiquito, Paraíso Grande." *Bohemia* 87: B16–B19.

———. 1995b. "Hablemos Francamente." *Bohemia* 87: B4–B7.

Rivkin-Fish, Michelle. 2000. "Health Development Meets the End of State Socialism: Visions of Democratization, Women's Health, and Social Well-Being for Contemporary Russia." *Culture, Medicine and Psychiatry* 24: 77–100.

———. 2005. *Women's Health in Post-Soviet Russia: The Politics of Intervention.* Bloomington: Indiana University Press.

Rodríguez, Félix and Meinardo Zayas. 1997. "Estudios para el perfeccionamiento del plan del médico de la familia." *Revista Cubana de Medicina General Integral* 13(1): 12–18.

Roemer, Milton. 1963. *Medical Care in Latin America.* Washington: General Secretariat, Organization of American States.

Rogers, Douglas. 2006. "How to Be a *Khoziain* in a Transforming State: State Formation and the Ethics of Governance in Post-Soviet Russia." *Comparative Studies in Society and History* 48(4): 915–45.

Roitman, Janet L. 1990. "The Politics of Informal Markets in Sub-Saharan Africa." *Journal of Modern African Studies* 28(4): 671–96.

———. 2004a. *Fiscal Disobedience: An Anthropology of Economic Regulation in Central Africa.* Princeton: Princeton University Press.

———. 2004b. "Productivity in the Margins: The Reconstitution of State Power in the Chad Basin." *Anthropology in the Margins of the State,* ed. Veena Das and Deborah Poole, 191–224. Santa Fe: School of American Research Press.

Rojas, Marta. 1986. *El Médico de la Familia en la Sierra Maestra.* Havana: Editorial Ciencias Médicas.

Rojas Ochoa, Francisco , and Cándido López Pardo. 1996. "Entorno socio-económico, voluntad política y situación de salud en Cuba." 9th Congress—International Association of Health Policy, Montreal, Canada.

Rose, Nikolas. 2006. *Politics of Life Itself: Biomedicine, Power and Subjectivity in the Twenty-First Century.* Princeton: Princeton University Press.

Rose, Nikolas, and Carlos Novas. 2004. "Biological Citizenship." *Global Assemblages: Technology, Politics, and Ethics as Anthropological Problem,* ed. Aihwa Ong and Stephen J. Collier, 439–63. Oxford: Blackwell.

Rosendahl, Mona. 1997. *Inside the Revolution: Everyday Life in Socialist Cuba.* Ithaca: Cornell University Press.

Ross, Oakland. 2003. "Wave of Repression Sweeps Cuba." *Toronto Star,* 13 April: A20.

Bibliography

Salmi, Anna-Maria. 2003. "Health in Exchange: Teachers, Doctors, and the Strength of Informal Practices in Russia." *Culture, Medicine, and Psychiatry* 27: 109–30.

Sandoval, Mercedes C. 1977. "Afro-Cuban Concepts of Disease and Treatment in Miami." *Journal of Operational Psychology* 8: 52.

———. 1979. "Santería as a Mental Healthcare System: An Historical Overview." *Social Science and Medicine* 13B: 137–51.

Santana, Sarah. 1987. "The Cuban Health Care System." *World Development* 15: 113–25.

———. 1990. "Whither Cuban Medicine? Challenges for the Next Generation." *Transformation and Struggle: Cuba Faces the 1990s*, ed. Sandor Halebsky and John M. Kirk, 251–70. Boulder: Westview.

———. 1997. "AIDS Prevention, Treatment and Care in Cuba." *AIDS in Africa and the Caribbean*, ed. G. Bond, I. Kreniske, Susan Vincent, and Joan Vincent, 65–84. Boulder: Westview.

Sawicki, Jana. 1991. *Disciplining Foucault: Feminism, Power, and the Body*. New York: Routledge.

Scheper-Hughes, Nancy. 1994. "AIDS and the Social Body." *Social Science and Medicine* 39: 991–1003.

Scott, James. 1969. "Corruption, Machine Politics, and Political Change." *American Political Science Review* 63: 1142–58.

———. 1985. *Weapons of the Weak: Everyday Forms of Peasant Resistance*. New Haven: Yale University Press.

———. 1990. *Domination and the Arts of Resistance: Hidden Transcripts*. New Haven: Yale University Press.

———. 1998. *Seeing Like a State: How Certain Schemes to Improve the Human Condition Have Failed*. New Haven: Yale University Press.

Scott, Rebecca J. 1985. *Slave Emancipation in Cuba: The Transition to Free Labor, 1860–1890*. Princeton: Princeton University Press.

Sharma, Aradhana, and Akhil Gupta, eds. 2006. *The Anthropology of the State: A Reader*. Malden, Mass.: Blackwell.

Shohat, Ella. 1993. "Notes on the 'Post-Colonial.' " *Social Text* 31/32: 99–113.

Shore, Chris, and Susan Wright. 1997. "Policy: A New Field of Anthropology." *Anthropology of Policy: Critical Perspectives on Governance and Power*, ed. Chris Shore and Susan Wright, 3–41. London: Routledge.

Skidmore, Thomas E., and Peter H. Smith. 1989. *Modern Latin America*. Oxford: Oxford University Press.

Skolbekken, John-Arne. 1995. "The Risk Epidemic in Medical Journals." *Social Science and Medicine* 40: 291–305.

Smith, Lois M., and Alfred Padula. 1996. *Sex and Revolution: Women in Socialist Cuba*. New York: Oxford University Press.

Song, Priscilla. 2010. "Biotech Pilgrims and the Transnational Quest for Stem Cell Cures." *Medical Anthropology* 29(4): 384–402.

Spack, Tracey Lee. 2001. *Medicine in the Special Period: Treatment-Seeking Behaviours in Post-Soviet Cuba*. Ph.D. diss., University of Alberta.

Spiegel, Jerry, and Annalee Yassi. 2004. "Lessons from the Margins of Globalization: Appreciating the Cuban Health Paradox." *Journal of Public Health Policy* 25(1):85–110.

Spiegel, Jerry, Annalee Yassi, and Robert Tate. 2002. "Dengue in Cuba: Mobilisation against *Aedes aegypti*." *The Lancet* 2: 207–8.

Spiegel, Jerry, M. Bonet, A. Ibarra, N. Pagliccia, V. Ouellette, and A. Yassi. 2007. "Social and Environmental Determinants of *Aedes aegypti* Infestation in Central Havana: Results of a Case-Control Study Nested in an Integrated Dengue Surveillance Programme in Cuba." *Tropical Medicine and International Health* 12(4): 503–10.

Spivak, Gayatri C. 1985. "Can the Subaltern Speak? Speculations on Widow Sacrifice." *Wedge* 7–8 (Winter/Spring): 120–30.

Stan, Sabina. 2005. *L'agriculture roumaine en mutation: La construction sociale du marché.* Paris: CNRS Éditions.

Stark, Evan. 1978. "Overcoming the Diseases of Poverty." *Cuba Review* 8(1): 23–28.

Stoler, Ann Laura. 1995. *Race and the Education of Desire: Foucault's History of Sexuality and the Colonial Order of Things.* Durham: Duke University Press.

——. 2009. *Along the Archival Grain: Epistemic Anxieties and Colonial Common Sense.* Princeton: Princeton University Press.

Stout, Noelle. 2008. "Feminist Queers and Critics: Debating the Cuban Sex Trade." *Journal of Latin American Studies* 40(4): 721–42.

Strout, Jan. 1995. "Women, the Politics of Sexuality, and Cuba's Economic Crisis." *Socialist Review* 25: 5–15.

Suárez, Julio. 1994. "Sistemas de vigilancia de situación de salud según condiciones de vida: Una propuesta desarrollada en Cuba." *Revista Cubana Salud Pública* 20: 20–51.

Sullivan, Stefan. 2002. *Marx for a Post-Communist Era: On Poverty, Corruption, and Banality.* London: Routledge.

Sunder Rajan, Kaushik. 2006. *Biocapital: The Constitution of Postgenomic Life.* Durham: Duke University Press.

Taussig, Michael. 1989. *Shamanism, Colonialism, and the Wild Man: A Study of Terror and Healing.* Chicago: University of Chicago Press.

——. 1992. *The Nervous System.* London: Routledge.

——. 2002. "The Genesis of Capitalism amongst a South American Peasantry: Devil's Labor and the Baptism of Money." *A Reader in the Anthropology of Religion,* ed. Michael Lambek, 472–92. Cambridge: Blackwell.

Thomas, Nicholas. 1995. *Colonialism's Culture: Anthropology, Travel and Government.* Princeton: Princeton University Press.

Treichler, Paula. 1987. "AIDS, Homophobia, and Biomedical Discourse: An Epidemic of Signification." *October* 43 (Winter): 31–70.

Trouillot, Michel-Rolph. 2001. "The Anthropology of the State in the Age of Globalization: Close Encounters of the Deceptive Kind." *Current Anthropology* 42: 125–38.

Tsing, Anna. 1997. *In the Realm of the Diamond Queen*. Princeton: Princeton University Press.

——. 2005. *Friction: An Ethnography of Global Connection*. Princeton: Princeton University Press.

Ubell, Robert. 1989. "Twenty-five Years of Cuban Health Care." *The Cuba Reader: The Making of a Revolutionary Society*, ed. Philip Brenner, William M. Leo-Grande, Donna Rich, and Daniel Siegel, 435–45. New York: Grove Press.

United Nations (UN). 1998. *Basic Indicators: Cuba*. United Nations Development Report (UNDP). New York: Oxford University Press.

Vallant, Armando. 2001. "I Am Not a *Jinetero*." *Qualitative Studies in Education* 14: 239–54.

Van-Dijk, Rijk. 1994. "Foucault and the Anti-Witchcraft Movement." *Critique of Anthropology* 14(4): 429–35.

Vaughan, Megan. 1994. *Curing Their Ills: Colonial Power and African Illness*. Stanford: Stanford University Press.

Vera Castillo, Teresa, Esther Iglesias Díaz, María Milían Montesino, Juan Torres Ruiz, and Victor Diaz Narváez. 1989. "Conocimiento del estado de salud de la problación antendida por el Médico de la Familia antes y después de implantado el nuevo modelo de atención médica integral." *Revista Cubana de Enfermeria* 5: 143–56.

Verdery, Katherine. 1991, "Theorizing Socialism." *American Ethnologist* 18(3): 419–39.

——. 1996. *What Was Socialism and What Comes Next?* Princeton: Princeton University Press.

——. 2002 "Whither Postsocialism?" *Postsocialism: Ideals, Ideologies and Practice in Eurasia*, ed. C. M. Hann, 15–28. London: Routledge.

Waitzkin, Howard, K. Wald, Ross Kee, R. Danielson, and L. Robinson. 1997. "Primary Care in Cuba: Low- and High-Technology Developments Pertinent to Family Medicine." *Journal of Family Practice* 45: 250–58.

Wedel, Johan. 2003. *Santería Healing: A Journey into the Afro-Cuban World of Divinities, Spirits, and Sorcery*. Gainesville: University of Florida Press.

Werner, David. 1983. "Health Care in Cuba Today: A Model Service or a Means of Social Control?" *Practicing Health for All*, ed. David Morley, Jon E. Rohde, and Glen Williams, 15–37. Oxford: Oxford University Press.

Whiteford, Linda M., and Laurence G. Branch. 2008. *Primary Health Care in Cuba: The Other Revolution*. New York: Rowman and Littlefield.

Whitney, Robert. 2001. *State and Revolution in Cuba: Mass Mobilization and Political Change, 1920–1940*. Chapel Hill: University of North Carolina Press.

Wilkinson, Richard G. 1997. *Unhealthy Societies: The Afflictions of Inequality*. London: Routledge.

Williams, Robin C. 1997. "In the Shadow of Plenty, Cuba Copes with a Crippled Health Care System." *Canadian Medical Association Journal* 157: 291–93.

World Health Organization (WHO). 1978. *Alma Ata Declaration*. Geneva.

——. 2000. *World Health Report 2000—Health Systems Improving Performance.* Geneva.

Yang, Mayfair. 1994. *Gifts, Favors, and Banquets: The Art of Social Relationships in China.* Ithaca: Cornell University Press.

Young, Allan. 1978. "Mode of Production of Medical Knowledge." *Medical Anthropology* (Spring): 97–124.

——. 1983. "Rethinking Ideology." *International Journal of Health Services* 13: 203–19.

Young, Allen. 1981. *Gays under the Cuban Revolution.* San Francisco: Grey Fox Press.

Young, Robert J. C. 1995. *Colonial Desire: Hybridity in Theory, Culture and Race.* London: Routledge.

——. 2001. *Postcolonialism: An Historical Introduction.* London: Blackwell.

Yurchak, Alexei. 1997. "The Cynical Reason of Late Socialism: Power, Pretense, and the *Anekdot.*" *Public Culture* 9(2): 161–88.

——. 2002. "Entrepreneurial Governmentality in Post-Socialist Russia: A Cultural Investigation of Business Practices." *The New Entrepreneurs of Europe and Asia*, ed. Victoria E. Bonnell, and Thomas B. Gold, 278–324. Armonk, N.Y.: M. E. Sharpe.

——. 2005. *Everything Was Forever, Until It Was No More: The Last Soviet Generation.* Princeton: Princeton University Press.

Zhang, Li. 2001. "Migration and Privatization of Space and Power in Late Socialist China." *American Ethnologist* 18(1): 179–205.

Page references in italics indicate illustrations. Unless otherwise indicated, all institutions and places are in Cuba.

biotechnology/pharmaceutical exports, 215n.5

birth control, 77, 213–14n.59

birth rate, 77

"black," use of term, 201n.26

black market (bolsa negra): crackdowns on, 197–98n.31; for currency, 200n.18; goods sold door-to-door, 36; before the período especial, 197n.25; physicians' handling of, 120; for prescription drugs, 2, 27–28, 39, 200n.21; for rations, 143; supplementing income by trading on, 195; for vitamins, *166*

Bohemia, 88, 134

boteros (illegal taxis), 23

Bourdieu, Pierre, 195n.10, 195n.14

bourgeoisie vs. proletariat, 64

breast cancer, risk factors for, 210n.21

brigadistas (public health brigades), 70

brujeros (witch doctors), 43, 47

bureaucracy, xix, 183

campesinos (people from the countryside), 103

cancer, 80

carcacoles (a form of divination), 40

Carlos F. Finlay Medical Detachment, 82

Castro, Fidel: and Barrio Adentro, 170; criticism of, 106; on Cuba as Third World medical bulwark, 10; on dengue fever, 128, 129, 211n.29; on dollarization of the economy, 147; economic changes by, 62; on exporting revolution, 199n.50; on family physicians, 119; on health care, 53; health crisis of, 7–8; on health welfare as a basic human right, 205n.36; "History Will Absolve Me," 61, 204n.16; on homosexuals, 135; Marxist-Leninist principles embraced by, 63–64; on MEF physicians, 83; messianic status of, 65, 205n.31; on the new currency, 193n.1; Regional Integration Project signed by, 174, *175*; retirement of, 197n.29; on the revolutionary government, 60, 205n.34; Santería, association with, 39, 202n.7; on socialism under siege, 33–34; speeches by, xx; on women in the workforce, 76–77

Castro, Raúl: community meetings urged by, 179; on la doble moral, 214n.62; economic changes by, 62; MEF reorganization announced by, 179–80; presidency assumed by, 197n.29; on social science research, 193n.2

Catholic Church, 37, 42, 139

CDRS (Comités de Defensa de la Revolución), 25; blood drive by, 70; community surveillance by, 143, 214n.63; decline of, 143, 214n.66; founding of, 64, 204n.25; programs of, 204n.25; records kept on individuals, 206n.44

census (2005), 208n.16

Center for Genetic Engineering and Biotechnology, 89

Central de Trabajadores de Cuba. *See* CTC

Central Havana, 102, 208n.15

El Cerro, 208n.15

Changó (warrior god), 38–39, 202n.7

Chávez, Hugo, 170, 174, 216n.13

Chernobyl disaster (1986), 169

childbirth, institutionalization of, 78

Chilean earthquake, 169

Chinese traditional medicine, 50–51

Christianity, evangelical, 42

cigarettes, xxii–xxiii

cigars, 102

CIMEX S.A., 150, 151

Cira García International Clinic, 152, *153*, 160

citizenship, 111

CITMA (Ministry of Science, Technology, and the Environment), 44

City of Havana Province, 209n.20

civil society, 64–65, 198n.32

class stratification, 60, 61, 66, 103–5, 143–44, 183, 203n.9, 204n.18

clinical medicine/intervention vs. public health, 200n.17

clinics. *See* consultorios

Los Cocos (near Havana), 134

Cold War, 63

collectives, 131, 212n.37

Colomer, Josep M., 214n.66

Comaroff, Jean, 217–18n.10

COMECON (Council for Mutual Economic Assistance), 17, 63, 199n.2

hepatitis, 72, *75*
herbal medicine (medicina verde), 44–51, 48, 205–6n.38. *See also* MTN
Hermanos Ameijeiras (Havana), 89, 95, 152, *153–54*, 208n.10
Hernández-Reguant, Ariana, 165
heroic sacrifice (numancia), 64
high blood pressure, 80
high school equivalency education, 204n.19
Hirschfeld, Katherine, 211–12n.36
history of the present, 5, 196n.18
HIV/AIDS: and condoms, 135–36, 138; conspiracy theories about, 137–38; drugs for, 213n.55; education about/prevention of, 132–38, 212nn.42–43, 213n.53, 213n.55; HIV testing, 133–34, 136, 212n.43; prevalence of, 134, 212n.42; and prostitution, 137; quarantine policy, 134–35, 136–37, 212n.43; and risky behavior, 138, 213n.58; transmission of, 10, 134, 137–38
homosexuality, 134–36, 212n.48, 213n.51
hospital beds, 156, 203n.10
housing, nationalization of, 64
housing exchange (permuta), 38, 202n.5
humanitarian aid/solidarity campaigns, 169–81; and ALBA, 176; and commodification of medicine, 174, *175*, 179; consultorios affected by, 176–78; as diplomacy, 172–73, 176; ELAM, 172, 216n.8; Integral Health Programs, 170, 173; MBA, 170–71, *171*, 174–75, 178, 216n.13; medical brigades, 169; medical internationalism, 170, 172–73, 180, 216n.2; Operación Milagro, 171, *171*, 176; overview of, 169–72; and political agendas, 173–76; public reception of, 171–72, 177–79, 180; as response to global health inequity, 172–73; *¡Salud!* 172; and surplus/deficits, 178–81
human rights. *See* health welfare as a basic human right
hurricanes, 169
hustling, xix, 7, 102, 179
hygiene campaigns, 70, 72, *73–74*, 89

ideology inscribed in assumptions, 217–18n.10
illiteracy. *See* literacy programs

immigration, 105
income disparity, 32
In Cuba I Was a German Shepherd (Menéndez), 187–88
India's technical excellence, 164
inequality, economic, 32
infant mortality rate, 10, 16, 19, 53, 66, 76, 78, 80, 203n.10
infant nutrition, 120
lo informal (informal economy): as cultural paradigm, 196n.20; as endemic, 141; during the período especial, 7, 185, 197n.25; socios' role in, 7, 22, 26, 164; vs. Soviet blat networks, 198n.42; and transition from socialism to liberal capitalism, 9, 198n.41. *See also* black market
informants, demographic makeup of, 195n.9
Instituto de Cardiología, 163
integral care of adults, 114
integral care of children, 209n.13
integral care of women, 114
Integral Health Programs, 170, 173
internacionalistas. *See* humanitarian aid/solidarity campaigns
International Monetary Fund, 10
Iraq, 174

jineterismo. *See* prostitution
John Paul II, pope, 42

La Covadonga Hospital (later named Salvador Allende Hospital), 25
Lage, Carlos, 17
Lancaster, Roger, 202n.8
land reforms, 62
laser eye surgery, 157
Las Vegas consultorio, 26–31, 160
Latin American School of Medicine (ELAM), 172, 216n.8
Law Number 723 (El Servicio Médico Social Rural), 206n.47
Law Number 949, 68
Leiner, Marvin, 212n.46
Lewis, Oscar, 37, 193n.2
Lewis, Ruth M., 193n.2
liberalism, 196n.20
liberal subject, conceptions of, 183–84

8370

P. SEAN BROTHERTON IS AN ASSISTANT PROFESSOR OF
ANTHROPOLOGY AT YALE UNIVERSITY.

Library of Congress Cataloging-in-Publication Data
Brotherton, Pierre Sean.
Revolutionary medicine : health and the body in post-Soviet
Cuba / P. Sean Brotherton.
p. cm.
Includes bibliographical references and index.
ISBN 978-0-8223-5194-8 (cloth : alk. paper)
ISBN 978-0-8223-5205-1 (pbk. : alk. paper)
1. Medical policy—Cuba. 2. Human body—Political aspects—
Cuba. 3. Medical care—Cuba. 4. Biopolitics—Cuba. I. Title.
RA395.C9B76 2012
362.1097291—dc23   2011030937